A Conservation Manual for the Field Archaeologist

THIRD EDITION

Catherine Sease

Archaeological Research Tools 4
Institute of Archaeology, University of California, Los Angeles
1994

ACKNOWLEDGMENTS: I would like to acknowledge my debt of gratitude to all those whose help made this book possible. The many friends and colleagues who were generous with encouragement, advice, information, and time are too numerous to mention individually, but I herewith thank them all.

Very special thanks are due to Kathryn Walker Tubb, Stephen Koob, and Lucia Nixon who read the entire manuscript at various stages and made invaluable suggestions and constructive criticism. I am also grateful to Jennifer Shay, Thomas Shay, David McCreer, Claire Dean, Monona Rossol, Carol O'Biso, and Brigid Sullivan for reading and commenting on various smaller sections of the text. Jennifer Shay, Stephen Koob, and Jane Cocking generously supplied photographs while Hillary Lewis did the line drawings and Ronald Testa printed the photographs. My thanks to them all.

I would like to acknowledge the generous support of the 1984 Foundation of the Mellon Bank, Philadelphia.

I would also like to express my gratitude to my husband, David Reese, for providing unflagging support and encouragement throughout this entire project, for reading, rereading, and commenting on the manuscript.

Most of all, I am indebted to the directors of all the excavations who employed me as conservator: Iain Crawford, David Bivar, Donald White, Nicholas Postgate, Cuyler Young, and Joseph Shaw. Quite simply, without them this book would not have been possible.

PHOTO CREDITS: Photographs were provided by: Stephen Koob, figure 4.17; Jane Cocking, figure 4.29; Jennifer Shay, figure 5.11; The Agora Excavations of The American School of Classical Studies in Athens, figure 5.43a. Figure 5.24 (U.C. 5207), figure 5.35 (U.C. 33204), and figure 5.38 (U.C. 28123) are courtesy of Petrie Museum, University College, London. Figure 5.16 is used with the permission of the Managing Committee of The British School of Archaeology at Athens. All other photographs were taken by the author.

Edited by Rita Demsetz, Marilyn Gatto, Beverly Godwin, Patricia Campbell Healy, Brenda Johnson-Grau, and Catherine Weinerth
Designed by Brenda Johnson-Grau
Production by Angie Hiltz, Wendy Lau, Pat Lin, and Tim Seymour
Index by Patricia Campbell Healy

Library of Congress Cataloging-in-Publication Data
Sease, Catherine, 1947-
A conservation manual for the field archaeologist/ Catherine Sease. -- 3rd ed.
p. cm. -- (Archaeological research tools ; 4)
Includes bibliographical references and index.
ISBN 0-917956-82-6 :
1.Archaeology--Field work. 2. Antiquities--Collection and preservation.
I. Title. II. Series: Archaeological research tools; v.4.
CC76.S4 1994
930.1'028--dc20 94-45393
CIP

Contents

TO MY PARENTS

Introduction

THIS BOOK is for the field archaeologist. It provides excavators with the techniques necessary to safeguard and protect artifacts from the moment they are unearthed until they are fully treated in a properly equipped conservation laboratory by professional conservators.

The techniques are basic, tending to be more first-aid treatments rather than full-scale conservation procedures—not because conservators want to prevent others from treading on their territory but out of a genuine concern for the well-being of the artifacts and the information they can give us. Field conservation is not easy and cannot be done by any or all members of the excavation team in their spare time. No matter how well intentioned, inexperienced hands can irreparably damage artifacts. Only those treatments and procedures that an untrained person can do competently are presented here. All others must be carried out by a professional conservator. Although it may sound tedious constantly to say "take it to a trained conservator," it is the soundest advice that can be given.

A minimum of actual treatments is, therefore, given here; instead, emphasis is placed on how to lift an object safely out of the ground, what materials are suitable to use on artifacts, and how to pack and temporarily store objects—all procedures that nonconservators can undertake to help ensure the safety of the objects until they can be treated by a conservator.

Wherever possible, more detailed information is provided. The conservation treatment done in the field—no matter how basic—is, however, often the only treatment these objects will ever receive. Follow-up treatment may be possible during subsequent seasons. Once objects are deposited in museums, access can be restricted, if not impossible. If it is clear that objects will not receive post-excavation treatment in a museum laboratory, a conservator should definitely be included in the excavation team so that the more detailed cleaning and conservation techniques not presented in this book can be undertaken to ensure maximum retrieval of information from the artifacts.

I do not condone or encourage the practice of not having a fully trained conservator on site as a permanent member of the excavation team. This book is not meant to be, nor can it attempt to be, a replacement for an on-site conservator, for there are countless variables involved in field conservation. No two objects are alike even though they are made of the same material and have been buried within inches of each other in the ground. Every object, of necessity, must be treated individually. Moreover, no two sites are exactly alike, because of different soil conditions and climate, for example. As a result, it is impossible for this book, or any other, to serve as anything but a treatment guide. Although every attempt has been made to make this book comprehensive, it is impracticable to attempt to take into consideration every eventuality that might be encountered.

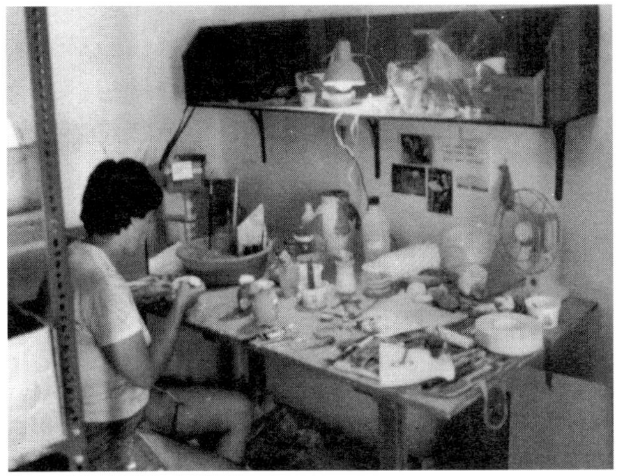

CATHERINE SEASE (shown above at work in field laboratory, Kommos, Crete) is a graduate of Bryn Mawr College and has a degree in conservation from the Institute of Archaeology, London. She has worked on excavations in Britain, the Mediterranean, and the Middle East. Currently she is the head of the Division of Conservation at the Field Museum in Chicago.

While all the treatments mentioned in this book are tried and true in the sense that they have been used with success for many years, unusual variations in what might otherwise be seen as a straightforward situation may cause a treatment not to work. Even trained conservators have this problem; for no apparent reason, some treatments simply do not work on one occasion when they have worked countless times before. A trained conservator, however, has the knowledge and expertise to take into consideration all variables presented by a site, as well as to cope with any unforeseen problems and devise suitable treatments.

The important principles of conservation, suitable supplies and materials for use in field conservation, safety procedures, and basic field techniques are discussed in the first four chapters. The fifth and final chapter deals with the treatment, packing, and storage of specific materials. Although this information will be of most interest to the excavator, it is imperative that the preceding chapters be read in full before any work is undertaken. Once you have read and fully comprehended the first four chapters, refer to sections in chapter 5 concerning individual materials. Be sure to read the entire section before attempting treatment.

Chapter One

Important Points

EVERY MATERIAL has a stable form in relation to the environment in which it exists. When it is buried, an object finds itself in a new microclimate, possibly one vastly different from its previous state. The material of which the object is made will begin to adapt to these new conditions. Assuming these conditions are reasonably constant, the material will undergo a process of modification to approach a stable relationship, or equilibrium, with the new environment. As the material approaches equilibrium, the rate of change will decrease and eventually stop when equilibrium is actually reached. This stability will remain constant as long as the object remains buried in the ground.

Impact of Excavation

In a burial environment, materials are broken down by physical, chemical, and/or biological processes. Physically, ceramics and stone can be modified by being broken by a cycle of freezing and thawing, or by abrasion, or by saturation with water-soluble salts. Glazes can be pushed off a ceramic vessel through the physical action of water-soluble salts or by freezing and thawing. If it has a calcareous filler, pottery can be modified chemically by acids in groundwater. Many kinds of stone will also be adversely affected by acids and other substances in the groundwater and soil. Glass, glazes, and metals are all very sensitive to chemical processes and can be modified drastically when buried. Although organic materials can be modified by chemical processes, they are also subject to biological decay which is indirectly both physical and chemical. The effect of soil types on materials is presented in table 1.1.

Just how much the material is modified from the original during burial depends mainly on the soil and climatic conditions that prevail and how the material behaves under those particular conditions. Organic materials, for example, rarely survive burial in the ground. Alkaline or slightly acidic soil conditions, along with the attack by organisms in the soil, contribute to the generally rapid decomposition of organic materials. The same organic materials, however, can survive surprisingly well when buried under very arid desert conditions, when waterlogged and buried in very fine silt or mud, or when frozen. In all of these extreme conditions, normal decaying mechanisms do not take place and the organic material survives.

Changes will resume as soon as an object is uncovered in the ground and is suddenly exposed to new environmental conditions. From the very moment the object is exposed to air, the processes of deterioration and corrosion begin again. Some materials are more sensitive than others to these changes. With organic materials, for example, this process can be very rapid, causing objects to disintegrate within hours. On the other hand, certain materials, such as well-fired pottery or stone, may deteriorate little, if at all. With the majority of materials, however, some form of deterioration will inevitably take place. It is important to point out that this deterioration is not necessarily immediately visible to the naked eye.

It is possible to slow down and, in some instances, arrest the deterioration process, thereby helping to safeguard the object. This preservation is part of the field conservator's job. In the absence of a conservator, the archaeologist can take certain positive preventive steps to ensure that an object will remain intact long enough to be taken to a trained conservator for proper treatment. It is essential for anyone undertaking this responsibility to have a good grasp of some basic concepts of conservation so that no irreparable damage is inadvertently done to the object.

The Least Done Is Best

The most important point to keep in mind at all times is that more often than not the best treatment is the least treatment. If an object appears to be sound and has a good chance of survival without having anything done to it, then nothing at

Table 1.1: Effect of Soil Types on Materials

	ACIDIC	ALKALINE	SALINE	Waterlogged ACIDIC	Waterlogged ALKALINE	DESERT	ARCTIC
METALS							
Iron	Bad corrosion	Good preservation	Bad corrosion	Good preservation	Good preservation	Good preservation	Good preservation
Copper alloys	Bad corrosion	Good preservation	Bad corrosion	Good preservation	Good preservation	Good preservation	Good preservation
Lead	Poor preservation	Poor preservation	Reasonable preservation	Good preservation	Good preservation	Good preservation	Bood preservation
Silver	Poor preservation	Good preservation	Slight salinity: good High salinity: poor	Good preservation	Good preservation	Good preservation	Good preservation
ORGANIC MATERIALS							
Bone, ivory, antler	Poor preservation	Good preservation	Poor preservation soluble salts	Poor preservation	Poor preservation	Good preservation	Good preservation
Horn, hair, wool, leather	Slow deterioration of protein	Poor preservation	Extreme: dehydration	Good preservation	Good preservation	Good preservation	Good preservation
Wood, cotton, linen	Poor preservation	Poor preservation	Extreme: dehydration	Good preservation	Good preservation	Good preservation	Good preservation
Shell	Poor preservation	Good preservation	Poor preservation soluble salts	Poor preservation	Poor preservation	Good preservation	Good preservation
CERAMICS	Reasonable pres-ervation; calcareous fillers will dissolve	Poor preservation; dissolution of basic structure; insoluble salt encrustations	Poor preservation soluble salts	Same as for acid soils	Same as for alkaline soils	Good preservation; possible wind erosion	Good preservation
GLASS AND GLAZES	Reasonable pres-ervation; leaching of alkalis	Poor preservation; dissolution of basic structure	Poor preservation	Reasonable preservation	Poor preservation	Good preservation; possible wind erosion	Good preservation
STONE	Good preservation; etching, dissolu-tion of marble and limestone	Good preservation; insoluble salt encrustations	Poor preservation soluble salts	Poor preservation	Insoluble salt encrustation	Good preservation; possible wind erosion	Good preservation
WALL PLASTER	Poor preservation	Good preservation	Poor preservation	Poor preservation	Poor preservation	Good preservation	Good preservation

all should be done. Understandably, many archaeologists find this concept difficult to follow. In this instance, patience and restraint are decided virtues. Impatience to see what lies under an encrustation, dirt, or a corroded surface can lead to drastic overcleaning or scratching of an object. It can also cause irreparable breakage if the object is not strong enough to withstand handling by untrained hands.

An object generally has a better chance of survival if it is handled as carefully but as minimally as possible and is packed and stored properly. For this reason, in the sections on specific materials in chapter 5, emphasis is placed on proper packing and storage materials and methods as a viable alternative to treatment.

If, in the course of excavation, one encounters a monumental conservation problem—wall paintings in situ, for example—or vast quantities of extremely fragile material for which one is not prepared, by far the best course of action is to cover it again immediately. Keep it well covered and protected while a conservator is found and consulted and a method of conservation or lifting is devised, even if this means delaying removal until a later season. Never act precipitously. Enough time should be taken to consider all aspects of the problem so as to work out the best solution. It is far better to take the time to devise a suitable treatment and have trained conservators carry it out than to rush into the job unprepared with inadequate supplies and risk the loss of the object altogether. Never be afraid to postpone action on a difficult problem and seek professional help.

What Is Done Generally Must Be Undone

When it is absolutely necessary to undertake a treatment, keep in mind that whatever is done in the field by a nonconservator almost certainly must be undone in the laboratory. This underscores the importance of the principle of reversibility, an important concept in any conservation treatment. This means that any treatment applied to an object must be reversible, that is, must be capable of being reversed or removed at a later date with no resulting damage or change to the object. It should make no difference whether the reversal process takes place several hours later, several days later, or as long as a year or more later. Reversibility is especially important for field conservation because one is often forced to carry out procedures under less than ideal conditions.

For this reason, only certain materials are acceptable for conservation use. These, and only these, should be used. In the following chapters, reference is made specifically to a variety of conservation materials which are of good quality and have withstood the test of time and reversibility. It is important that only these materials be used. Do not use something else that looks or sounds the same without first

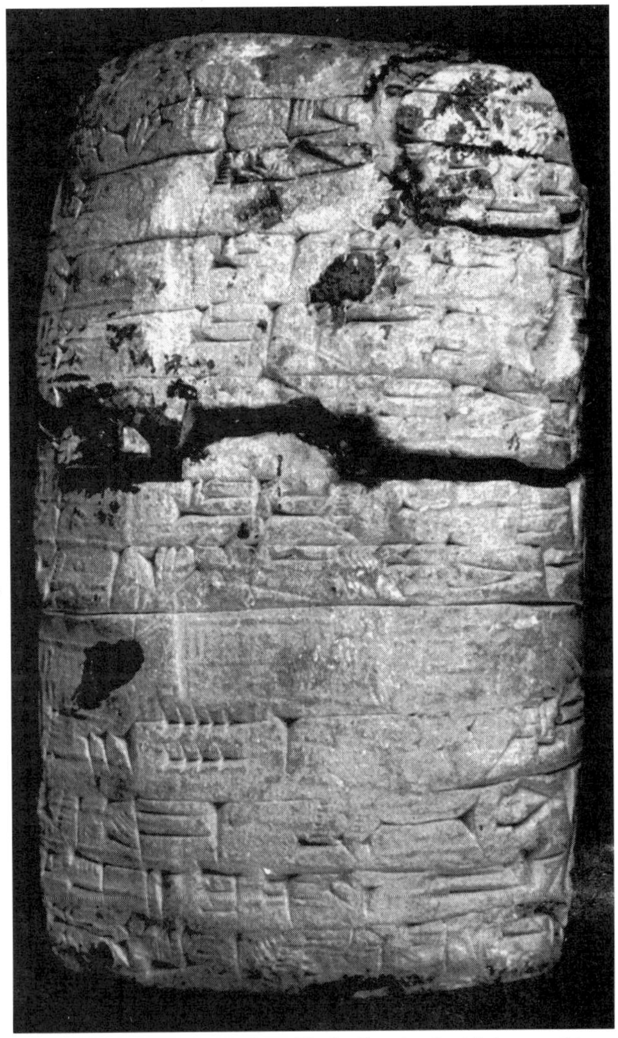

FIGURE 1.1 Mesopotamian clay tablet badly joined with irreversible adhesive.

consulting with a conservator. If improper materials are used, even professional conservators may not be able to reverse the treatment and undo the resulting damage. In such a case, compromises have to be made, and it is invariably the object that suffers. A case in point are the pieces of clay tablet shown in figure 1.1 which were joined with an adhesive that sagged before it hardened, allowing the two main pieces of the tablet to separate. Over time, the adhesive has discolored badly and become insoluble. It is now impossible to remove the adhesive without badly damaging the tablet; the pieces cannot be properly aligned nor the stains removed. Had a reversible adhesive been used, a problem would not now exist.

In keeping with this principle of reversibility, it follows that, if treatment is absolutely necessary, materials applied to an object should be used sparingly. Only the smallest possible quantities needed to ensure the safety of the object should be used. It is mistakenly thought by nonconservators that if a little adhesive or consolidant is good, then a great deal is better and a very thick layer is best of all. A thick layer of consolidant or too much adhesive only means a more difficult and time-consuming job for a conservator back in the museum or laboratory, possibly to the detriment of the object.

Analysis

It must always be kept in mind that any treatment applied to an object, including mere cleaning, can contaminate it and invalidate any subsequent analysis, whether it be for dating purposes or elemental analysis. If any kind of analysis will be required at a later date, representative samples of the material should be taken carefully and set aside. Even if analysis is not immediately envisaged, it is wise to set aside samples automatically so that testing can be done later. Moreover, the experts doing the analysis should be given a copy of the complete conservation record of the object.

Know Your Site

A great deal of wasted effort and damage to objects can be avoided if archaeologists know their site well. That is, if the soil conditions, local climate, and depth of deposits are known, as well as the kinds of materials and objects likely to be found, it is then possible to predict with a degree of accuracy the condition in which objects are likely to be found and to anticipate basic conservation problems. Forearmed with this information, the archaeologist can consult with professional conservators to work out methods of treatment and handling appropriate for that particular site. The archaeologist can then go into the field with suitable equipment and supplies and thus be better prepared to deal adequately with whatever is found.

In countries where supplies are readily available, obtaining supplies ahead of time may seem unnecessary, although it can save considerable time later in trying to locate suppliers. In other areas, however, it is essential to plan ahead because suitable supplies are difficult, if not impossible, to find. Precious time can be wasted trying to track down items. When found, their purity and, therefore, their suitability cannot always be assumed.

Knowing the climate of the area can be just as important as knowing the site itself. Knowledge of climatic conditions will enable a conservator to anticipate problems that might arise when using certain materials. For example, when the weather is very hot and dry, acetone is difficult to use as the solvent for a consolidant. Being very volatile, it will evaporate before the consolidant has a chance to penetrate sufficiently to be effective. Toluene, which is less volatile, would be a better choice of solvent; since it is generally more difficult to find than acetone, it might have to be brought to the site with the excavation team.

Common Sense

No book can regulate the amount of common sense employed by the person treating an object. Unfortunately, good field conservation relies heavily on the common sense, competence, and imagination of the person doing the work. These qualities, along with patience and restraint, although vital for any successful treatment, cannot be given or ensured by any book. The success or failure of any treatment undertaken must, of necessity, rest with the person doing the work.

Chapter Two

Safety

ALL THE MATERIALS cited in these pages are chemicals and should be used and handled with the utmost care at all times. Some chemicals are highly flammable, while others are corrosive and will destroy almost everything, except plastic, with which they come in contact. Almost all chemicals are toxic to varying degrees and, if improperly handled, can cause serious medical problems.

The disposal of chemicals and chemical waste is a complex problem. Every country and state has its own laws concerning the disposal of such materials. These laws are complicated and can change frequently. It is the responsibility of excavation staff to find out what these laws are for their particular area and fully understand them before disposing of any chemical waste.

For excavations in the United States, it is necessary to have on file and readily accessible Material Safety Data Sheets (MSDS) on each chemical used.

The following safety precautions are offered as general guidelines. In some instances, detailed safety procedures for handling individual chemicals can be found under the appropriate sections in chapters 3 and 5.

Transportation of Chemicals

The transportation of chemicals can be difficult and dangerous. If an overland trip is planned, it is necessary to be aware of and comply with the laws governing the transport of chemicals in each country traversed. Advice on these regulations can be obtained from embassies or consulates.

Chemicals must be packed as safely as possible for transport. Flammable liquids and acids should be kept in nonbreakable plastic containers. For obvious reasons, the use of glass jars, bottles, and other breakable containers should be avoided. Plastic-coated glass containers are now available and are recommended. If breakable containers must be used, they can be employed safely in conjunction with polyethylene acid/solvent carriers designed especially to transport acids and other chemicals. Even if nonbreakable containers are used, it is always wise to use these carriers as well.

If acid carriers are not available, chemicals should be packed in sturdy cardboard boxes or wooden shipping crates. For further protection, the box can be lined with thick polyethylene sheeting. Fill the cavity surrounding the containers with vermiculite to absorb any leakage that might occur. Label the boxes clearly with the name of the chemical inside along with pertinent information about it; for example, that it is flammable or corrosive (fig. 2.1).

When packing the vehicle, place the chemicals where they will not be exposed to extreme heat or sunlight. If they are stored in the passenger compartment, prohibit smoking and make sure there is good ventilation to prevent the buildup of vapors.

The driver and passengers should be apprised of the nature of the chemicals they are transporting and be familiar with basic safety precautions. It is also wise to provide the driver with an official letter itemizing the chemicals and authorizing their carriage for conservation purposes.

Storage of Chemicals

The following guidelines should be followed when storing chemicals:

- The amount of chemicals stored on site should be kept to an absolute minimum. Bring only what you are likely to use in a season and store as few chemicals as possible from one season to the next.
- Store all solvents in well-ventilated, cool areas away from large concentrations of people.
- Keep the storeroom locked and secure at all times.
- Keep acids and bases separate. Do not store oxidizing agents with solvents. For example, nitric acid should be kept away from acetic acid, acetone, and alcohol.

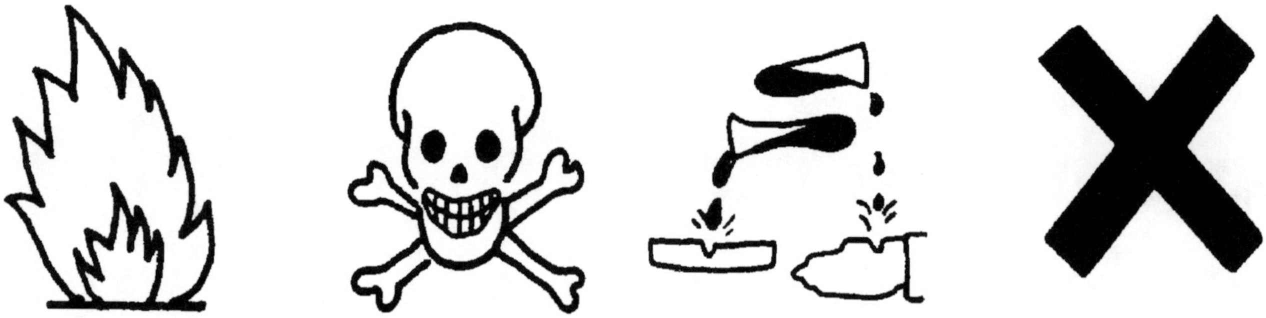

FIGURE 2.1 Standard hazard symbols

- All containers should be well sealed and nonbreakable. Avoid glass containers whenever possible. If glass containers must be used, keep them in safety bottle carriers. Plastic-coated containers are recommended.
- Clearly label all containers of chemicals, solutions, acids, and fungicides. For solutions,indicate not only the concentration, but also what the solvent is. If appropriate, use bilingual labels.
- If containers are reused, remove all old labels.
- Where appropriate, the standard hazard symbol should be used (fig. 2.1).

Use of Chemicals

Follow these guidelines when using chemicals:

- Do not smoke or eat when working with chemicals. Do not allow others to smoke or eat around anyone working with chemicals. Not only are chemicals flammable, but some, when inhaled through cigarettes, are converted into poisonous gases.
- Do not use solvents near open flames.
- Do not use chemicals, especially solvents, near motors that can cause sparks. Keep in mind that it is possible for solvent vapors to be ignited by a spark some distance away.
- Do not keep large amounts of solvents or acids in the work area.
- Clearly label all containers of chemicals, solutions, acids, and fungicides in the work area. Use bilingual labels and/or hazard signs when appropriate.
- Keep all chemicals out of the reach of children, animals, and people who cannot read labels.
- Keep containers of all chemicals away from the edges of tables or shelves where they can be easily knocked off.
- Wear chemical splash goggles whenever pouring acids, caustics, or solvents.
- Do not use acids unless there is a source of running water close by.
- When diluting an acid, always add the acid to water; never add water to the acid. Large amounts of heat can be generated when water is added to acid, causing it to sputter and spit.
- Thoroughly wash all containers used for chemicals, especially acids and fungicides, immediately after use. Do not leave them around with the remains of the chemical still inside.
- Make sure that artifacts packed with a fungicide are meticulously labeled to that effect so that people will take the necessary precautions when handling them.

Disposal of Chemical Waste

The disposal of chemical waste is a difficult problem. Since the situation at every site differs, it is not easy to generalize. Certainly, common sense plays a major role in waste disposal. Consideration must be given not only to the nature of the material being disposed of but also to the safety of the local human and animal populations. One must also be aware of the unforeseen problems that can be caused by waste disposal. Large quantities of solvents, for example, should never be disposed of down the drain. Flammable vapors can collect in traps and standpipes, creating fire and explosion hazards. Other chemicals poured down the drain can damage the sewer system by killing off the bacteria which is introduced to treat raw sewage. Any chemical dumped on the ground in large quantities will filter down to the water table; this process might take years, but eventually the chemical will pollute the water below.

Waste solvents should never be burned. Some compounds, when burned, can form persistent intermediate products that can be toxic.

Small amounts of chemicals, roughly speaking less than a pint or half liter, can be disposed of in the following manner.

ACIDS: Thoroughly dilute the acid by adding it to water, then neutralize it by adding baking soda (sodium bicarbonate) or soda ash (sodium carbonate). The acid has been neutralized when the foaming and effervescing stop. The liquid can then be flushed down the drain with copious amounts of water. If no baking soda or soda ash is available, dilute the acid thoroughly with water and then dump it in a deserted area along with copious amounts of water. The soil, if it is very saline, will serve to neutralize the acid. Small amounts of acid can be flushed down the drain after first being thoroughly diluted with water. Let the water run while pouring the acid down the drain; keep the water running for five to ten minutes afterward.

SOLVENTS: Small amounts of solvents can be allowed to evaporate by leaving the top off their containers or by pouring the solvent into a shallow dish. This process should be done in a well-ventilated area, preferably outside, far removed from any open flames or sources of sparks. It is also important to do this in a secluded or secure place where children and animals cannot get at the open container.

RESIN SOLUTIONS: Allow the solvent to evaporate as in the solvent disposal procedure above and then throw away the container with the hardened resin inside. It is wise to break the container or render it unusable before disposing of it.

EMULSIONS: Thoroughly dilute the emulsion with water and then flush it down the drain with copious amounts of water. Allow the water to run for five minutes afterward. It is extremely important to dilute the emulsion and flush it down with a great deal of water to prevent the resin from forming deposits and hardening inside the drain, which will eventually block it.

FUNGICIDES: Small amounts of fungicide should be thoroughly diluted with water and then flushed down the drain with copious amounts of water. Allow the water to run for five minutes afterward. If there is any question that even dilute amounts of fungicide could damage the local sewage system, dispose of it by dumping it in a deserted area along with copious amounts of water. The fungicide should be thoroughly diluted before being dumped.

Disposal of Solid Waste

The disposal of solid waste can also cause problems. Local villagers and children can be skillful scavengers who, unbeknownst to the staff, thoroughly rummage through excavation waste. Plastic containers, for example, especially if unavailable locally, are prized items and will vanish from garbage containers and dumps unless they have been rendered unusable. If scavenging is likely to be a problem, some waste may be better disposed of by burial. Use the following procedures when disposing of solid wastes:

- Swabs, cotton, tissue, and toweling containing solvents should not be thrown away immediately. Place them in a glass container and set them aside in a well-ventilated area away from the workplace, people, sparks, and flames to allow the solvent to evaporate. Once the solvent is gone, they can be thrown away.
- Swabs, cotton, tissue, and toweling containing acid should be thoroughly rinsed in running water to remove all traces of the acid before being thrown away.
- Carefully wrap used scalpel blades and other sharp utensils in the foil envelopes in which they came or in a thick piece of paper or cardboard before discarding them. They can also be embedded in surplus plaster of Paris or resin before it hardens and can then be thrown away. If scavenging is a problem, sharp waste may be better disposed of by burying after it has been wrapped or embedded.
- Any glass bottles, jars, or other containers used to hold chemicals, including photographic chemicals, should be washed thoroughly to remove all traces of chemicals before being thrown away. If it is not possible to remove all traces of the chemical, it is best to break the vessel carefully and wrap the pieces in toweling or newspaper before discarding them.
- All plastic containers used to hold chemicals should be rendered unusable before being discarded. This precaution is taken because it is much more difficult to remove all traces of chemicals from plastic. Perforate the bottom of the vessel or cut large holes in the bottom before throwing the container away.

Personal Safety

Take the following measures to ensure personal safety:

- Wear chemical splash goggles while pouring solvents and acids.
- Don't wear contact lenses when using with chemicals.
- Always wear protective clothing when using chemicals. For example, wear thick rubber gloves when handling acids and polyurethane foam. Make sure the gloves are not too big or else they can be very clumsy, constituting a hazard in themselves. Plastic gloves should be worn when handling solvents.
- Always wash your hands thoroughly after using chemicals, and especially before eating.
- Work in well-ventilated areas when using chemicals.
- Avoid breathing solvent vapors or acid fumes.

Emergency Procedures

These procedures are meant only to be used as a quick reference to first-aid measures applicable to handling and using chemicals. All excavations should have a first-aid book on hand. Anyone handling chemicals should be familiar with the relevant first-aid procedures.

SPLASHES OF CHEMICALS ON THE SKIN

1. Flood the splashed area with copious amounts of running water. Continue until you are satisfied that none of the chemical remains on the skin. If the chemical is not miscible with water, soap will help to remove it.
2. Remove any clothing that has been splashed. Thoroughly wash the clothes before wearing them again.
3. If the splashing is acute, especially with acids, seek medical attention. Be prepared to provide information on the chemical involved and the first-aid already given.

SPLASHES OF CHEMICALS IN THE EYE

1. Remove contact lenses.
2. Flood the eye with copious amounts of gently running water. Continue this process for at least fifteen minutes. Gently pry open the lids and hold them apart during the irrigation to ensure that the entire eyeball is bathed.
3. All eye injuries require medical attention. Be prepared to provide information on the chemical involved and first-aid given.

INHALATION OF CHEMICAL VAPORS

1. Remove the victim from the contaminated work area.
2. Loosen the victim's clothing.
3. If the victim is unconscious, place the victim face down and watch to see if breathing stops.
4. If breathing stops, administer artificial respiration.
5. If the victim's condition is acute, seek medical attention. Be prepared to provide information on the chemical involved and first-aid given.

INGESTION OF CHEMICALS

1. If ingestion is confined to the mouth, rinse the mouth thoroughly with copious amounts of water, making sure that the chemical is not swallowed.
2. If the chemical is swallowed, make the victim drink copious amounts of water or milk to dilute the chemical in the stomach.
3. Do not induce vomiting.
4. Seek medical attention. Be prepared to provide information on the chemical involved, the quantity and concentration ingested, and first-aid given.

SPILLAGES

Chemical supply houses have spill kits designed to deal with spillages of specific kinds of chemicals. If large amounts of chemicals are to be used, it is wise to obtain spill kits for those particular chemicals.

Of Liquids Miscible in Water (acetone, alcohol, ammonia)

1. Shut off any sources of ignition or sparks if a flammable liquid is involved.
2. Mop up the spill using plenty of water and dispose of it down the drain, diluting it further with copious amounts of water.
3. Before reentering the area, ventilate it until all traces of the smell are gone.

Of Liquids Immiscible in Water (toluene)

1. Shut off any sources of ignition or sparks.
2. Sprinkle the spill liberally with vermiculite or sand, allowing the solvent to be absorbed. Then shovel the vermiculite or sand into a metal bucket and take it to a safe, open area where the solvent can evaporate.
3. Before reentering the area, ventilate it until all traces of the smell are gone.

Of Acids

1. Wear rubber gloves and goggles.
2. Spread soda ash (sodium carbonate) or baking soda (sodium bicarbonate) liberally on the spill to neutralize the acid. Add enough water to make a thoroughly mixed slurry, using a shovel to mix it. The acid has been neutralized when the foaming and effervescing stop.
3. Mop up the area using plenty of water and dispose of the liquid down the drain, further diluting it with copious amounts of water.

Chapter Three

Supplies and Materials

ALL MATERIALS listed here are mentioned in chapters 4 and 5. Not all these materials are required at any given site. Because so many variables are involved, it is impossible to state which materials are essential for which sites. If one has a reasonably good idea of what is likely to be found, a list of suitable materials and supplies can be easily compiled.

It is important to use only the materials cited here, even if it means bringing them with you over long distances. All these materials are recommended because they meet the conservation requirements of stability, durability, and reversibility. Do not use something else that looks or sounds the same without first consulting a trained conservator. Under each material listing, information is given about the qualities of the material and its conservation uses. Details of such uses are found under the appropriate listing in chapter 5.

Information is also given on the toxicity and safety hazards of each material and on any special safety precautions. This information is not meant to scare people unduly, but rather to give one a healthy respect for these chemicals to ensure that they are not used unnecessarily or carelessly.

Some of the materials listed are available in many places, but the main source listed below is recommended because it supplies a wide range of acceptable conservation materials, all in small quantities. This vendor also keeps abreast of new developments in conservation materials and treatments, will also pack materials for shipping anywhere in the world by air freight, and is knowledgeable about the safety requirements for shipping. Unless otherwise indicated, all materials mentioned are available from:

Conservation Materials, Ltd.
1395 Greg #10
Sparks, Nevada 89431 USA
(702) 331-0582

A complete list of manufacturers and distributors can be found in appendix III.

Acids

Acids are extremely corrosive liquids that will destroy almost everything with which they come in contact except plastic; most will not destroy glass. Contact with the skin can cause serious burns, and the inhalation of acid fumes can result in severe damage to the eyes and the respiratory system. Acids can be very dangerous when handled by inexperienced people and should be used only when absolutely necessary. Strict safety precautions must be observed at all times when handling acids. For detailed safety precautions, see chapter 2 and the pottery section in chapter 5.

The transport of acids can be dangerous and is not recommended over long distances. If the carriage of acids is unavoidably, see chapter 2 for the appropriate safety measures. The acids cited here are available in most countries from chemical or medical supply houses or pharmacies. It is generally easier and safer to obtain them as close to the site as possible.

GLACIAL ACETIC ACID: A colorless, fuming liquid with a pungent, acrid odor, glacial acetic acid is flammable and corrosive, causes burns (especially severe to the eyes), and its vapor can be an irritant to the eyes and the respiratory system. It should be kept away from nitric acid because violent reactions might occur if they interact with each other. This acid is only suitable for removing bones from a calcareous matrix.. Although it can be used to remove insoluble salts from pottery, other acids are faster acting and much more efficient.

HYDROCHLORIC ACID: A colorless or yellowish fuming liquid with a pungent smell, hydrochloric acid (muriatic acid) is very corrosive. Dilute solutions will irritate the skin, while stronger solutions can burn the skin and will severely burn the eyes. Its vapor will irritate the eyes and the respiratory system. Hydrochloric acid should be used only for the removal of insoluble salts from pottery. It should never be used on or near metal artifacts because chlorides in the acid are the major cause of corrosion of iron, silver, copper, and copper alloys. It will also severely damage all organic materials.

NITRIC ACID: A colorless or pale yellow fuming liquid, nitric acid is highly corrosive and caustic. The liquid will severely burn the skin and eyes, and its vapor irritates the eyes and all parts of the respiratory system. It should be kept away from acetic acid, acetone, and alcohol because violent reactions might occur if they interact with each other. If nitric acid comes in contact with combustible materials, it may cause fires spontaneously.

This acid is used to remove insoluble salts from pottery. It will dissolve a wider range of salts than hydrochloric acid, and, in general, its reaction time is faster. Although its use is slightly preferable to hydrochloric acid, it is more difficult to find in some countries. Nitric acid should not be used on ceramics with lead glazes. It will dissolve the lead causing the glaze to opacify.

pH INDICATOR STRIPS: pH indicator strips are useful for determining when the acid used to remove insoluble salts has been thoroughly rinsed out of pottery. These strips come in convenient small packets, generally of 100, that either cover the entire pH scale of 0 to 14 (with 7 being neutral) or only a portion of it. It is not necessary to have the full range, although it is helpful to have it on hand; however, the scale from 0 to 7 will be the most useful. (These strips can also be used to test whether distilled water is contaminated with sulfuric acid.) To take a reading, quickly dip a portion of a strip into the water. Within seconds, the strip will change color. Compare the color of the strip to the color range provided to determine the pH of the water.

Solvents

Solvents are liquids capable of dissolving another substance. Like acids, they can be extremely dangerous chemicals and should always be handled with caution. Most solvents are highly volatile; that is, large quantities of them evaporate quickly, filling an enclosed space with vapors and causing both a health and a fire hazard. Because they are highly flammable, solvents should never be used in a room with any kind of spark or open flame, including cigarettes and heaters, even though the flame may seem to be well separated from the area where the solvent is being used. It is possible, in fact, for solvent vapors to be ignited by a spark some distance away from the solvent itself.

Solvents should be stored in as cool a place as possible away from direct sources of heat. Because of their extreme flammability, solvents are difficult to transport, so it is best to obtain them as close to the site as possible. They can be bought at chemical and medical supply houses and, in small quantities, from pharmacies.

All solvents are toxic to varying degrees. Exposure to them can result in serious damage to vital organs, such as the central nervous system. Some solvents act as narcotics, causing drowsiness, light-headedness, and confusion; thus, they are more likely to cause accidents. Solvents should be used only in well-ventilated areas, and care should be taken not to inhale their fumes. All solvent containers should be stoppered at all times.

Avoid direct contact of solvents with the skin. They can directly or indirectly cause local skin irritations, skin allergies, or skin cancer. Solvents are absorbed through the skin if the skin is broken or irritated; certain solvents will be absorbed even through unbroken skin. Wash your hands with soap and water after exposure to solvents. Since many solvents remove oils from the surface of the skin, it is wise to use a skin moisturizer frequently.

Solvents should be selected in conjunction with the consolidants and adhesives taken into the field to ensure that there is at least one solvent for each. Ideally, it is best to have more than one solvent for each resin because the choice of solvent can be used to increase or decrease the resin's drying time.

ACETONE: A colorless liquid with a characteristic odor, acetone is extremely flammable and, as a result, is difficult to transport. It is best to obtain it as near the site as possible. This liquid will cause skin dryness and may cause dermatitis. It can also severely damage the eyes. Inhalation of large amounts of the vapor may cause dizziness, narcosis, and coma.

Acetone is a good, all-purpose solvent for field conservation because it dissolves a wide range of resins. It is a solvent for polyvinyl acetate, acrylic resins, and cellulose nitrate adhesives. It is more difficult to use in a hot, dry climate than are other solvents because it is very volatile and evaporates quickly. Keep it away from nitric acid; violent reactions might occur if they come in contact with each other.

Acetone bought in pharmacies in many countries often contains varying amounts of water. Such acetone is not suitable for use with consolidants because the water will cause the consolidant film to turn milky white. Try to obtain as pure a grade as possible for use with consolidants. Any water present can be removed by using small pellets called molecular sieves. (See the section on molecular sieves below.)

ALCOHOL: Commonly used to mean "ethanol," alcohol properly refers to a large group of chemical compounds. For the purposes of this book, either ethanol (ethyl alcohol) or isopropanol (isopropyl or rubbing alcohol) can be used. Both can be readily obtained in a local pharmacy.

Both alcohols are colorless, highly flammable liquids that can damage the eyes. Inhalation of high concentrations of vapor or ingestion can result in headache, dizziness, drowsiness, and damage to the central nervous system.

To prevent human consumption, alcohol bought in many countries is often colored pink or purple to indicate the presence of various additives. This coloring agent can be removed by filtering the alcohol through powdered charcoal, although for the purposes of this book, this step is not necessary. (Filtering will not render the alcohol suitable for consumption.)

In the field, alcohol is used to clean and soften lumps of dirt when water cannot be used. It should not be used on moisture-sensitive materials such as ivory, wood, or leather because it may cause excessive drying, resulting in warping and cracking.

TOLUENE: A colorless, flammable liquid, toluene (toluol) has a characteristic odor. Inhaling the vapor can cause dizziness, headache, nausea, and mental confusion. If it contains benzene as an impurity, vapor inhalation over long periods may lead to leukemia. Both liquid and vapor will irritate the eyes and mucous membranes; inhalation of vapor can damage the liver, kidneys, and central nervous system. Prolonged skin contact may result in dermatitis; absorption through the skin and ingestion can cause poisoning.

Toluene, a solvent for acrylic resins and cellulose nitrate adhesives, is useful in field conservation because it is less volatile than acetone. It makes a good alternate solvent for consolidants, especially in hot, arid climates. Because toluene is not miscible with water, the problem of contamination with water does not arise.

AMMONIA: A colorless liquid with a strong, pungent odor, ammonia is used only as a solvent for rubber latex. It is generally bought as a 33% solution in water. In a more dilute form, it is commonly available as a household cleaner, usually containing some detergent with the water. Both strengths of ammonia can be used for the purposes mentioned in this book.

Ammonia causes severe burns to the skin and eyes while its vapor irritates all parts of the respiratory system. If ingested, ammonia can cause severe internal damage.

In warm weather, a strong solution of ammonia will cause pressure to develop inside its container, and so the cap must be released with care.

Consolidants

A consolidant is a resin in a liquid solution that is applied to a soft, friable material or object to strengthen it. Consolidants used in conservation are available in two main forms: as the pure resin or as an emulsion. The pure resin generally comes as pellets which are dissolved in a solvent. Emulsions are formed by suspending a resin/solvent solution in water, resulting in a liquid with a characteristic milky white color. Before an emulsion dries, it is soluble in water. Once it has fully dried, however, it is only soluble in the solvent in which the resin is soluble. For example, brushes containing liquid polyvinyl acetate (PVA) emulsion can be cleaned with water. If the PVA emulsion is allowed to dry on the brush, it can only be cleaned with acetone or toluene.

In general, emulsions are used to consolidate damp material, whereas pure resins can only be used on thoroughly dry material.

Caution should be taken with the use of emulsions. All emulsions have a tendency over time to change chemically, or cross-link, which renders them less readily soluble. This condition is caused by, among other things, the presence of additives necessary for keeping the resin in suspension. If extensive cross-linkage takes place, the resin will become insoluble. Many emulsions will also turn yellow upon exposure to sunlight.

ACRYLOID B72: Known as Paraloid B72 in Britain, Acryloid B72 is an acrylic resin that is a good, all-purpose consolidant. It is a colorless, durable, stable resin that achieves good penetration and, when applied properly, should not appreciably alter the appearance of the material to which it has been applied. It is soluble in acetone and toluene and is readily reversible.

Acrylic resins are available in emulsion form as well. In the United States, Rhoplex AC33, and in Britain, Primal AC33, are recommended. In both countries, the resin involved is very similar to, but not exactly the same as, Acryloid B72. They are both soluble in acetone and toluene, but, as with all emulsions, may become insoluble over time.

Colloidal dispersions are similar to emulsions in appearance. They are also acrylic resins dispersed in water, but the particle size is smaller than in an emulsion. Acrysol WS24 in the United States and Primal WS24 in Britain are very similar to, but not exactly the same as, Acryloid B72. They are durable and readily soluble in acetone and toluene, but sometimes have less tack, or stickiness, than the emulsions.

POLYVINYL ACETATE (PVA): Widely used in field conservation, polyvinyl acetate (PVA) has generally been supplanted by Acryloid B72, which is harder, stronger, and less flexible, and which usually achieves better penetration. PVA is soluble in alcohol and acetone. A major drawback to PVA is that it softens when hot and then tends to flow; so, it can be difficult to use in a hot climate. PVA forms a more flexible film than Acryloid B72, which can be a disadvantage if a rigid support is needed to lift an object. It can be advantageous, however, when treating flexible organic materials.

PVA, in both the resin and emulsion form, is available under a wide variety of trade names and grades, all of which are different and have different properties. Not all PVA is suitable for conservation purposes. In the United States, Union Carbide's AYAF is a good, general purpose PVA, and CM Bond M3 is a good PVA emulsion. In Britain and Europe, Mowilith 50 and the emulsion Mowilith DMC2 are recommended. In Britain, Vinamul 6815 can also be used, although it has a tendency to turn yellow over time.

ELVACITE 2013: An acrylic resin that is soluble in acetone and toluene but not in alcohol, Elvacite 2013 is used to consolidate the surfaces of wall paintings when PVA emulsion will be used as the facing adhesive before removing the painting from the wall.

POLYSTYRENE: Polystyrene's only use in field conservation is as a surface coating for bone when the bone is being removed from a calcareous matrix.

Adhesives

The temptation with adhesives, probably more than with any other material used in field conservation, is to rely on whatever is available locally. It is dangerous to use many proprietary adhesives because they contain plasticizers and stabilizers intended to extend its range of properties and shelf life. These additives can prove harmful not only to the material adhered but also to the long-term life of the adhesive itself. White glues are not suitable for field use because, as emulsions, they are subject to cross-linkage.

POLYVINYL ACETATE: Readily available in the resin form, known around the world under the trade name UHU, polyvinyl acetate (PVA) is a good, all-purpose adhesive that sets quickly and is soluble in acetone and toluene. It is packaged in easy-to-use small yellow tubes. In the United States, Union Carbide's AYAF can be used as an adhesive when in a very viscous solution with toluene or acetone. Made up this way, PVA can be difficult to apply neatly to the surfaces to be joined. A polyethylene squeeze bottle can be used to more easily apply the adhesive. Make very sure, however, that the bottle is made of polyethylene and not some other plastic that might be soluble in the solvent used with the PVA.

The major disadvantage of PVA as an adhesive is its tendency to soften when it becomes hot. It is not a suitable adhesive for use in very hot climates because joins made with it will sag and creep unless storage conditions can be kept quite cool.

CELLULOSE NITRATE: A good all-purpose, quick-setting adhesive that is soluble in acetone, cellulose nitrate usually comes in easy-to-use small tubes. It forms a harder film than PVA and, since it does not have a tendency to flow when hot, is suitable for use in hot climates. It does have a tendency, however, to dry out over time and become brittle. It is also highly flammable. It is available in the United States as Duco Cement, in Britain under the trade names HMG and Durofix, and in Europe as UHU Hart. UHU Hart comes in a blue tube and should not be confused with UHU in the yellow tube, which is PVA.

ACRYLOID B72: Listed under consolidants, Acryloid B72 is also a good all-purpose adhesive. It forms a clear, stable film more rigid than PVA. It cannot be purchased ready for use as an adhesive and must be made up individually.

Dissolve the resin solids in acetone or ethanol to make a 50% solution. Add approximately 1 level teaspoon of fumed silica for every 100 ml of solution. The fumed silica improves control of the flow of the adhesive. Once the resin is completely dissolved, remove the lid from the container to allow some of the solvent to evaporate. When the solution is quite viscous, roughly one half its original weight, cover the container. The adhesive can then be used out of the container with a brush, or it can be poured into aluminum tubes with nasal tips and solvent-proof caps.

Lifting Materials

PLASTER OF PARIS: Calcined gypsum in a white powdery form, plaster of Paris is almost universally available and is cheap and easy to use. It forms a rigid support for fragile objects, but if used in too large a section must be reinforced with bandage or thin rods to prevent it from cracking. Its major disadvantages are that it is heavy, and therefore requires mechanical means to remove it, and that it generates a considerable amount of heat as it sets, and therefore cannot be used on heat-sensitive materials. Plaster should never come in direct contact with an object; a separating layer of aluminum foil, plastic cling film, or cloth should be used under it at all times.

PLASTER BANDAGE: Ordinary gauze bandage impregnated with dry plaster of Paris, plaster bandage can be obtained from pharmacies and medical supply houses and is available in a variety of widths. Although expensive, it is extremely helpful for lifting objects because it is quick and easy to use and is much less messy than making your own material with plaster of Paris and bandage.

GAUZE BANDAGE: Used to wrap an object to give it support once it is out of the ground, gauze bandage is also used in conjunction with plaster of Paris or consolidants to reinforce fragile objects prior to lifting them from the ground. It is readily available at pharmacies in most countries and also from medical supply houses. Having a variety of different widths on hand is useful.

POLYURETHANE FOAM: Polyurethane foam comes as two liquid components that, when mixed together, produce a foam. When cured, the foam is hard, providing a rigid, lightweight encasing material. Although it is not reversible, it can be cut down and removed easily as long as a separating layer of aluminum foil or plastic cling film is used between it and the object.

Polyurethane foam is a dangerous material and should be used only when absolutely necessary, preferably when a person experienced in its use is present. It generates a considerable amount of heat and gives off toxic fumes as it cures. Exposure to these fumes can cause conjunctivitis, and inhalation can cause a tightening of the chest and difficulty in breathing which may not occur immediately. Inhalation can also cause severe lung problems, such as asthmatic attacks and chronic bronchitis. One can also become permanently sensitized to further small doses of the fumes. Avoid skin contact with both the uncured components and the partially cured foam.

Stringent safety precautions must be observed when using polyurethane foam. It should only be used in a well-ventilated area, preferably outside, while protective clothing, including impermeable rubber gloves and goggles, is worn. Unfortunately, there are no air-purifying respirators effective against polyurethane foam vapors. Although the toxic vapors cease to be produced once the foam is cured, they will still be present within the cavities of the foam. Subsequent cutting or trimming of the cured foam will release them. The rigid cured foam should never be openly heated, burned, or cut with a hot wire, and should be stored away from sources of ignition.

ANIMAL GLUE: A general term for hide glue, extracted bone glue, and green bone glue, animal glue is the traditional adhesive for facing wall paintings and mosaics prior to removing them from their wall support or mortar. It is soluble in warm water, is applied hot, and bonds upon cooling. Animal glue shrinks considerably when it dries; so, it is only suitable as a facing adhesive when lifting wall paintings or mosaics.

FACINGS: Facings for the removal of wall paintings and mosaics are available from fabric shops. For wall paintings, two kinds of facings are needed: one of a fine muslin with a tight weave and the other of a heavier fabric such as linen scrim, hessian, or canvas. For mosaics, the sectional method requires only one facing of a fine cotton, gauze, or linen. The fabric should be strong, but thin enough to enable one to see the mosaic design through it. The rolling method requires several facings depending on the size of the mosaic and the tesserae. If the mosaic is small, the innermost facing should have a loose weave, such as gauze or veterinary bandage, to enable it to be worked into the cracks between the tesserae. The second facing should be of a tighter, stronger weave, such as thin cotton or linen. For large mosaics or mosaics with big tesserae, two or more thin facings followed by at least two thicker facings may be necessary.

Before they are used, all facing materials should be carefully washed to remove any dressings on them. More detailed information on the preparation of the facing material can be found in the sections in chapter 5 regarding wall paintings and mosaics.

PLASTIC NETTING: Plastic netting or *nylon tulle* is used to backfill a mosaic or wall painting. If netting is used, a very tight mesh of approximately 0.5 mm is necessary. Since organic materials will rot in the ground, the netting must be made of plastic. Such netting or tulle can be obtained from some fabric stores and from plastic suppliers.

PAINT SPRAYERS: Paint sprayers can be used to spray a consolidant on wall paintings prior to lifting them. An expensive electrical sprayer is good but not necessary. Small sprayers operated with detachable power packs are available from conservation suppliers and art stores and are ideal for field conditions. It is wise to have a supply of power packs and extra jars on hand.

Molding Materials

DENTAL PLASTER: A fine quality plaster that produces especially fine, detailed casts for items such as gemstone seals and coins, dental plaster is available from dental and medical supply houses, but perhaps not in the small quantities available from conservation suppliers. Plaster of Paris can be used for most other casts.

MODELING CLAY: Modeling clay is available under a variety of trade names. Klean Klay in the United States and Plasticine in Britain and Europe are recommended for field purposes. Since they both contain oils, they should never be placed in direct contact with an object for more than a few minutes. Plasticine is available from some art and toy stores as well as from conservation suppliers. Klean Klay is available from the manufacturer. Substitutes for these products can be used as long as they are fine grained and not too oily.

These modeling clays tend to dry out slowly, especially in hot climates, becoming stiff and difficult to use; so, store in a sealed plastic bag when not in use.

MODELING COMPOUNDS: Modeling compounds that can be hardened are available under a variety of trade names. These claylike compounds harden when heated in an oven. Because they are fine grained and shrink little upon curing, they are useful for taking impressions of seals, incised gemstones, and cylinder seals. After curing, they can be easily handled without harming the impression. In the US, Sculpy Modeling Compound is available from art and sculpture supply houses; in Britain, Fimo Modeling is available from conservation suppliers.

RUBBER LATEX: A suspension of natural isoprene in ammonia containing about 35% rubber solids, rubber latex is useful for making impressions and squeezes, although it shrinks considerably as it dries and can pull off bits of the surface being molded if the surface is friable. Latex is available from art and sculpture supply houses and conservation suppliers under a variety of trade names. Latex squeezes and impressions are susceptible to deterioration from atmospheric pollutants; so, obtain as pure a grade of rubber as possible. Latex squeezes should be stored away from light.

TALCUM POWDER: Talcum powder is used as a separating agent when taking an impression. It is readily available at pharmacies all over the world.

SOAP/DETERGENT: Liquid soap or detergent is used as a separating agent when making a cast of a coin or taking a plaster impression on a potsherd. It is readily available in most stores as dishwashing liquid.

PAPER: Paper suitable for taking squeezes, or impressions, can generally be found in most countries. Large sheets of blotting paper work satisfactorily, but most epigraphers favor some form of filter paper. Chromatography paper and the filter paper used in making beer are especially good. They can be obtained from scientific supply houses, some stationers, and brewery supply firms.

BRUSHES: A brush with densely packed bristles is needed to make a paper squeeze. It is helpful if the brush has a long, sturdy handle to facilitate the beating process. An adequate brush should be found in any store carrying a wide variety of brushes.

Packing Materials

POLYETHYLENE BAGS: Polyethylene bags of varying size and thickness are generally available throughout the world. Self-sealing (also called ziplock or mini-grip) bags are extremely useful for the packing of samples and small objects. Make sure that the bags are made of polyethylene. Many less-expensive bags are made of polyvinyl chloride (PVC), which gives off hydrochloric acid in the presence of moisture. PVC has the very distinct odor associated with all vinyl materials, one that polyethylene does not have. Polyethylene bags are available from plastic and conservation suppliers.

POLYSTYRENE BOXES: Polystyrene boxes with hinged lids are excellent for the storage of delicate objects. These boxes may be obtained in a variety of sizes from plastic suppliers. Although more expensive than polyethylene bags, they are recommended, especially for fragile objects, because they are rigid and sturdy. They can also be stacked one on top of the other.

PLASTIC FOOD CONTAINERS: Plastic food containers with snap-on lids are useful for packing waterlogged material that must be kept wet or material that must be kept dry with silica gel. They are not readily available throughout the world and may need to be brought with the excavation team. In the United States and Europe, they are available in most supermarkets and hardware stores.

MASON JARS: Mason jars with rubber seals are ideal for storing unstable metal objects requiring a very dry environment. When used in conjunction with silica gel, a very dry environment can be maintained for a long time. If a jar has been in use for a long time, check to make sure that the rubber seal is still good. Replace the seal when necessary or a good seal will not be achieved. Mason jars are available in most hardware stores. A supply of rubber seals should be kept on hand.

POLYETHYLENE FOAM: Polyethylene foam is a good, inert packing material that can be used for both wet and dry material. It is also a good packing material for transporting objects since it is a good shock absorber. It is available from plastic suppliers in a variety of thicknesses. For packing purposes, it is most useful in sheet form, approximately 3 mm to 6 mm thick. Ethafoam, manufactured by Dow Chemical, is recommended.

POLYURETHANE FOAM: Polyurethane foam is used to pack waterlogged materials. Unlike polyethylene foam, it has an open-cell structure that enables it to act like a sponge and hold water. Gray polyurethane foam is recommended over the white form. It is sometimes referred to as gray padding foam and is available from plastic suppliers.

ACID-FREE TISSUE: Acid-free tissue is used to cushion and pack objects, especially those made of metal and organic materials. It is recommended over newspaper, facial tissue, and toilet paper because it contains no harmful acids. As well as being available from conservation suppliers, it can usually be ordered from a good stationer.

PAPER ENVELOPES AND BAGS: Paper envelopes and bags are recommended for the packing of carbonized material because they will allow samples to dry out. Small pottery and stone objects can be stored in them as well. They should not be used, however, for storing metals, glass, or organic materials because the acid in them can harm these materials. They can be used as temporary packing to take an object from the site to the dig house. Envelopes can be bought at stationers, and paper bags can be bought at most supermarkets and hardware stores.

LAYFLAT POLYETHYLENE TUBING: Layflat polyethylene tubing can be used in conjunction with a heat sealer to make polyethylene bags of varying sizes and shapes. Such tubing is useful for packing large amounts of wet or waterlogged material of varying shapes. The tubing is clear, seamless, and comes in several different thicknesses and widths. After cutting the tubing to the desired length, seal the ends with the heat sealer to make a tight bag. Layflat tubing is available from plastic or industrial suppliers.

HEAT SEALER: A heat sealer is used to seal layflat tubing to form polyethylene bags. Several different kinds of sealers are available, depending on your needs. A simple, portable type is best because it is lightweight and can be taken into the field as long as there is a source of electricity. Since sealers are made for different kinds of plastic, be sure to obtain one for use with polyethylene. Heat sealers are available from industrial suppliers.

SILICA GEL: A pure, amorphous, chemically inert material, silica gel is a desiccant (drying agent) used to pack and store moisture-sensitive materials. Its ability to absorb moisture results from the millions of tiny pores on each crystal. Although available in two forms, the self-indicating (or blue) crystals are best for field conservation. These crystals slowly change in color from blue to pink as they absorb moisture. Silica gel must be checked periodically. When it is fully saturated and pink, it must be regenerated by being heated in an oven until it becomes blue again. Silica gel is effective only when used in a sealed, airtight container. If only small amounts of the self-indicating form are available, a little of it can be added to the regular grade to act as an indicator.

To regenerate either grade of silica gel, spread it out in a large metal or enamel tray. Heat it in an oven at 150° C (300° F) for approximately three hours. Stir it frequently to make sure that all the crystals have dried out. (The inhalation of silica gel dust can cause damage to the lungs.)

Silica gel is available in brick form measuring approximately 15 x 15 x 1 cm. Each brick consists of an acrylic grid filled with silica gel covered on both sides with Gore-Tex. The brick can be used as is or cut down with a saw to fit into smaller containers. To recondition the brick, heat it in an oven at 90° C (194° F). These bricks are available from the manufacturer, Gore and Associates. (See appendix III.)

STORAGE TINS: Metal cookie or cake tins are useful for storing metal objects requiring a dry environment. When used with silica gel, a very dry environment can be achieved for quite a long time. These tins are available in many supermarkets, hardware, and department stores.

FUNGICIDES: Fungicides should be added to any material packed damp or wet. By their very nature, fungicides are toxic and should be handled with extreme care. In general, they can irritate the skin, eyes, and upper respiratory system and can affect the central nervous system, the circulatory system, and the liver and kidneys. Neoprene or butyl rubber gloves should be worn when handling fungicides, and all containers should be thoroughly washed after use. Avoid contact with the skin, and wash hands thoroughly after handling fungicides.

Sodium orthophenyl phenate, available as Dowicide A, is suitable for use with wet wood, basketry, bone, ivory, and textiles. It is soluble in water and should be used in a 0.2% solution. It is not suitable for use with wet leather because it is too alkaline. Panacide, also called Dichlorophen, can be used for wood and basketry, although only the disodium salt should be used.

Orthophenyl phenol, available as Topane WS and Dowicide 1, is suitable for use with all materials, especially wet leather. A solid at room temperature, it is soluble in alcohol and organic solvents and should be used in a 0.2%

solution. For use with water, dissolve it first in a small amount of alcohol and then add it to the water. Nonfoaming Lysol spray, available in most supermarkets in the United States, is a dilute solution of orthophenyl phenol in alcohol that is suitable for short-term use when storing wet material. Orthophenyl phenol is not absorbed through the skin and is not a skin irritant. It can irritate the eyes, however, and inhalation of the powder can lead to upper respiratory irritation. Chronic exposure can cause kidney damage.

Fungicides available on the market and the laws governing their sale and use are changing constantly. If in doubt about the suitability of a fungicide, consult a conservator.

VERMICULITE: Vermiculite is an alteration product of biotite and other micas used as heating insulation and as a medium for starting plant seeds and cuttings. In field conservation, it is used for backfilling a mosaic or wall painting and is available in bulk from florists and garden suppliers. It is also good for packing chemicals for transport and for mopping up spilled chemicals. Vermiculite can contain asbestos; so, be careful when buying it.

Water

Water used to clean objects should be as pure as possible. Distilled water is preferred for conservation use and, if available, should be used at all times. In most countries, it is usually available at pharmacies and supermarkets, although not in large quantities. It can also be obtained at garages, but there is always the danger of contamination with sulfuric acid. Contamination can be tested easily by using pH indicator strips. Distilled water left standing has a pH of about 5.5; if a lower reading is obtained, the water is contaminated and should not be used.

If the local water is relatively pure, it can be used without worry. In many places—the Middle East, for example—the local water can be extremely saline. If large numbers of potsherds are to be cleaned in these areas, use the local water but, if possible, soak them in at least one bath of distilled water before drying them.

Various kinds of water-purifying apparatus are available, but they are expensive and can be cumbersome to use in the field, especially when facilities are limited. They are generally not worth the trouble unless the local water is extremely salty, large quantities of material need washing, and the excavation will be of long duration. If there are any questions about the water and its suitability for use, consult a trained conservator.

Tools

SCALPELS: Scalpels are useful for cleaning dirt and encrustations off objects. The most useful handle size is number 3, for which a wide variety of blade sizes and shapes is available. The most useful blade sizes are numbers 10 and 15. Blades and handles are available from medical and dental supply houses and conservation suppliers.

SHARPENING STONES: Hard Arkansas sharpening stones, made from the siliceous fine-grained rock novaculite, can noticeably extend the life of scalpel blades. Before using to sharpen the blade, lubricate the stone with a little all-purpose oil.

DENTAL TOOLS: Dental tools come in all sizes and shapes and can be very useful in lifting and cleaning objects. They are available from dental supply houses but are very expensive. Dentists will, however, frequently donate old tools that are no longer useful. A variety of similar tools can be obtained from sculpture and art suppliers.

BRUSHES: Brushes are always in demand on a site, and it is useful to have a wide variety of sizes and shapes on hand. Toothbrushes are good for cleaning robust objects and are readily available throughout the world at pharmacies and supermarkets. Paintbrushes, as well, are generally readily available. When 2 cm to 5 cm wide, they are especially good for cleaning objects still in the ground and for removing dirt from around them. A variety of small artist's paint brushes should also be on hand for use with consolidants. Very fine artist's brushes should be available if tablets, cylinder seals, or other delicate objects are likely to be found.

If only a limited supply of artists' brushes is available, considerable variety in size and shape can be achieved by partially or completely cutting off some of the bristles (fig. 3.1). For example, if a small but stiff brush is needed, the bristles can be cut off straight across; the shorter the bristles are cut, the stiffer the brush will be. If a very fine brush is needed, all but a few of the bristles can be removed.

It is important to remember that any brush to be used with solvents must have natural hair bristles. Most synthetic, plastic bristles will dissolve in solvents. Brushes to be used with acids, however, should have plastic bristles since the acid will attack natural hair as well as the metal ferrule holding the bristles in place.

Safety Equipment

Gloves should be worn when handling many chemicals, but it is important to note that gloves, in themselves, can pose serious safety hazards if a chemical gets inside. Instead of protecting the skin, the glove will keep the chemical in close contact with the skin, allowing for greater absorption through the skin. It is important to check gloves frequently for leakage and to change them if leakage is suspected. It is wise

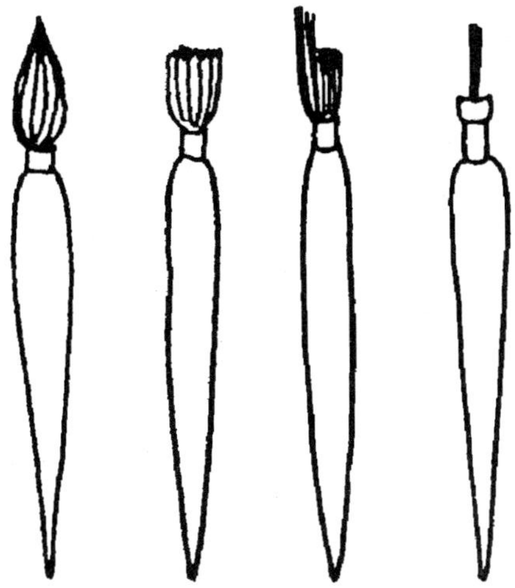

FIGURE 3.1 Three possible ways to alter brushes

to wear two gloves, one inside the other, if prolonged use of chemicals is necessary. Gloves should never be too large because they can make the wearer clumsy and more likely to cause an accident.

Gloves are made from a variety of different materials especially suited to resist particular solvents or chemicals. Before buying gloves, check to make sure they will be resistant to the chemicals that will be used. Disposable gloves can be obtained from conservation suppliers.

RUBBER GLOVES: Neoprene or butyl rubber gloves should always be worn when handling acids, solvents, and polyurethane foam. Unfortunately, they are not available in many countries and must be brought with the excavation team. They are available at stores dealing with protective apparel, chemical supply houses, and conservation suppliers. It is always a good idea to bring a fresh supply of gloves each season, especially in hot countries, because heat can cause the gloves to disintegrate over time.

VINYL GLOVES: Vinyl or copolymer disposable gloves should be worn to prevent the contamination of radiocarbon samples. Although resistant to many chemicals, vinyl gloves do not afford sufficient protection against acids and polyurethane foam.

DUST MASKS: NIOSH-approved dust masks are lightweight, disposable masks that filter out dust, powders, and sprayed paint particles. The mask will not filter out chemical fumes. Martindale masks, while slightly less effective, are also available. These masks hold a thick gauze filter over the nose and mouth to prevent the inhalation of dust and particulate matter. Refills should be kept on hand to replace those filters that have become filled with dust. Dust or filter masks should be worn when doing any job that produces large quantities of dust.

RESPIRATORS: A dual cartridge respirator should be worn when handling large quantities of solvents. The cartridges are made for use with specific chemicals (organic solvents, for example). Be sure to indicate which chemicals will be used when buying the cartridges. For the purposes of this book, the two cartridges needed would be for all acid gases (except nitric) and organic vapor. The respirator and cartridges are not available everywhere and may need to be brought in by the excavation team.

GOGGLES: Goggles for protection against chemical splash can be obtained in most countries and are available from conservation suppliers. Goggles should always be used when handling acids, caustics, or solvents and when involved in dust-producing jobs.

ACID/SOLVENT CARRIERS: Acid/solvent carriers, also called *safe packs*, are polyethylene containers designed especially for transporting acids and other dangerous chemicals. They should always be used when transporting dangerous liquids, especially if the liquids are in glass containers. Carriers can be obtained from chemical supply houses.

PLASTIC-COATED GLASS CONTAINERS: Plastic-coated glass containers are now available from most chemical supply houses and are ideal for the storage and transportation of chemicals. Even if the glass is shattered, the plastic coating will continue to hold the contents until the container can be replaced.

SPILL KITS: Spill kits are designed to clean up spillages of specific kinds of chemicals, such as solvents immiscible in water. If large quantities of chemicals are used, the appropriate spill kit, available from chemical supply houses, should be on hand.

Miscellaneous

MOLECULAR SIEVES: Molecular sieves are synthetic crystals used for drying, purifying, and separating liquids. They are available from chemical supply houses as powder, beads, or pellets in which the crystals are held together by an inert clay binder. They are porous, consisting of a network of tiny internal cavities interconnected by openings of a fixed diameter. The sieves work by allowing the desired molecules (those of water, for example) to enter the pores where they are trapped; larger molecules are excluded. In this way, water is removed from the liquid. After having been used to remove water, the pellets can be regenerated by being heated in an oven or by being spread out in the sun to dry in a hot, dry climate.

Molecular sieves are available in a wide range of pore sizes. For our purposes, the sieves should be able to adsorb molecules with critical diameters up to 3Å. Pellets are the easiest form to use on an excavation. Because molecular sieves are powerful desiccants, gloves should be worn when handling them. Care should be taken not to inhale any dust from the sieves or their container.

WOODEN TONGUE DEPRESSORS: Useful for removing dirt around objects prior to lifting them out of the ground, wooden tongue depressors can also be used for other purposes such as stirring solutions of consolidants and rubber latex. They are readily available from pharmacies and medical supply houses.

WOODEN TOOTHPICKS: Wooden toothpicks can be used with cotton wool to make swabs for delicate cleaning work. The advantage to making your own swabs is that you can vary their size and shape; ready-made swabs come in only one shape. Rounded toothpicks are stronger and more suitable than flat ones. They are readily obtained from supermarkets and pharmacies. Do not use plastic toothpicks because solvents will dissolve them.

COTTON WOOL: Used for making cotton swabs, cotton wool is readily available all over the world. Be sure, however, that it is indeed cotton and not a synthetic equivalent which will dissolve in solvents. The cotton need not be sterile.

COTTON SWABS: Used for delicate cleaning work, cotton swabs are readily available from pharmacies, but make sure they are not made of plastic or synthetic fibers. Frequently, the stem is plastic as well and will be dissolved by solvents. It is cheaper and sometimes better to make your own swabs with wooden toothpicks and cotton. See the above paragraphs concerning wooden toothpicks and cotton wool.

PLASTIC WRAP: Plastic wrap or cling film serves as a separator when using plaster of Paris or polyurethane foam for lifting objects out of the ground. It is available from most grocery, variety, and hardware stores.

ALUMINUM FOIL: Used as a separator when using plaster of Paris and polyurethane foam to lift objects out of the ground and for packing radiocarbon samples, aluminum foil is available from supermarkets and hardware stores.

CLEAR NAIL POLISH: Clear nail polish can be used as a substitute for Acryloid B72 when marking objects. If the objects to be marked are very dark in color, it may be easier to read the number if white nail polish is used. Nail polish is available at pharmacies, markets, and department stores.

INDIA INK: India ink is used to mark objects. If black ink will not show up on a dark-colored object, white ink can be used instead. Neither should be applied directly to the surface of the object, but rather on- to a patch of lacquer painted onto the object. India ink is readily available at stationers and art supply stores.

SPUN-BONDED POLYETHYLENE LABELS: These labels are recommended for labeling and packing any waterlogged material because they will not disintegrate in water. They can be obtained from plastic suppliers and garden supply stores.

FELT-TIPPED INDELIBLE MARKERS: Used to mark all labels, markers should be fade-proof and waterproof. They can be obtained at stationers and conservation suppliers.

MASKING TAPE: Masking tape can be used to hold the joins of an object together, especially pottery joins, while the adhesive sets. While a helpful aid, tape should never be left on longer than absolutely necessary because it can leave an indelible stain. Masking tape comes in a variety of widths and is available all over the world.

HAND LENS: A hand lens or magnifying glass can be useful in examining the surface of an object. These items can be obtained fairly inexpensively from conservation suppliers, stationers, or optical supply houses.

BULB SYRINGES: Bulb syringes or blowers can be useful for blowing dust off objects either in situ or after they have been removed from the ground. They can be found at photographic supply stores but may not be available in some countries.

HUMIDITY INDICATOR CARDS: Humidity indicator cards provide an inexpensive and readily portable means of monitoring approximate relative humidity levels in storage areas. The cards are small enough that they can be placed inside sealed storage containers.

PLASTIC BUCKETS: When using acid to remove insoluble salts from potter, use plastic buckets. They are useful for all kinds of conservation jobs, and a good supply should be on hand. They are readily available in markets all over the world in a variety of sizes and shapes.

Chapter Four

General Treatment Techniques

SEVERAL FIELD CONSERVATION procedures are used for all materials: record keeping, handling, lifting, consolidating, cleaning, marking, joining, packing, storing, and transporting. While the supplies used may vary slightly from material to material, the basic principles and procedures remain the same and are set out here in detail. Any modification of a procedure necessary for a specific material will be dealt with under the appropriate entry in chapter 5.

Record Keeping

When any conservation treatment is undertaken, whether in the field or in the laboratory, it is imperative to make detailed and accurate records of everything done to the object. To the archaeologist, the treatment applied may seem obvious, but it may not be so to the conservator in the laboratory who will eventually work on the object. Considerable time and effort on the part of the conservator, not to mention possible damage to the object, can be avoided if proper records are made in the field.

Treatment reports need not be long or elaborate. Depending on the object and treatment, several lines or half a page in a notebook can be sufficient as long as all relevant information is provided. A treatment report should include a brief but clear description of the object, the material(s) of which it is made, and the condition in which it was found. Any weak areas, cracks, and the like that might not be readily visible should be indicated. It is always helpful to include sketches and, if possible, photographs to indicate these weak areas and the position of cracks.

Clearly record what was done to the object, how it was done, and under what conditions. State what specific materials were used, including the full trade name and grade, and the solvents used and in what concentrations. Even when the relevance of information may seem questionable, include it because it is always best to err on the side of too much information. Samples of typical treatment reports are shown in figure 4.1.

Make sure that these records accompany the treated objects and that the conservator is given all relevant treatment information. This same information should also be incorporated in the excavation's cataloging or archival system so that there will be a permanent treatment record.

Handling

All excavated materials have suffered some degree of deterioration which has weakened them in one way or another. Important structural components may have been partially or completely leached out or, if still present, may have been rendered unsound through desiccation, corrosion, or attack by biological, chemical, or physical agents. No matter what the cause, the important point is that archaeological material is generally in a fragile and weakened condition. It should be handled, therefore, with the utmost care at all times.

As a general rule, always assume that every excavated object is extremely fragile. The condition of an object is not necessarily readily apparent. Some objects may appear quite robust and strong but can actually be riddled with cracks and fissures hidden by dirt and/or corrosion. Microscopic cracks, although they are not visible to the naked eye, render some objects extremely brittle and fragile. It is always better, therefore, to err on the side of being overly cautious.

All objects should be subject to a bare minimum of handling, not only when they come out of the ground but also during cleaning, processing, studying, and packing. By placing objects carefully in rigid containers prior to studying and processing, much unnecessary handling can be avoided. Only authorized staff should be allowed to handle objects. If certain objects must be available for showing to

C 1279

Ceramic sherd, low fire with painted dec. edges very soft, paint flaking badly, lots of fine cracks.

Consolidated in situ with 5% Acryloid B72.

C. 1285

Large fragment of painted jar, smashed and broken into many small pieces.

Backed entire fragment with gauze bandage and Vinamul 6815 (PVA emulsion) undiluted. Lifted as one piece.

B. 356

Bronze dagger with bone/ivory handle, 20 cm long. Handle badly fragmented and detaching from blade. Blade badly corroded; cracked in 4 pieces - see sketch.

Lifted in block using a wooden frame and plaster. Dagger isolated with 2 layers of plastic film, 1 layer foil.

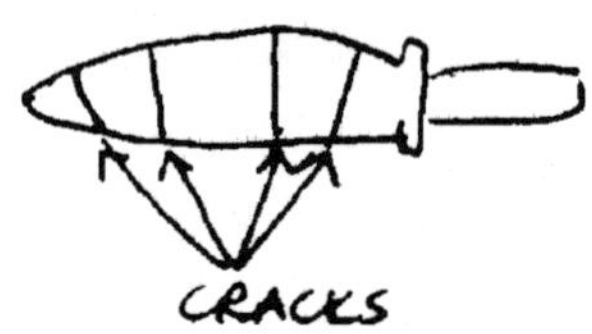

In lifting, the wooden frame cracked, so reinforced it by wrapping with bandage.

P62 1984 T 4 Room B

Fragment of fallen wall plaster 15 x 25 cm. Found in association with P 63-9. Found face up; three colors visible. red, blue, black. Red paint extremely fugitive. Surface badly cracked and soft (see photo. Roll 4. frames 10 – 18.)

Faced with gauze bandage and CM Bond M3 (PVA emulsion) undiluted.

FIGURE 4.1 Examples of treatment records

visitors, pack them carefully in well-padded, rigid containers so that they can be viewed easily without being picked up or touched. Always insist that visitors and staff look with their eyes, not their fingers.

Although handling is mostly a matter of common sense, the following points should be observed when handling is absolutely necessary. Always pick up an object lightly, but firmly. Too tight a grip can snap objects; too loose a grip can allow them to fall out of your hands. If the object is small and light, pick it up in one hand while cradling or supporting it in the other. If it is large and heavy, grasp it firmly in both hands, being careful not to damage it by using too much pressure on vulnerable areas.

As a general rule, pick up objects at the thickest, strongest part in such a way as to distribute the weight of the object evenly. Never pick up pottery or metal vessels by their handles; rather, place both hands on the lower half of the body and lift. Always keep one hand underneath the vessel when holding and turning it. Do not pick up vessels by the rim or any object by only the outer edges. The rim or edge may not be able to bear the weight of the entire object and can snap off in your fingers. If the vessel or object is being held when this happens, it will fall and possibly break. The same principle holds true for long, thin objects. Metal or bone pins, for example, should be picked up in the middle not by one end.

When handling objects, always hold them over a table or soft surface, such as your lap, and try to keep the distance between the object and the table to a minimum. Not only have objects been broken by being dropped long distances onto a hard floor, but the broken fragments have been lost as they shattered or bounced into dark or inaccessible corners. If you must examine an object closely, it is best to keep it close to the tabletop and bring your eyes down to the object.

Do not try on rings, bracelets, or other pieces of jewelry, especially those made of silver. The pressure necessary to get them on and off can easily cause them to crack or break.

Avoid bending flexible materials such as textiles, fibers, and metals. Repeated flexing, even if done inadvertently, can result in irreparable breakage. For this reason, these materials should be handled as little as possible. To facilitate handling, place them on a sheet of acid-free tissue or polyethylene foam so that they can be picked up and moved without being handled.

When putting an object down, always place it securely on a table or shelf and do not remove your hands until you are sure that the object is securely positioned. This process is especially necessary for tall, unwieldy objects or pots with rounded bottoms or very small bases. If an object is extremely unstable when set down upright, lay it on its side, using crumpled tissue paper or foam to hold it securely in place. It can also be placed in a cardboard box or other rigid container that will hold it securely. Never leave objects close to the edge of a table or shelf where they can easily be swept off onto the floor.

Unnecessary breakage can be avoided if the activity in a room where objects are out in the open is kept to a minimum. The workroom should not be a major thoroughfare, nor should it be a general common room for the excavation staff. People carrying large, unwieldy objects such as shovels, stadia rods, or ranging poles can inadvertently knock over objects. Boisterous play can be equally dangerous and should not be permitted in the workroom.

Lifting

Lifting refers to the process of removing objects from the ground. Generally, this is a straightforward process requiring the use of only common sense and patience. Sometimes, however, objects are too fragile and weak to be picked up unaided. These objects require the help of strengthening materials that either render the object rigid or encase it. The choice of a lifting method depends on the strength, size, weight, composition, and condition of the object to be lifted as well as on the soil conditions.

Do not lift an object before examining it carefully to ascertain its surface condition. Make sure there is no paint layer or applied decoration that has already become or will become detached from the object when it is lifted. It is also wise to photograph and/or sketch an important object in situ prior to lifting it. Such records can be extremely helpful to the conservator later, especially if many pieces are involved.

Most objects can be removed from the ground unaided by following simple rules. The most important rule is never pry or flick objects out of the ground. Before lifting an object, carefully remove all dirt surrounding it so that the object sits on top of a pedestal of dirt, and its size and shape are fully determined. Paintbrushes, wooden tongue depressors cut to form a point (fig. 4.2), or spatulae are especially good for cleaning around objects in the ground; metal tools and trowels can scratch and abrade their surfaces. Most freshly uncovered materials—for example, pottery—can be very soft and friable while still in the ground.

From the nature of the object, it should be possible to tell whether or not protruding portions of the object are extending down into the ground. If the object is flat—a potsherd, for example —lifting should be very straightforward. With pressure evenly distributed around the object, gently dislodge it. Pick it up carefully, making sure that it is adequately supported, and place it directly into a polyethylene bag or rigid, padded container, whichever is appropriate.

If there are likely to be protruding portions of the object

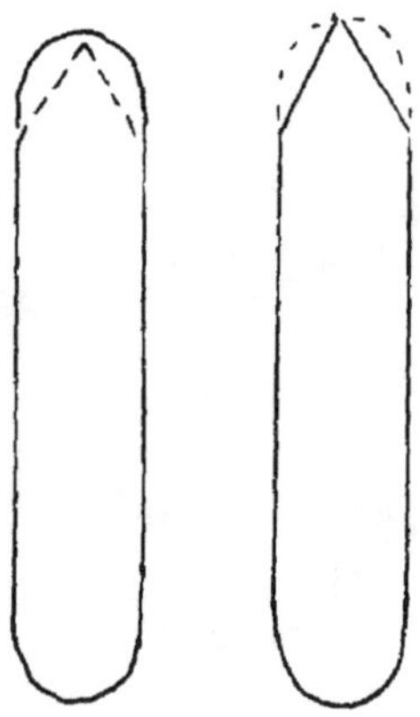

FIGURE 4.2 Wooden tongue depressor altered to make a tool

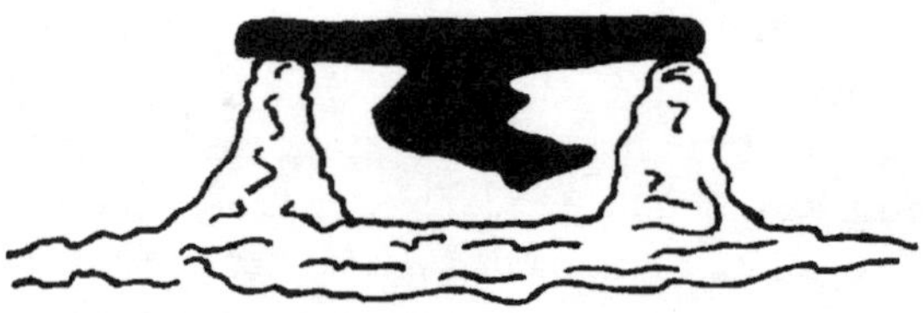

FIGURE 4.3 In situ object supported by two pedestals of dirt while the contours of the object are determined.

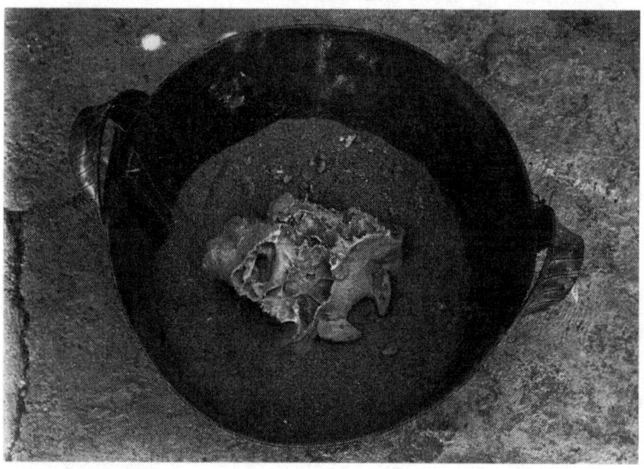

FIGURE 4.4 Sand-filled rubber bucket supporting an animal skull

extending into the ground or if the dirt is very hard, more excavation will be necessary to free these portions before lifting can be attempted. If not freed, these portions can easily be snapped off when the object is lifted. Using a wooden tool, carefully begin to remove dirt from underneath the object until the full contours of the underside of the object are known. If necessary, support the undercut areas of the object with pedestals of dirt or some material that is firm yet soft (fig. 4.3). Once the protruding portions are free, the object can be lifted as outlined above.

If the dirt surrounding an object is extremely hard and dry, the pressure necessary to remove the dirt can damage the object. Drops of water or alcohol can be applied locally with a brush to soften the dirt and facilitate lifting. Be very careful, however, not to moisten the object when doing this. Water can damage certain materials, such as metals, ivory, and wood, while alcohol can cause moisture-sensitive organic materials—for example, ivory—to dry out too much, leading to possible warping and cracking.

When objects are still in the ground or have just come out of the ground, avoid the temptation to clean them on the spot by scraping, brushing, rubbing, or washing. Impatience to see the design or color of the plaster, for example, can result in needless damage to the object: decoration can be removed or added, surfaces can be defaced, and edges can be badly abraded making for poor joins later on.

When an object is found in pieces, make sure that all the pieces, including the smallest, most insignificant-looking ones, are lifted and kept together. Tiny sherds, flakes, and crumbs *are* worth bothering about. In the hands of a conservator, their places can be found once major pieces are positioned, resulting in a more complete object. If an inscription is involved, a small piece could be of the utmost importance. When a large concentration of sherds, for example, is found, it is not always possible to tell immediately whether they all belong to the same pot. It is safer, therefore, to collect and keep together all sherds found together. Later, sherds can be returned to the general pottery lot or batch if they do not belong to the pot.

If a vessel or large object such as a skull is found intact, it can generally be lifted out after carefully removing all dirt from around it. Once out, if support is needed, the object can be placed in a bucket and carefully surrounded with dirt or sand (fig. 4.4). The contents of any vessel should be carefully excavated and sieved and possibly a portion of it set aside as a sample. Intact vessels can contain the remains of their original contents or faunal evidence that might give clues to the possible contents.

Bandaging

If a vessel is intact but has major cracks or breaks, it is usually possible to lift it out whole with the aid of bandaging. Remove the dirt surrounding the object, but leave the dirt inside to support the pot. For further support, wrap the vessel firmly with strips of gauze bandage or cloth in the following manner. Take a long, rolled-up strip of bandage and wrap it tightly around the vessel in a gradual spiral, being careful to overlap the strips (fig. 4.5A). Approximately one-third of each strip should overlap the preceding one and, in turn, be covered by the succeeding one. When one strip ends, fasten it securely with tape or a small straight pin,

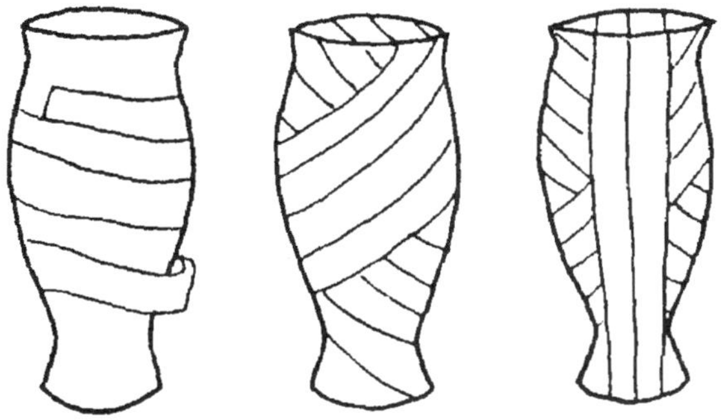

FIGURE 4.5 Method of bandaging an object. A, first layer of bandage; B, second layer of bandage at right angles to first; C, third layer.

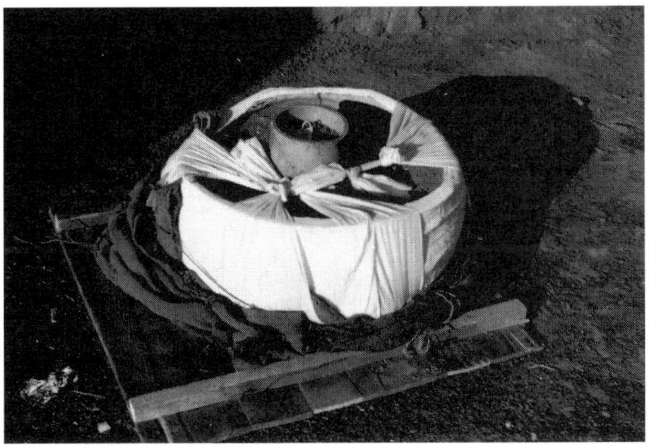

FIGURE 4.6 Pot encased in plaster bandage. Note the additional reinforcing with strips of bandage over the top. The pot is sitting on a wooden pallet cushioned with sacking for transport to the dig house.

making sure it will not dig into the surface of the vessel. Continue wrapping the vessel in this way until it is adequately supported. It may not be necessary to bandage the whole vessel. On the other hand, it may be necessary to add successive layers on the diagonal opposite to the first layer of bandage (fig. 4.5B) and then vertically (fig. 4.5C). Depending on the shape of the pot, it may not be possible to wrap the bandage in neat spirals with all the gauze strip flat against the pot. The important thing is to support the vessel. If a different method of wrapping appears to be easier and just as effective, use it.

This same bandaging procedure also can be used on a broken pot when the sherds are still held in place. If the pot is large and if sherds are loose, the bandaging may have to be applied piecemeal as the dirt is slowly removed from around the pot.

If bandaging does not provide sufficient support, further wrapping the object with plaster bandage or bandage impregnated with a resin can help. If the object does not already have a layer of bandaging, a separating layer of foil or plastic film should be applied first to prevent the surface of the object from absorbing any plaster or resin.

To apply the plaster bandage, quickly dip a strip in water and wrap it around the object as outlined above, following as closely as possible the contours of the object. It is not necessary to secure the ends of each piece, but make sure that they overlap at least 1 or 2 cm and that they are pressed well into the plaster. Be sure to allow the plaster to dry thoroughly before lifting the object. The pot shown in figure 4.6 has been wrapped in bandage followed by plaster bandage, and further supported with pieces of bandage tied vertically around it.

If ready-made plaster bandage is not available, it can easily be made by mixing a watery plaster of Paris solution into which strips of gauze bandage are dipped. Remove excess plaster by drawing the strip of bandage lightly through the fingers. Wrap the strip around the vessel as outlined above. If plaster is not available, the same method can be employed using undiluted PVA emulsion.

If it looks as though the sherds or pieces of an object will move and rub against each other in spite of bandaging or that the object will collapse, it is better to forgo the bandaging procedure. Instead, carefully take the pieces apart, sketching their relative positions first. Be sure to keep all the pieces together.

Backing

The process of backing an object is useful when a fragile object or piece of material, such as fallen wall plaster, is flat and needs support but does not require rigid encasement. It is also useful when an object or large piece of material—for example, bone or pottery—is found badly crushed into a myriad of cracks, breaks, small chips, and fragments. In such a case, it is desirable to keep all the pieces and chips together in their relative positions and to prevent their almost certain loss, which would result if they were lifted individually.

To back an object, carefully remove the dirt surrounding it, being sure to expose its sides. With a soft brush, clean as much as possible of the exposed surfaces, being careful not to abrade them. Using a different brush, coat a strip of the surface with undiluted PVA emulsion; it is not necessary for the coating to be very thick. Take a strip of gauze bandage slightly longer than the object and place it on the area. With a stiff brush, gently tamp the bandage down into the PVA. Add more PVA, if necessary, to ensure that the bandage is thoroughly saturated and is in close contact with the object. Apply additional strips in the same manner, overlapping them at least 1 cm on each edge, until the entire surface of the object is covered (fig. 4.7A). Be sure to include the sides of the object, pushing the bandage well down along them. Apply a second layer of bandage at right angles to the first in the same manner (fig. 4.7B). Allow the PVA to dry

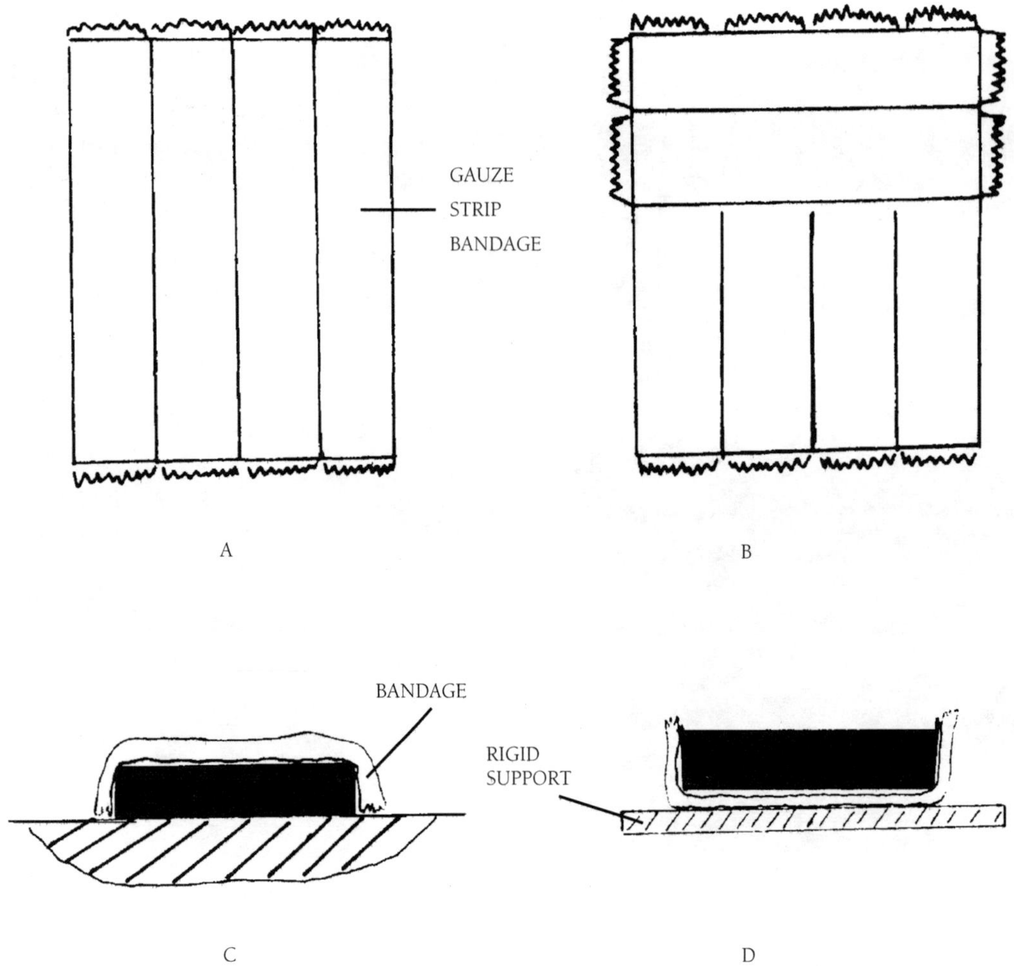

FIGURE 4.7 Method for backing an object. Top view: A, first layer of bandage strips; B, second layer of bandage strips perpendicular to first layer. Side view: C, undercutting of object; D, lifted object placed on rigid support.

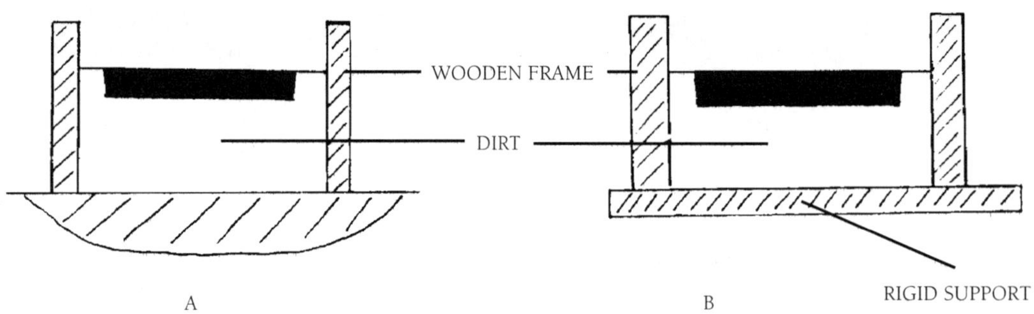

FIGURE 4.8. Block lifting method 1. A, object encased in dirt surrounded with wooden frame (hatched area underneath is dirt to be removed); B, lifted object on a rigid support.

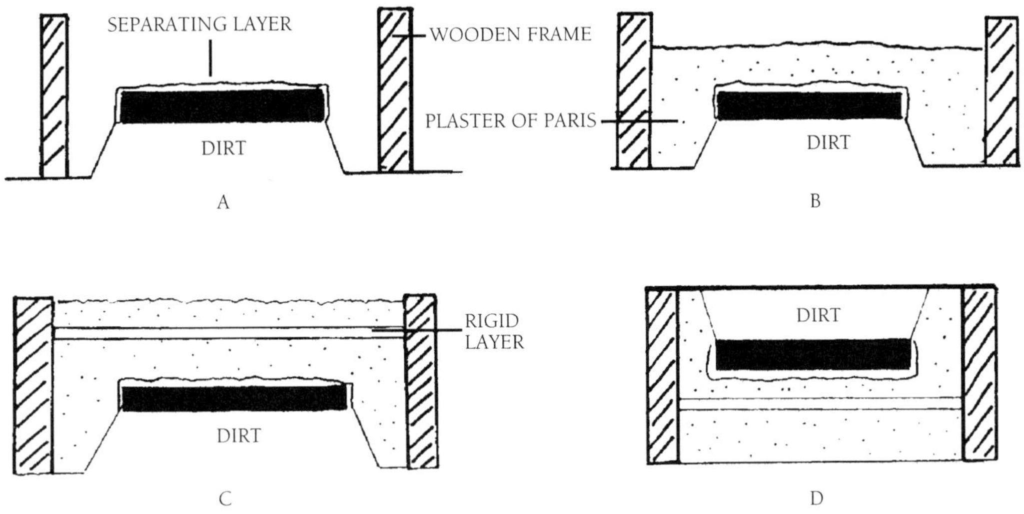

FIGURE 4.9 Block lifting method 2. A, object on a pedestal surrounded by a wooden frame; B, area inside frame filled with plaster; C, placement of a rigid layer and final plaster; D, lifted object.

thoroughly; it is dry when it has lost its milky color and become clear.

When the bandage is thoroughly dry (no longer tacky to the touch), carefully excavate underneath the object (fig. 4.7C) leaving a section of dirt directly under it. When the object is completely free, place your hand under it with fingers spread and carefully invert it so that the bandage is on the bottom. Store the object inverted (fig. 4.7D) and well supported in a rigid container. Do not attempt to remove any adhering dirt or to clean the object; instead, take it to a conservator for treatment.

When backing an object made of metal, use Acryloid B72 instead of PVA emulsion. The object, on being uncovered, has already been subjected to drastic environmental changes, and the addition of water from the emulsion could easily start or exacerbate the corrosion process.

PVA, being a fairly flexible resin, may not be rigid enough to back some objects, especially those that are long and thin. Undiluted Acrysol WS24 forms a more rigid film and is water soluble. A 10% to 12% solution of Acryloid B72 can also be used to provide a more rigid support, especially when a nonaqueous system is needed.

An alternate form of backing can be used with plaster of Paris. Carefully clean around the object, being sure to expose the sides. Cover the object with several layers of plastic cling film and/or aluminum foil to act as a separating layer. This layer must be tight and have no holes through which the plaster can reach the surface of the object. Mix up the plaster until it is thick and will remain where it is placed. Then spoon or pour a thin layer of plaster (about 1 cm) over the object. Place a piece of gauze bandage or netting on top of the plaster while it is still wet. Pour another thin layer of plaster followed by more bandage until the object is evenly covered with reinforced plaster. If the area to be covered is large, wooden splints can be incorporated into the wet plaster for greater rigidity and strength. Once the plaster has set fully, excavate the object as described above.

Block Lifting

Removing objects in a block of dirt can be a useful technique for lifting extremely fragile and less flat objects. Keep in mind that blocks of dirt can be quite heavy, especially when wet. The larger the object, the larger the block and consequently the heavier it will be. Be well aware of your limitations about how large a block can be successfully handled. Lifting too large a block without professional help can be very dangerous to the object as well as the staff.

METHOD 1: For extremely fragile and less flat objects, it is better to use a block lifting method. If the surrounding soil is cohesive, lifting can be done by isolating a block of dirt containing the object. Then tightly surround the block with a wooden frame (fig. 4.8A). If it is not possible to construct a wooden frame, flat splints of wood held firmly in position with bandage will suffice. It is also possible to wrap the block tightly with long strips of plaster bandage. If plaster bandage is used, first carefully cover the object with a layer of aluminum foil or plastic cling film to prevent any plaster from getting onto the object. Allow the plaster to dry thoroughly before proceeding to the next step. Then slowly undercut the block and, when free, slide it onto a rigid piece of wood or metal (fig. 4.8B). The undercutting can be done with a thin sheet of metal which can then be used as a rigid

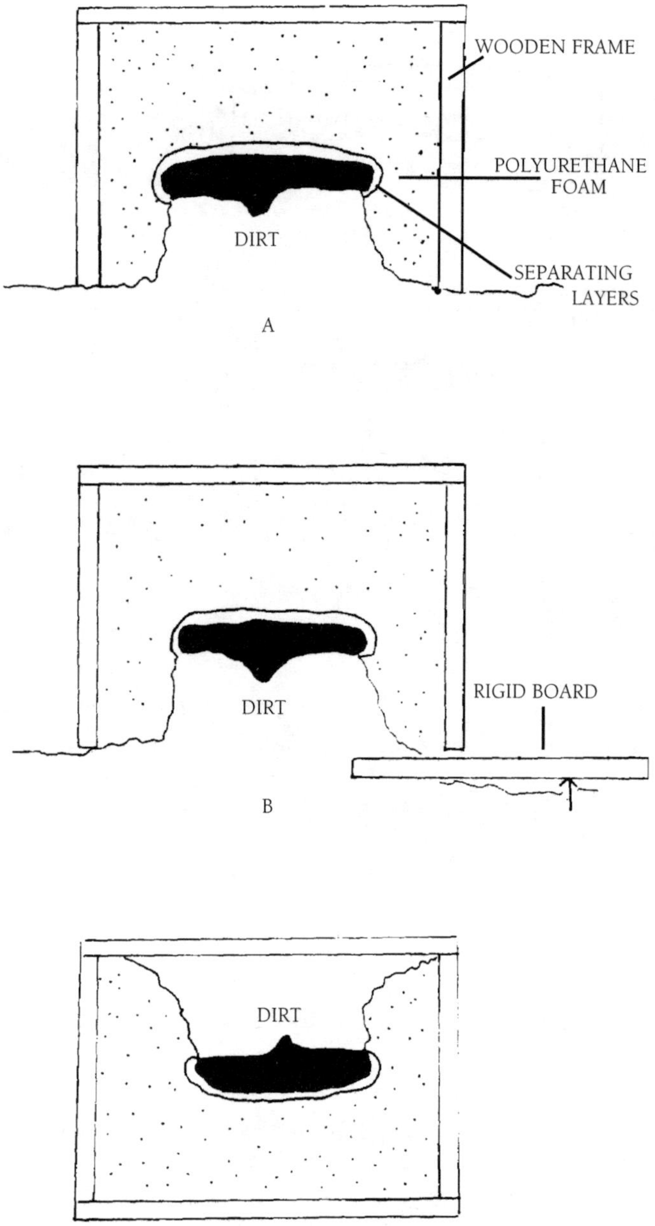

FIGURE 4.10 Block lifting method 3. A, object encased in polyurethane foam inside wooden box; B, object is undercut using a rigid board; C, lifted object encased in polyurethane foam.

support, or with a sharp knife, saw, or piece of wire. This method can be used in wet conditions because wet soil is generally extremely cohesive, and plaster will set in the dampest, most adverse conditions. After removing the block from the ground, further support it, if necessary, and take it to a conservator.

METHOD 2: A more elaborate method for lifting objects in blocks is necessary when the surrounding soil is not cohesive. If this is the case, remove all dirt from around the object, leaving it sitting on a pedestal of dirt at least 5 cm high. Cover the object with a layer of aluminum foil or plastic cling film to conform to its contours, then place a thin wooden frame around the object, allowing for at least a 2 to 3 cm margin of dirt all around (fig. 4.9A). Cover the object and partially fill the surrounding space with plaster of Paris (fig. 4.9B). When the plaster has set, place a grid of thin wooden strips or other rigid material on top of the plaster and pour a final layer of plaster to fill the entire space. Try to make the top of the plaster as flat as possible (fig. 4.9C). When the plaster is completely dry, undercut the pedestal and invert the block (fig. 4.9D). The dirt on top of the object can then be shaved down flush with the edges of the frame. Keep the block on a rigid support until it can be treated by a trained conservator.

METHOD 3: It is not practical to use plaster when large objects need to be lifted in block. The combined weight of the object, dirt, plaster, and frame would make it difficult, if not impossible, to handle the block without machinery. Lifting large objects in a block can only be attempted if a lightweight encasing material is used. Polyurethane foam, being both rigid and lightweight, can be used for this purpose. It is, however, an extremely dangerous material and should only be used when absolutely necessary, preferably when a person experienced in its use is present. Strict safety measures must be observed when using the foam. For more detailed information, see the section on polyurethane foam in chapter 3. If polyurethane foam is used, do not allow anyone who has a history of allergies, heart problems, or respiratory difficulties to be even peripherally involved.

Remove the surrounding dirt as described above, leaving the object sitting on a pedestal of dirt. Construct a wooden frame to fit around the pedestal, allowing a generous 10 cm to 15 cm margin all around it (fig. 4.10A). The frame must be extremely sturdy because the foam can exert a surprising amount of pressure.

Carefully cover the object with a layer of plastic cling film followed by a layer of aluminum foil. When joining two pieces of film or foil together, be very careful to fold the joining edges over together twice to seal the seam. It is also wise to further seal the seam with masking tape. Make very sure that there are no holes in either separating layer where the foam can get through to the object. It is always best to err on the side of overprotecting the object when using polyurethane foam.

Follow the mixing instructions that come with the polyurethane. Vigorous mixing together of the resin's two components is required before foaming starts. As soon as the foaming begins, work quickly because the whole mixture will seem to explode into foam. Pour the foaming mixture into the area between the wooden frame and the dirt pedestal. Depending on the ambient temperature, it will take approximately 15 minutes for the foam to cure after the initial foaming begins. Polyurethane foam does not work well in cool temperatures and will not foam below 10° C.

It is best to mix up the foam in relatively small quantities because small amounts of the resin will produce copious amounts of foam. Also, the foam contracts as it cures and may pull away from the object, leaving gaps where the object is not supported. Applying the foam in small quantities will serve to fill in any of these gaps.

Once cured, the rigid foam can be cut across the top with a sharp knife or saw to make a smooth surface flush with the edges of the frame. Then cover the top of the frame with one or more pieces of wood to form a solid lid (fig. 4.10A). Once this is done, excavation under the box can start. Carefully undercut the pedestal. Insert a rigid board or piece of metal, if necessary, to facilitate the process (fig. 4.10B). When the box is free, carefully invert it. If the dirt is flush with the edges of the box, a wooden lid can be secured in place and the box removed from the site (fig. 4.10C). If there are large holes where the dirt has crumbled away, it will be necessary to use more foam or dirt to fill them. Before pouring in any foam, make very sure that the object is not exposed. If it is, carefully cover it with layers of foil and cling film as described above; then fill the space with foam. After the foam cures, shave it off level with the edges of the box, and seal the box with a lid as described above for the bottom of the box.

The encased object should be stored away from open flames and taken to a conservator as soon as possible. An object should not be kept encased in polyurethane foam for any length of time because the cured foam can give off fumes that can reach the object even with an airtight, inert separating layer.

Consolidation

Frequently, objects buried in the ground lose their adhesive constituents through leaching, ion exchange, or other chemical and physical processes. As long as they remain in the ground, the objects maintain their shape and bulk, but disintegrate if removal from the ground is attempted. Consolidation is the process by which these fragile materials are joined and strengthened by the addition of a foreign substance that allows them to be lifted and handled safely. Consolidants must meet conservation requirements. It must have good adhesive and cohesive properties; achieve good penetration; be durable, stable, and reversible; and not alter the appearance of the material being consolidated.

Do not consolidate any sherds or material to be used for dating or other forms of analysis because the consolidant will contaminate the sample.

Although consolidants are required to be reversible, it is generally impossible to remove all traces of them from a material. For this reason, consolidation should be undertaken only when absolutely necessary. Also, it is difficult to fully clean objects in situ before consolidation, which can result in a messier and more tedious cleaning job later in the laboratory.

Always remember that any excess consolidant will have to be removed in the laboratory, possibly to the detriment of the object; so, always apply it sparingly. There should never be a thick, glossy layer of consolidant on the surface.

Make sure to record the kind of consolidant used, including the trade name and grade. A copy of this information should be kept with the consolidated object for the benefit of the conservator.

If, after careful scrutiny, an object is deemed too fragile to be lifted from the ground without additional support, and simple bandaging will not prove sufficient, the object should be consolidated. The choice of consolidant depends on the condition of the material. If the material is dry, a resin/solvent solution should be used; if it is damp, an emulsion must be used. Good penetration will be achieved with an emulsion because, being water-based, it will be pulled into and dispersed easily throughout the damp material. If the material is too wet or completely waterlogged, however, consolidation might be impossible to achieve. Because of the damp conditions, the consolidant will not be able to dry out sufficiently to impart any strength to the object. The drying out of the consolidant, in addition, entails the drying out of the object. If the object is not totally impregnated, irreparable damage can result from drying out because stresses develop at the interface between consolidated and unconsolidated areas. Consolidation, therefore, should not be attempted on an extremely fragile, waterlogged object. Block lifting should be used instead. See the section in this chapter concerning waterlogged materials.

Regardless of the type of consolidant used, it is critical that it be allowed to dry completely before any attempt is made to lift the object. A material still wet with a consolidant is more fragile than it was before the consolidant was applied.

Before applying a consolidant, clean the object as thoroughly as possible with a soft brush or air blown from a bulb syringe. Be sure to remove the dirt from around the edges of the object to prevent large lumps from adhering to it. If the object is damp, clean it with great care because even a soft brush can scratch or damage the surface and thereby obscure surface detail. If the object is dry with large lumps of dirt adhering to it, drops of water or alcohol applied locally with a brush can help soften the lumps and facilitate their removal. Be careful not to moisten the object itself.

If the object is damp, a PVA emulsion diluted 1 to 4 with

water should be used for consolidation. If the material being consolidated is very dense, it may be necessary to dilute the emulsion further to achieve more than just surface consolidation. Apply a small amount of the 1:4 emulsion first with a brush and see how readily it is absorbed into the material. If it just sits on the surface and shows no sign of soaking in after a few minutes, remove it by drawing it up onto a piece of toweling or other absorbent material and try a more dilute solution. In general, it is more effective to apply several thin coats of consolidant rather than a single heavy coat.

Apply emulsion sparingly to the cleaned object with a brush, allowing it to soak in. The best procedure is to touch the full brush to the surface of the object, allowing capillary action to pull emulsion off the brush and into the material. In this way, there is little, if any, damage to the surface. It is also possible to apply consolidant with a medicine dropper, although it can be a little more difficult to control the flow. Keep applying the emulsion, waiting a few minutes between each application, until it is no longer absorbed by the material. Try to avoid a surface buildup of the consolidant.

With emulsions, it is especially important to allow the consolidant to dry thoroughly before lifting the object. The evaporation rate of water is much slower than that of acetone or toluene, and it is often difficult to determine precisely when the emulsion is dry. Therefore, err on the side of too much rather than too little drying time.

If the material to be consolidated is dry, a solution of Acryloid B72 or PVA resin in toluene or acetone can be used. After cleaning the surface and sides of the object as carefully as possible, apply the solution with a brush. Start with a low (3% to 4%) concentration for the first few applications; then increase the concentration to 7% to 10%. The application method is the same as for an emulsion. Allow the solvent to evaporate somewhat between applications, but do not let it evaporate completely because penetration of subsequent coats of consolidants will be impeded. Applying the solvent alone first can help to increase penetration.

In hot, arid climates, acetone may be too volatile to be used effectively as a solvent because it can evaporate before the consolidant has a chance to penetrate; thus only superficial consolidation is achieved. Under these conditions, toluene is a better choice of solvent because it is less volatile. If only acetone is available, it may be necessary to carry out the consolidation process at a time when the air and material being consolidated are as cool as possible as, for example, in the early morning. Loosely covering the object with a piece of aluminum foil after applying the consolidant will also help to slow down the evaporation rate of the acetone. It is also possible to bypass the problem altogether by using a dilute (2% to 4%) solution of Acrysol WS24. A dilute (1 to 4) solution of PVA emulsion could also be used. Emulsions, however, should be used only as a last resort since they have a tendency to change chemically, or cross-link, thereby becoming insoluble over time.

When a resin/solvent consolidant is applied, a white bloom may appear on the surface of the object as a result of one of two things. Either the material being consolidated is not thoroughly dry or the solvent has been contaminated with water. The cooling effect of the evaporating solvent results in the precipitation of moisture in the resin film, causing it to whiten. This bloom can usually be removed later with applications of uncontaminated solvent.

If a large object requires consolidation, try to do the consolidating all at one time. If the consolidation is done piecemeal after a small area has been cleaned, stresses can be set up in the material where the consolidated areas meet unconsolidated areas, leading to warping and cracking. Quickly but carefully apply a coat of consolidant to the whole object; then apply additional coats in the same manner. If necessary, cover the consolidated areas loosely with foil as you work along the object in order to slow down the evaporation rate of the solvent. Evaporation can also be reduced by carrying out the consolidation when the air and material being consolidated are as cool as possible.

While the consolidant is drying, try to keep the area around the object as dust-free as possible. Windy days should be avoided because dust, sand, and other debris will be blown onto the consolidated surface. A piece of aluminum foil sitting lightly on top of the consolidated object can exclude airborne dust; alternatively, a box can be placed over the object. Do not use a sheet of plastic as it might be dissolved onto the object by the solvent.

After the consolidant has dried thoroughly, the object can be removed from the ground following general lifting procedures. Pack a consolidated object carefully in a well-padded container. If cotton wool is used, always keep a layer of acid-free tissue, plastic, or foil between it and the object, especially if PVA has been used as the consolidant. PVA softens when it becomes warm, causing the cotton fibers to stick to the surface of the object. Consolidated material should be stored in as cool and dry a place as possible and be taken to a trained conservator for further treatment.

The fact that an object has been consolidated should never lull one into a false sense of security. Although stronger than it was before, a consolidated object is still fragile and should be treated accordingly. Handle it as minimally as possible; when handling is necessary, be careful and gentle. Support the object carefully at all times.

Cleaning

Unless a conservator is present, the only cleaning that should be undertaken in the field is the removal of superfi-

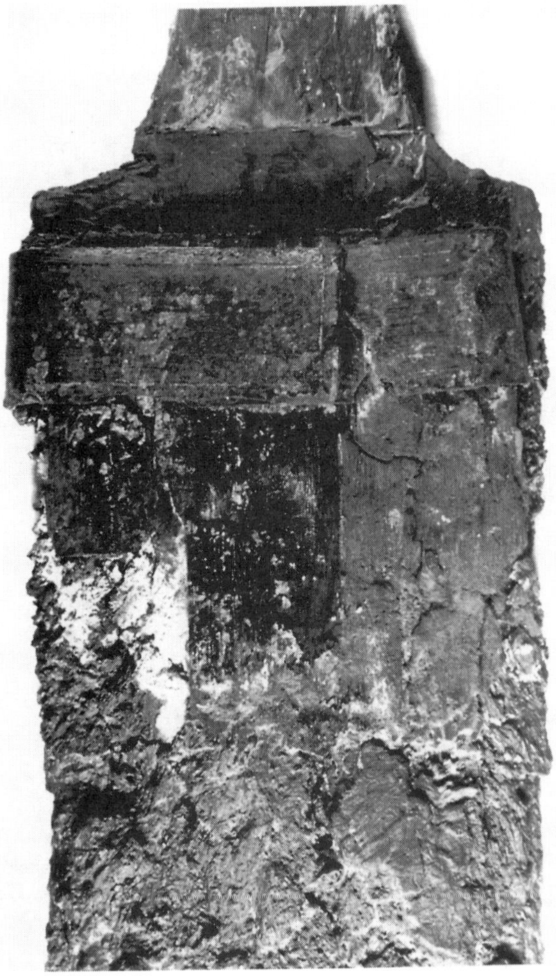

FIGURE 4.11 Detail of an Anglo-Saxon sword. Wood, leather, and fleece have been preserved by the iron corrosion products.

cial dirt. Unless otherwise noted in the instructions concerning specific materials, more extensive cleaning procedures should be left for a trained conservator.

When objects first come out of the ground, avoid the temptation to clean them on the spot by scraping, rubbing, or immersing them in water. It is extremely easy to remove decoration and paint in this way and to scratch the surface of an object. Since water is a primary cause of metal corrosion, contact with water, which may not be free of contaminants, can initiate the corrosion process. In the Middle East, for example, water can be very saline or heavily chlorinated; both conditions could seriously damage metal objects.

Metal objects should not be cleaned by an untrained person in the field. The removal of corrosion products can be a difficult process and should be undertaken only by a trained conservator. Metal surfaces can be scratched very easily by untrained hands, and surface detail can be obliterated. In badly deteriorated pieces, corrosion is frequently only a thin shell encasing what remains of the metal of the object, which can be powdery or mineralized. Attempts to remove such corrosion can result in the shattering of the object. Injudicious cleaning, as well, can easily damage and destroy not only surface detail but also organic and environmental evidence preserved by or in the corrosion. Figure 4.11 shows an iron sword blade with the wood, leather, and sheepskin of its scabbard preserved in the corrosion. Corrosion products from the iron and the bronze crosspiece have prevented the biological deterioration of two strips of wood running parallel to the blade. A third strip on the top edge has been completely permeated and replaced by iron corrosion products, preserving exactly the shape and grain of the wood. To the right of the wood and along the edges of the blade, the corrosion products have also replaced the sheepskin lining the scabbard, preserving the bumpy surface of the fleece. The smooth areas along the center of the blade, between areas of fleece, are leather that has been replaced. This leather once formed the outside surface of the scabbard. Had this sword been cleaned by someone not trained to notice such detail, much, if not all, of this information would have been lost. For these reasons, no attempt should be made to clean dirt or corrosion products from metal objects.

Cleaning an object need not involve the use of water. In fact, whenever possible, the use of water should be avoided. If the soil is sandy or not tightly compacted, dry brushing may be sufficient to clean most excavated material. The hardness of the brush used will depend on the nature of the material being cleaned. Use the softest brush possible that will still remove the dirt. Do not scrub the object too vigorously as this can damage its surface. If the dirt does not come off easily, it may be mixed with insoluble salts that will require special treatment to remove. Leave any persistent dirt because it can always be removed at a later date; areas of the object or paint scrubbed away can never be replaced. If a fine, persistent dust remains on an object after dry brushing, it can be blown off with a bulb syringe or removed by light dabbing with a slightly damp sponge. The latter should be done only to materials, such as pottery or stone, that are not sensitive to moisture.

If hard lumps of dirt adhere to the object, do not flick or pry them off because they can easily pull off some of the surface. Instead, touch the lumps with a brush containing either alcohol or water, allowing the dirt to pull the moisture off the brush. The lumps should then be soft enough for easy removal with a brush or wooden tool. Be very careful, however, not to moisten the object when doing this. Water can damage certain materials, such as metals, ivory, and wood, and alcohol can cause moisture-sensitive organic materials, such as ivory and wood, to dry out too much, leading to possible warping and cracking. If there is any question as to the suitability of this treatment, allow a conservator to remove the lumps.

If cleaning with water is absolutely necessary, try to use as little as possible. If only part of the object is dirty, clean only that particular area. The amount of water needed can be controlled by using cotton swabs or a damp piece of sponge. If swabs are used, be extremely careful not to abrade the surface of the object. Do not rub with the swab, but rather gently roll it back and forth over the surface to be cleaned. As soon as the swab becomes dirty, discard it for a new one; dirty swabs can be extremely abrasive. If a piece of sponge is used, squeeze it out quite well to remove most of the water before touching the object. As with swabs, do not rub the surface of the object with the sponge; rather, dab at it. Rinse the sponge frequently in fresh water to remove any abrasive dirt adhering to it.

Some materials—potsherds, for example—can be washed by being immersed in water. If a large batch of sherds is involved, examine it carefully first and remove painted or fragile sherds that will not withstand immersion. Fragments of alabaster vessels frequently become mixed in with potsherds. They, too, should be separated out because alabaster is soluble in water and can be damaged by washing. When the pieces are immersed, a soft brush can be used to remove the dirt from them, but do not scrub too vigorously. Change the wash water as frequently as possible because the dirty water, itself, can be abrasive.

To protect the sherds from the sludge of dirt that will build up on the bottom of the wash basin, place them on a rack made of plastic mesh or screening that either raises them off the bottom or suspends them from the rim of the basin (fig. 4.12). They can also be placed in a sieve or piece of netting and be suspended or swirled gently in the wash water.

After washing an object, allow it to dry thoroughly before proceeding further. Carefully remove excess water with absorbent toweling, and then allow the object to dry evenly and uniformly away from direct sources of heat, including sunlight. Most pottery can just be spread out in the sun to dry.

Sometimes it is necessary to use acid to remove encrustations on pottery. The removal procedure, set out fully in the section on pottery in chapter 5, should be used only on pottery. Even with pottery, cleaning with acid is an extremely harsh treatment and should be used only when absolutely necessary. It is important to soak pottery in water for a minimum of one hour before treating it with acid to prevent the acid from being drawn into the fabric of the pot. Pottery that has been treated with acid must also be thoroughly rinsed afterward to remove all traces not only of the acid but of the soluble salts which are products of

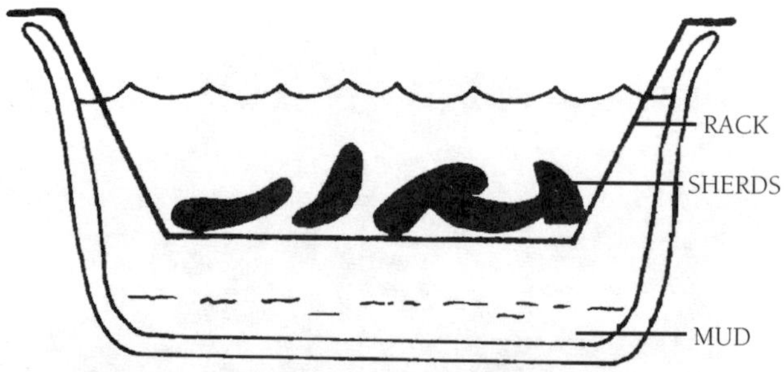

FIGURE 4.12 Basin with rack for washing pottery

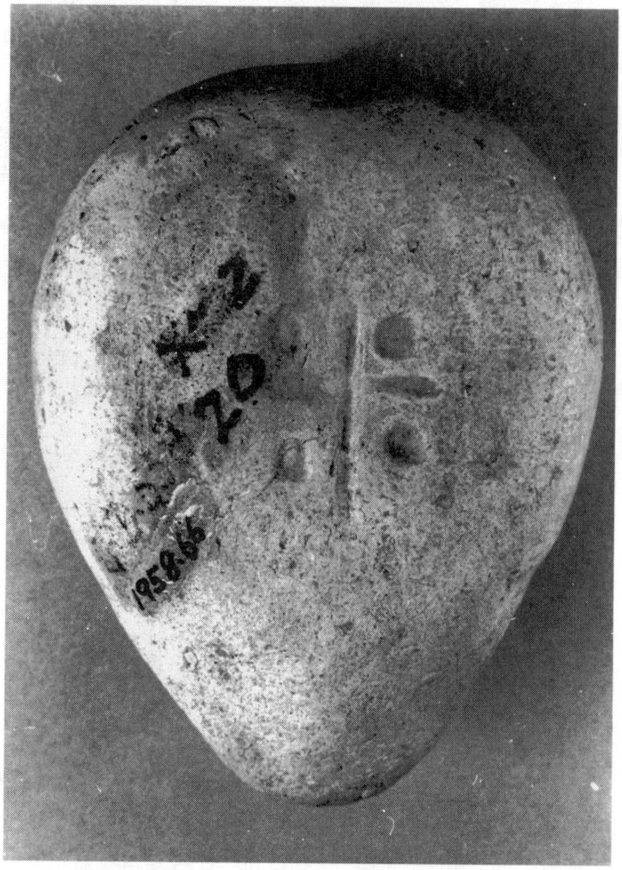

FIGURE 4.13 Pottery lamp illustrating correct and incorrect methods of marking objects

dissolving insoluble salts. Considerable damage will be done to the pottery if these steps are omitted.

Marking

When objects have been lifted and cleaned, the standard excavation procedure is to mark them with their register number and/or their site location numbers. Unless a certain procedure is followed, the marking ink will soak into the fabric of the object and will be impossible to remove completely at a later date. Such was the case with the number "X-2, 20," written in indelible ink directly on the bottom of the ceramic lamp shown in figure 4.13. Despite repeated attempts with various solvents to remove the

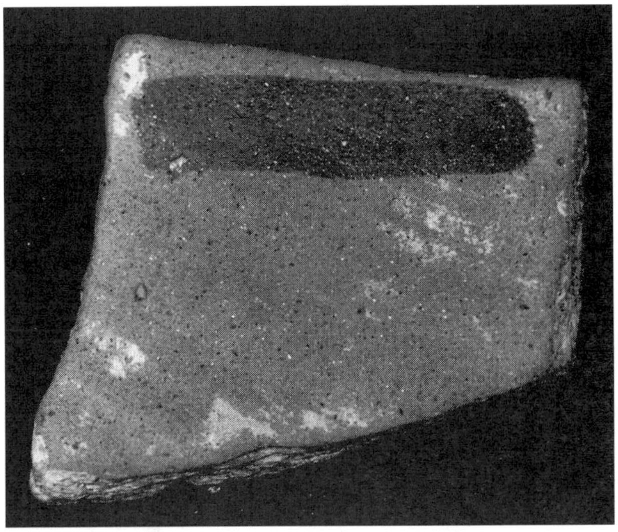

FIGURE 4.14A Proper method for marking objects: lacquer patch painted onto surface.

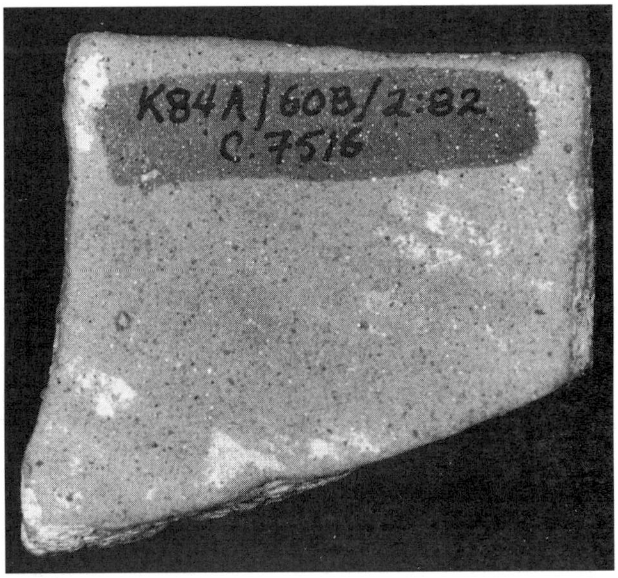

FIGURE 4.14B Proper method for marking objects: number written on lacquer patch.

number, it remains permanently on the lamp. In contrast, the new number, "1958.66," has been written on properly and can be removed easily at any time. It is also possible for the marking pen itself to indelibly incise the number into the surface of the object.

When deciding where to place the number, use common sense and choose an area on the object where the number will be inconspicuous but not impossible to find. Avoid decorated and painted areas; do not mark on any surface that is flaking or heavily encrusted with dirt or corrosion. Do not use the front or sides of an object if it has a base. If an object, especially a pot, is broken into many fragments that will eventually be joined together, it is not necessary to label each individual piece. Label only the base sherd on the bottom and a few body sherds on their inside surface, then pack all the sherds together to prevent them from becoming mixed up with others.

Before marking, be sure that the area to be marked is thoroughly clean and dry. Use a damp swab, if necessary, to make sure that all dirt has been removed. When the area to be marked is dry, coat a strip of it with a layer of 10% Acryloid B72. The size of the strip should be commensurate with the quantity and size of the markings (fig. 4.14A). When the lacquer is completely dry, write the number on the lacquer with India ink. It should not be necessary to apply pressure when writing the number. Allow the ink to dry thoroughly before covering it with another layer of lacquer (fig 4.14B). In this way, the number is not easily removed or smudged inadvertently, but can be removed readily, if necessary, with swabs of acetone.

A layer of clear nail polish also works well and can be used instead of Acryloid B72. Nail polish is soluble in acetone and is readily available almost everywhere. If an object is very dark in color, it can be helpful to use white (rather than clear) nail polish to make the number more visible. One may also use white ink.

Joining

The joining of broken objects, especially pottery, is best done by a conservator. If pottery profiles are needed for drawing or broken objects are needed for photography, join only what is absolutely necessary. Joins made by inexperienced people in the field almost always must be taken apart in the laboratory, to the detriment of the object. Every time a join is taken apart and old adhesive removed, small amounts of the edges are lost, making subsequent joining more difficult and unsightly.

Never join objects while they are damp. If the adhesive turns milky white, the material is still too damp. The adhesive may never dry properly, and the resulting joins will be weak and more likely to give way.

Always use a reversible adhesive, such as HMG, UHU, UHU Hart, Duco Cement, or Durofix; all are soluble in acetone. See the section on adhesives in chapter 3 for more detailed information on these products. Avoid white glues, such as Elmer's, because they are emulsions and can become insoluble over time. It is best to avoid any local proprietary adhesives as well because they may contain substances harmful to the objects and/or become insoluble over time (fig. 1.1). These adhesives can also discolor badly (fig. 4.15). All objects joined with UHU should be kept away from extreme heat and sun or they will sag and/or collapse.

Before applying the adhesive, use a brush to thoroughly clean the edges to be joined. Then apply adhesive to one of the edges and gently press the two edges together. Run a finger across the join to make sure that the joined pieces are properly aligned. If a bump or unevenness is felt, reposition the pieces until the join feels smooth. Then set the joined pieces aside to allow the adhesive to dry. The pieces should be set down in such a way that no pressure is put on the join. Generally, the most efficient way to do this is to position the pieces one on top of the other in a tray or plastic basin filled with sand until the adhesive dries. If a sand tray is used, make sure that the joins are well above the sand to prevent sand from getting into them (fig 4.16).

A sufficient amount of adhesive should be applied to achieve good contact, but not enough for excess to squeeze out along the joins. If seepage does occur, do not wipe the excess off; this will serve only to smear it. Instead, allow the adhesive to dry until it becomes rubbery (about 5 to 10 minutes) and then either rub it off gently with a finger or scrape it off carefully with a knife or scalpel.

When working with an adhesive, always make sure that your hands are clean. Any adhesive on the fingers should be wiped off immediately or large smears and fingerprints of adhesive will be transmitted to the surface of the object being joined.

If a pot is to be joined, lay out all the sherds and determine their relative positions before applying any adhesive. This procedure helps one to determine the order in which sherds should be joined and to prevent sherds from being locked out. As a general rule, it is best to start with the base and work slowly up and around the pot in a big spiral rather than haphazardly join groups of sherds together to form several large segments. Any misalignments, even if only slight, will prevent these segments from joining together smoothly; they will have to be taken apart and rejoined. Misalignments are cumulative and can completely throw off the assembly of the pot. Therefore, before applying any adhesive, position the sherd and feel the join with a finger to assess whether it is properly aligned.

For some materials whose surface is very durable and hard, like pottery or stone, pieces may be held in position with masking tape while the adhesive dries. Test first to make sure that the tape will not pull off small pieces of the surface when removed. It must be stressed that the taping of joins must only be done as a temporary measure; the tape should be removed as soon as the adhesive dries. If left on, tape can leave a stain that is difficult, if not impossible, to remove. The pot shown in figure 4.17 has been held together with tape for a long time. Where the tape was removed on the lower portion of the pot, adhesive has left a sticky stain that will be impossible to remove completely; a dark shadow will always be there.

Never rip off the tape because this action can severely damage the surface. If the tape does not come off easily with gentle pulling, it can be dissolved with a solvent. Lift one

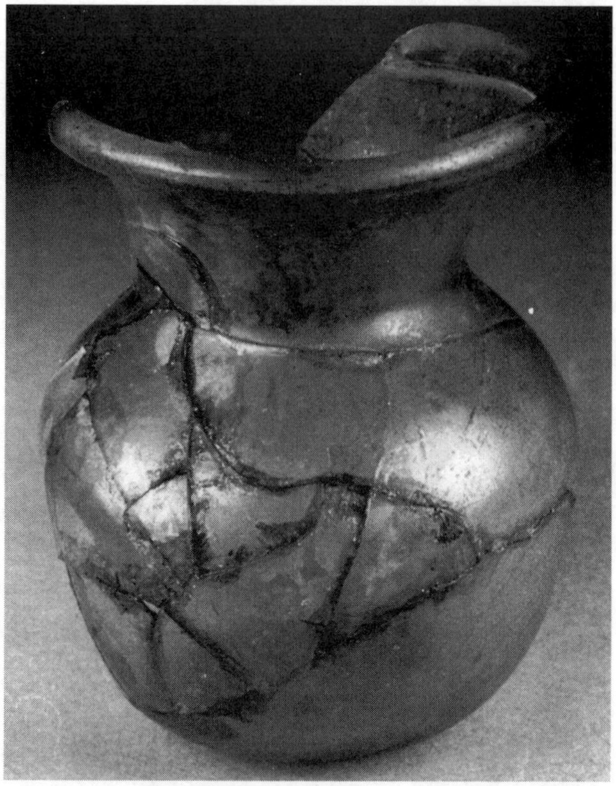

FIGURE 4.15 Roman glass jar with adhesive that discolored badly. Adhesive is also smeared over the surface of the jar.

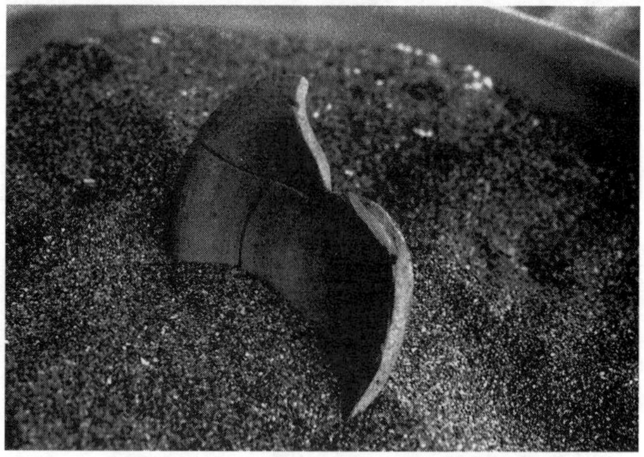

FIGURE 4.16 Proper use of a sand tray. Note that the join lines are well above the sand.

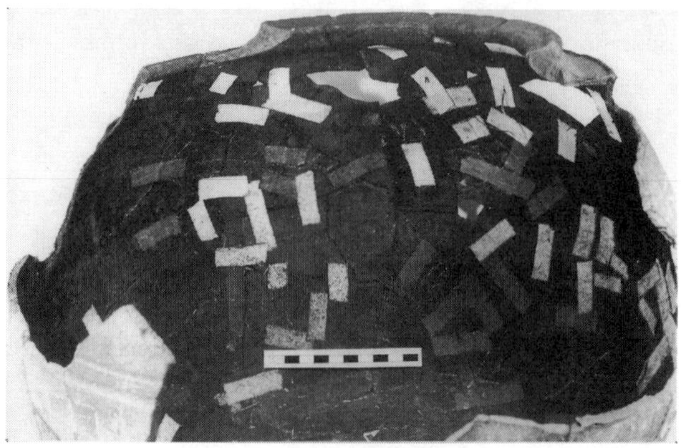

FIGURE 4.17 Adhesive stains from tape on a Roman pot

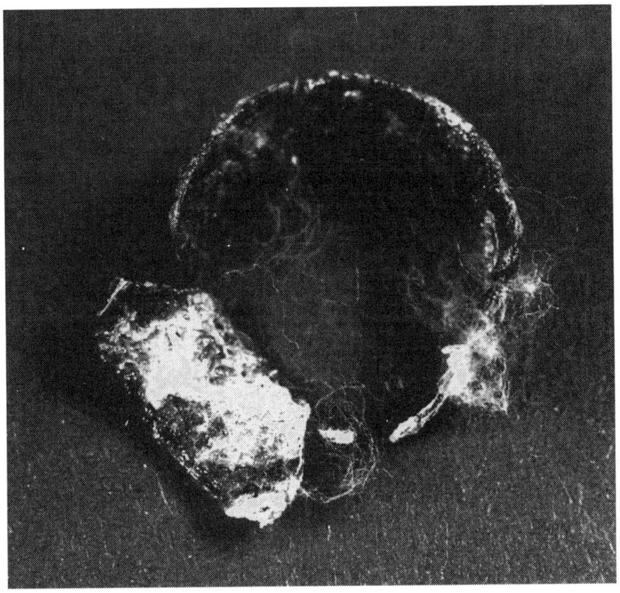

FIGURE 4.18 Bronze ring broken when removing cotton wool fibers in which it was packed. Note the fibers still caught on the rough surface of the bronze.

corner of the tape with a scalpel blade or fingernail; then, with a swab or brush, apply either acetone or toluene to the underside of the tape, allowing capillary action to pull it under the tape. Apply more solvent to saturate the tape. It should then be possible to pull up the tape easily or to roll it off gently with a wooden toothpick. Use more solvent, if necessary, to free stubborn areas of the tape. Any traces of the tape adhesive can be removed with swabs of acetone.

Always keep a record of the adhesive used with the object, and give it to the conservator.

Packing

The packing of archaeological materials, whether for storage or transport, is really a matter of common sense as long as a few important points are kept in mind. The most important points will be mentioned here. Specific information regarding each individual material will be found in the appropriate section in chapter 5.

All packing materials should be selected with care. Although some materials may be readily available, they may not be suitable because they can cause considerable damage if they remain in contact with certain objects for a long period of time. Only inert materials such as acid-free tissue or polyethylene should come in direct contact with the object, especially if it is made of organic materials or metals. Dyed and perfumed tissue and toilet paper should be avoided because they contain possibly harmful additives. Newspaper—because it is highly acidic, deteriorates rapidly, and is extremely dirty—should never come in direct contact with any object. It can be used, however, to pad out boxes filled with individually wrapped objects or smaller boxes in preparation for transport.

Cotton wool is readily available worldwide and is a useful packing and cushioning material. It should never come in direct contact with objects, however, especially those with extremely fragile or flaking surfaces. The cotton fibers will stick to or snag on the objects, especially if they have a rough surface, and be difficult to remove. Any snagged fibers must be removed extremely carefully to prevent the removal of flakes of paint, or the object's surface, or even the breakage of the object. The bronze ring shown in figure 4.18 was packed in cotton, and the fibers stuck to the rough, corroded surface. The fragile ring broke when an attempt was made to remove these fibers.

If cotton wool is used for packing, always keep a layer of tissue between it and the object. Plastic film or sheet can also be used as a separator for most materials. If the object has a very powdery or flaky surface, however, plastic should not be used because its static charge can be sufficient to pull off flakes and powder.

Cotton can be very useful if pads of various sizes and shapes are needed to support objects when packing them. Such pads can easily be made by wrapping an appropriate amount of cotton in acid-free tissue or a piece of polyethylene and securing it with tape.

Polyethylene expanded foams are also extremely useful packing materials. They have good shock-absorbing qualities while being soft, clean, and flexible. They are also very useful for packing and storing waterlogged material.

Polyethylene bags are invaluable for packing objects on excavations, but they must be used with care. Always make sure that objects are thoroughly dry before putting them in bags and sealing them. Once objects have been placed in plastic bags, make sure they are never left to sit in the sun. After a few minutes, the bags will begin to sweat, wetting the objects inside. To protect a flaking or powdery surface or paint layer from the static charge associated with plastic, carefully wrap objects in acid-free tissue before placing them in these bags.

Polyethylene bags come in a wide variety of sizes and thicknesses. It is best to have a good selection on hand so that a bag appropriate for the size and weight of the object can be used. If one bag is not sufficiently thick to hold sharp pieces of bone, for example, use a bag made of thicker plastic or use two bags, one inside the other.

Since polyethylene bags filled with excavated material are likely to be opened many times in the course of study, it is wise to seal the bags in such a way that they can be easily unsealed and resealed. Self-sealing or zip-lock bags are ideal and come in a variety of sizes. Unfortunately, they are not available in the extremely large sizes suitable for quantities of pottery or animal bones. For sealing regular poly-

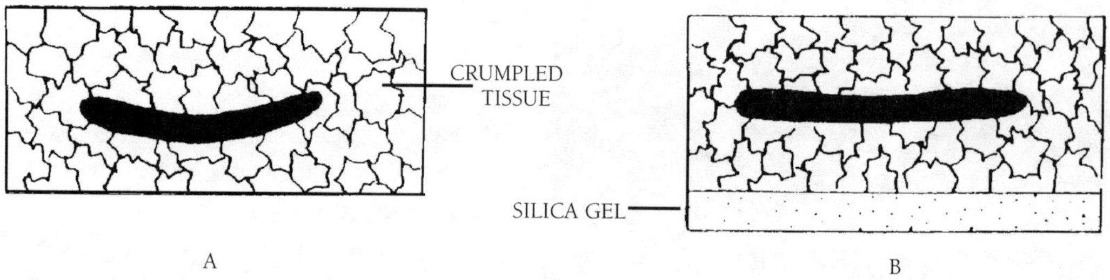

FIGURE 4.19 The object should float in the packing container. A, object surrounded by packing material; B, metal objects packed with silica gel.

ethylene bags, plastic-coated paper clips or wire ties are extremely useful because they do not rust. Paper-coated wire ties, however, will rust and eventually disintegrate. Avoid using string, metal staples, rubber bands, and uncoated paper clips because they deteriorate readily.

Brown paper envelopes can be used for the short-term packing of objects to transport them from the site to the dig house. If nothing else is available, they can also be used to pack pottery and stone objects. Paper envelopes are recommended for packing carbonized material because they allow the sample to dry out. Since they contain considerable amounts of acid, paper envelopes should not be used for the permanent packing of any metallic or organic materials or objects made of glass.

There are other major disadvantages to using paper envelopes for storage, even for pottery and stone. Certain insects—for example, silverfish—feed on paper, and rodents like it for nesting material. Although the actual objects may not be harmed, animals can wreak havoc in a storeroom by obliterating important information written on the envelopes or by completely destroying them. Such damage can also occur if the envelopes get wet.

When packing archaeological objects, always separate the different materials. This holds true for uninventoried as well as inventoried materials. Do not pack iron, for example, in the same box or bag with glass. Not only will the heavier iron break the glass, but one or the other will not be kept under the proper storage conditions since each material has different packing and storage needs. If all items of one particular material are packed together, it is much easier to store them and provide the proper environmental conditions to ensure their safety. Also, when any part of the material is studied at a later date, experts will not have to sort through and disrupt all objects to find their own particular items.

To be stored, most objects should be packed individually in well-padded, rigid containers. Polystyrene boxes are ideal, as are plastic food containers with snap-on lids. For many materials, sturdy cardboard boxes can be used as well. Carefully pad the container with polyethylene foam or crumpled acid-free tissue, leaving a well in the shape of the object in the center. When placed in the well, the object should be in the middle of the container, completely surrounded by packing material (fig. 4.19A). Finally, cover the object with a wad of packing material thick enough to prevent the object from moving inside the container. If the object is thin, a flat wad of packing will suffice. If the object is much thicker—for example, a vessel—it may be necessary to use several thicker wads of packing to fill up the container. In any case, the wad should not be so thick that undue pressure is exerted on the object when the lid is closed.

When packing metal objects (with the exception of lead), a layer of moisture-absorbing silica gel should be placed in the bottom of the box before putting in the padding (fig. 4.19B). Silica gel is an indispensable material for helping to keep moisture-sensitive materials dry. Since it is only effective when used in an air-tight container, tape the crack between the halves of the box to seal it. It is important that the silica gel not come in direct contact with the object. If it does touch the metal, it will hold the moisture against the object rather than protect it by keeping the moisture away.

One way of ensuring the separation of silica gel from the object is to make a packet to hold the gel. Place the silica gel in a sealed polyethylene bag and then pierce the bag all over with a needle or other small, pointed object. If a smaller or odd-sized packet is needed, cut up a polyethylene bag to obtain a piece of plastic of the required dimensions and wrap the silica gel in it like a package. Use tape to seal the packet and then perforate it as described above.

Once silica gel has become fully saturated and pink, it will no longer be effective unless regenerated by being heated in an oven until it again becomes blue.

Robust metal objects can be packed in polyethylene bags, but make very sure that the objects are thoroughly dry

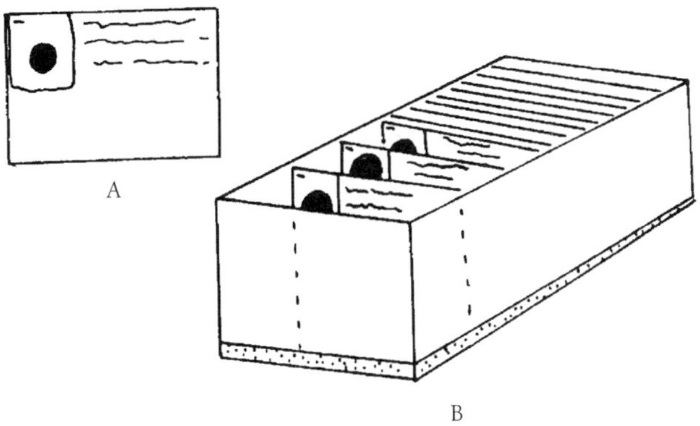

FIGURE 4.20 Small objects stored on file cards. *After Singley 1981*

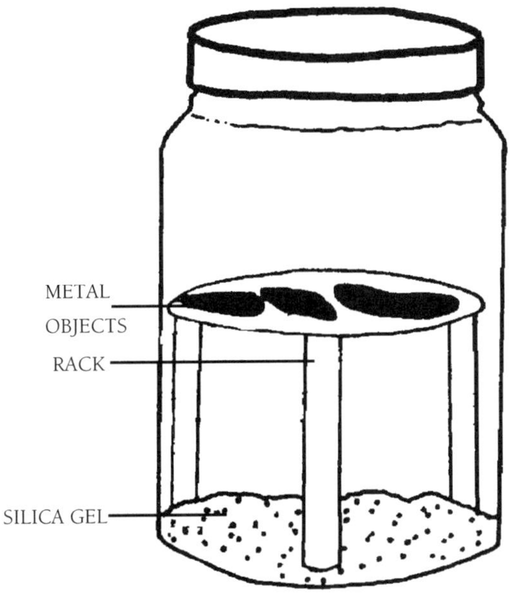

FIGURE 4.21 Mason jar used to store metal objects

before placing them in the bags. A packet of silica gel should be placed in the bag before sealing it. If silica gel is not available, polyethylene bags should be perforated to allow air to circulate around the object, and the bags should not be sealed. The bags of objects should be kept in a well-padded, rigid box or container.

An alternate method of packing robust metal objects is to place them in unsealed, perforated polyethylene bags, together with a packet of silica gel, and then put them into a metal or plastic container with a tight-fitting lid. A metal cookie tin or a plastic food container with a snap-on lid is ideal for this purpose. The container can be further sealed with tape. This method provides an effective means of keeping metals safe even in a damp storeroom.

Bags holding small objects like coins or rings can be kept in order by being stapled to a file card. The card can then be filed, along with silica gel, in an airtight container (fig. 4.20).

Another excellent means of packing metal objects, especially unstable ones, is to use a glass Mason jar (fig. 4.21). Fill the bottom of the jar with 4 to 5 cm of silica gel. Insert a rack or other device into the jar which will not allow the metal to touch the silica gel, then place the object on the rack. The rubber seal makes the jar airtight and will keep the object safe, even in a damp storeroom.

If airtight containers are not available, metal objects (with the exception of lead and pewter) can be packed in cardboard boxes. The box, however, must then be placed, along with a perforated packet of silica gel, inside a thick gauge polyethylene bag (fig. 4.22).

Objects made of lead and pewter should be packed only in acid-free tissue or plastic. The vapors given off by organic materials will attack lead; therefore, paper, cardboard, and wood—especially when freshly cut—should always be avoided.

Many robust materials, such as potsherds or bones, can be packed together in cloth or plastic bags. If plastic bags are used, make sure they are of a thick gauge which will not split or be punctured by the contents. Whether cloth or plastic bags are used, make sure that they are not too heavy when filled. Although it may be more convenient to keep all the material from one large deposit together in one bag, it is safer to use several smaller bags to prevent these materials from being crushed by their own weight if the bags are too full. The bags can also be extremely unwieldy and difficult to handle when they are too big and heavy.

The greatest harm to objects being transported comes from shock and vibration. A shock applied to the outside of the box will be transmitted directly through it to the object inside; this virtually undiminished force will break an improperly packed object. Therefore, when packing objects for transport, use large amounts of packing materials to cushion them and absorb any shocks. Think of the object as floating in the center of the box, surrounded by shock-absorbent materials (fig. 4.19A). The more layers of cushioning material the shock must pass through, the more it will be dispersed and the less force it will exert on the object.

The container should be large enough to accommodate the object comfortably and allow for adequate cushioning material. The object should never directly touch any internal surface of the container or any other object in that container. The amount of cushioning material needed will depend on what happens to the box. Obviously, when packing for storage on shelves it is not necessary to have as much cushioning material as when packing for air or vehicle transport. Use common sense in deciding on the amount of cushioning to use, but remember it is always better to err on the side of too much rather than too little. A general rule of thumb for storage is to surround an object with approximately 5 cm of padding; for transport, as much as 15or 20 cm of packing may be necessary around each object.

For a cushioning material to be an effective shock absorber, it must be resilient. If it is too soft or compresses too readily, it will not prevent shocks from being transmitted to the object. Rubber foam, polyethylene, and polystyrene expanded foams are excellent shock-absorbing materials. Styrofoam chips or peanuts can also be used; however, even when tightly packed, they have a tendency to shift and settle. These chips can be put into sealed plastic bags to minimize settling. Sawdust is not recommended because it compresses when used as a packing material.

Many of these packing materials may not be readily available in out-of-the-way places. Paper, by contrast, is generally readily available worldwide and acts as a very good shock absorber when crumpled; in this instance, newspaper can be safely used. Two or three sheets of crumpled paper have good shock-absorbing qualities, while the same few sheets smoothly wrapped around an object have virtually none. Crumpled cloth or sacking serves the same purpose.

The size and strength of the container needed will depend on the weight and size of the material to go into it and on the type of journey to which it will be subjected. Cardboard boxes are suitable for short, relatively easy trips, while wooden boxes or crates are necessary for longer, more rugged journeys. The lids of wooden containers should be secured with screws rather than nails. Shocks caused by hammering in nails can damage objects inside the box, and there are known instances of nails being driven into objects.

The size of the container should be commensurate with the size of the object(s) or boxes being packed in it: it is important not to crowd or overpack a container. The contents should fit comfortably together with copious amounts of crumpled paper to absorb shocks. If the paper or cushioning material is jammed in too tightly, it will no longer act as an efficient shock absorber. It is always better to have fewer boxes in a container and more packing material than vice versa.

When packing for transport, it is best to keep together objects or boxes of similar size, shape, weight, and material. Certainly, any materials that might require special handling at some point during the journey should be packaged separately before being packed together; for example, all soil samples should be wrapped separately. Then, if inspection by agricultural authorities is necessary, only one box with all the samples need be opened and disturbed.

The general principle for packing objects for transport is to first pack them individually or in small groups in small, well-padded boxes (fig. 4.23). Several of these small boxes are then placed together in larger, well-cushioned boxes which, in turn, are packed in larger containers. Enough cushioning material should be provided by this double or triple boxing system to ensure the safety of the material.

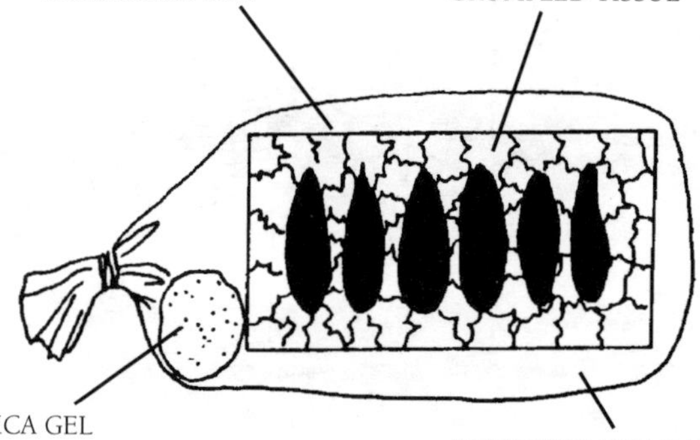

FIGURE 4.22 Packing metal objects in a cardboard box with silica gel

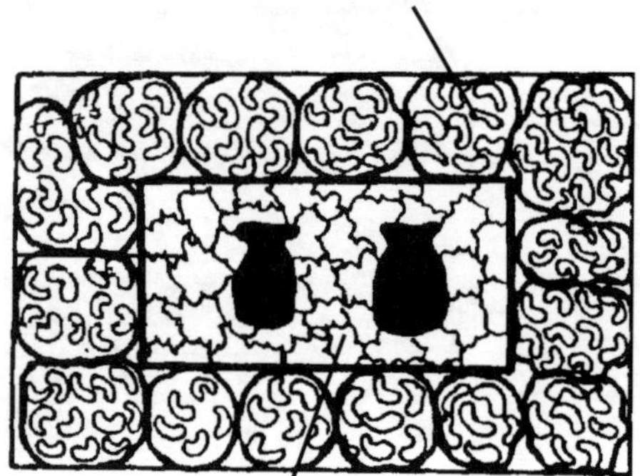

FIGURE 4.23 Box within a box system of packing for transport

Before packing for transport, make sure that all objects are well packed in their individual boxes. Generally, objects should not require repacking if they have been carefully packed following the guidelines set forth in the beginning of this section and in the sections in chapter 5. Some packing arrangements, however, might require minor changes. For example, bronzes in unsealed plastic bags may not fill the entire plastic container in which they have been placed. To prevent them from rattling around inside the container during transport, fill the empty spaces with polyethylene foam or crumpled acid-free tissue. The bottom of the container should be padded, as well. Whole, robust pots, kept in boxes without any packing to make them more readily accessible for study, must be well wrapped with tissue or soft polyethylene foam before being placed in a well-padded box for shipment.

Smaller boxes of objects can be packed in larger containers in the following manner. Put a thick layer of crumpled

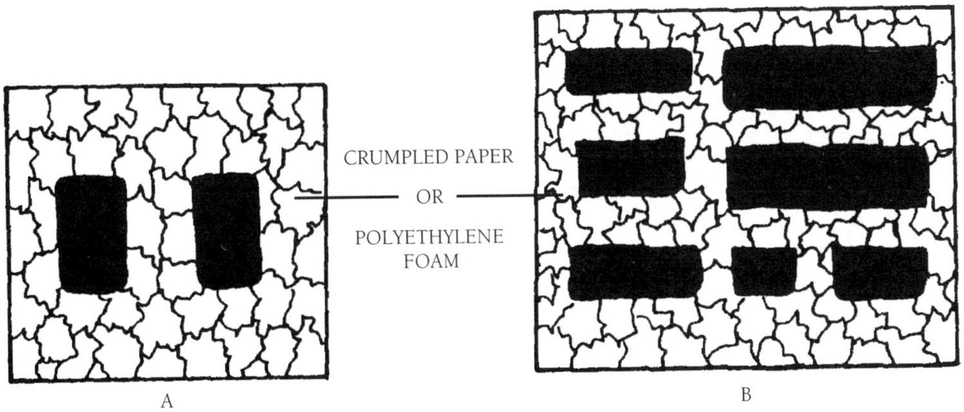

FIGURE 4.24. Packing boxes in boxes for transport. A, one layer of boxes; B, two or more layers of boxes.

paper or cushioning material on the bottom of the container. After being compressed by the weight of the boxes of objects, this layer should be no less than 10 cm thick. Then place the boxes of objects on top of the cushioning, making sure there is at least a 5 cm space around the sides of each box; individual boxes should not touch the sides of the container nor any other box. Fill the spaces around the boxes with more crumpled paper to ensure that they will remain separate and immobile. If only one layer of boxes will fit, they should sit more or less in the middle of the container, with the remaining space filled with more crumpled paper or cushioning material (fig. 4.24A). There should be enough paper so that there is slight resistance when the lid is closed. Tape the lid securely shut.

If more than one layer of boxes will fit in the container, place a layer of crumpled paper on top of the first layer after filling in around the sides. Then pack the second layer of boxes in the same manner as the first (fig.4.24B). Finish off the packing and seal the container as outlined above.

When packing bags of sherds or bones in a container for transport, make sure that the heavy bags are placed on the bottom. Do not fill the box too full or make it too heavy. Not only will the box be difficult to handle, but the material on the bottom is likely to be crushed by the weight of the material on top. Start by lining the box with a thick layer of cushioning material as described above. Then place a layer of bags on top of the cushioning. Try to put bags of the same size and weight together to form an even layer. In this instance, it is not necessary to keep the bags from touching one another; they should fit snugly together. Any excess plastic or cloth at the top of the bags will serve as additional cushioning material. After putting in a layer of bags, place a rigid piece of cardboard or expanded foam on top of them to help distribute the weight of the next layer (fig. 4.25). If bags of different size are in the same layer, it may be necessary to put additional packing material underneath the cardboard or foam to even out the layer.

Storage

The maintenance of stable environmental conditions in the storeroom throughout the year is the main concern when storing excavated material. No matter how hot and dry the storeroom may be in the summertime, it will undoubtedly be very damp during the rainy winter months unless, of course, it is centrally heated. Dampness can damage archaeological materials in three ways, causing a change in size and shape, a chemical reaction within the components, and biodeterioration.

All organic materials are sensitive to moisture and will react physically to fluctuations in relative humidity. They take on moisture and swell when the relative humidity rises, and give off that moisture and shrink when it falls. Such changes cause warping. Abrupt fluctuations in relative humidity also set up stresses in the material, leading to cracking and warping. In an object composed of different materials or of joined pieces, free movement of the different pieces can be restrained resulting in cracking, warping, or breaking. Even objects made of pieces of the same material can be damaged in this way because each piece can swell in different directions, restricting the movement of adjacent pieces.

High relative humidity also affects any porous material that is saturated with water-soluble salts, including pottery, stone, and wall plaster, and organic materials. Fluctuations in relative humidity cause these salts to exert physical pressure against the surface of the object, eventually resulting in the complete loss of the surface. For more information on soluble salt damage, see the section at the end of this chapter.

Moisture reacts chemically with metals, most particularly iron as well as copper and its alloys, causing corrosion. When this occurs, fluctuations in relative humidity are not

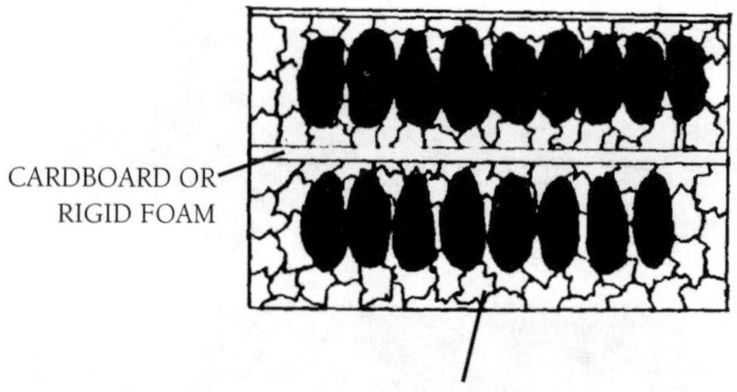

FIGURE 4.25 Packing bones or sherds in boxes for transport.

at issue, but rather overall high levels of relative humidity. Certain glass compositions are also sensitive to moisture because they are slightly soluble; in the presence of high relative humidity, some of their components can be leached out, causing tiny cracks to appear in the glass. Eventually, the glass becomes opaque. Little droplets of moisture also form on the glass, hence the name "weeping glass" applied to this condition.

Fungi, mold, bacteria, and most insects attack and damage organic materials at high humidities. Fungal and mold growth appear if the relative humidity exceeds 65%, and bacteria require even higher humidities.

For all these reasons, the relative humidity of a storeroom should be kept as low as possible. Fluctuations in relative humidity should also be kept to a minimum. Therefore, the building should be structurally sound and properly maintained year-round to prevent damage from leaking or flooding as well as to discourage infestation by insects and/or animals. For the same reasons, the building should be inspected regularly, including during the nonexcavation period, and any needed repairs made as soon as possible.

When objects are kept on site or in small local museums, it is generally difficult, if not impossible, to control storage conditions. Dampness is always a problem in the winter in countries where central heating is not common. In such places, however, if packing materials are chosen carefully and the proper packing procedures are used, much can be done to counter adverse circumstances.

Most materials should be stored in as dry a place as possible. While an acceptable humidity range is between 40% and 60% with as gradual fluctuations as possible, 45% to 55% is better. Temperature can range from 5° to 30° C. Direct sunlight on any organic material should be avoided because most radiant energy transforms into heat. In addition, organic materials should not be stored near any direct sources of heat or light. Both can cause these materials to dry out and become brittle, while light will initiate certain deterioration processes in most organic materials and also cause pigments to fade.

Such moisture-sensitive materials as glass, bone, ivory, wood, leather, and textiles require more strict control of the relative humidity. The range should fall within 45% to 55% with as little fluctuation as possible. Metals require drier conditions yet, ideally not above 30%. They should be packed in sealed, airtight containers with silica gel or be stored in a museum office or similar room that will be heated during the winter months. Glass known to be unstable should be kept below 40% relative humidity. If necessary, pack it in an airtight container with silica gel. Any material suspected or known to contain soluble salts should be stored in as dry a place as possible, using silica gel whenever necessary. Ideally, any sensitive material such as those mentioned should not be stored from one season to the next but taken to a conservator at the end of the digging season.

Store small boxes or bags containing objects in larger cardboard containers to avoid the loss or breakage of objects and to keep the storeroom tidy. So that they can be closed and sealed properly, make sure that the boxes will withstand the weight of heavy objects. If necessary, reinforce the bottom and seams of the box with strong tape.

For convenience, large robust objects, such as complete pots or stone objects, can be stored unboxed on open shelving. They should either be placed in plastic bags or covered with plastic sheeting to keep them clean. All boxes, especially those of cardboard, should be loosely covered with plastic sheeting at the end of each season. This helps to keep dirt out and to protect them from possible leaks.

All boxes and bags should be carefully labeled so that the contents are immediately clear. Boxes should be packed neatly with an accompanying list or diagram setting out the order. This process will save considerable wear and tear on objects since each box will not be needlessly disrupted every time an object must be located and examined.

For labeling boxes, use only indelible markers and labels that will not disintegrate or attract insects or rodents. Plastic or wooden labels survive best. Many excavations use plastic garden tags that can be written on with indelible felt-tip pens. Paper and cardboard labels placed inside plastic bags are not necessarily safe because rodents have been known to chew through plastic to get at them. Also, if the contents are not thoroughly dry, paper labels can disintegrate and encourage fungal growth.

Waterlogged Material

The packing of waterlogged material need not be any more difficult or complicated than the packing of dry objects as long as the proper materials are on hand. The primary aim is to prevent such materials from drying out; therefore, a good supply of sturdy polyethylene bags and plastic containers with tight-fitting lids is needed. If large quantities of odd-shaped pieces require packing, it may help to have polyethylene layflat tubing in several different widths. The tubing can be cut to fit the object and the ends heat-sealed to form a neat bag. Although moderately expensive, a heat sealer can be extremely useful for dealing with quantities of waterlogged material. Polyethylene foam and sheeting should also be on hand.

Waterlogged material should only be wrapped and padded with damp polyurethane foam. Paper and cloth should never be used because they are apt to rot before the object reaches a conservator. They will also encourage fungal growth.

Special labeling materials are required for packing waterlogged objects. Labels must be able to physically withstand a wet environment for an extended period of time and not encourage fungal growth. White spun-bonded polyethylene tags are the most suitable. A waterproof and fadeproof marker is needed. Many spirit-based felt-tip pens are readily available, and some ballpoint pens can be used. Any marker used should be tested first to make sure that it is indeed waterproof. Labels should be attached to the bags with plastic cord. String and metal wire should not be used because the former is biodegradable and the latter will corrode. If large timbers are involved, it may be necessary to attach the label directly to the wood with stainless steel tacks. Do not use any form of string or cord because it can very easily cut through the soft wood.

To prevent objects from drying out in their bags, use more than one bag per object. Place two or three bags inside each other; this procedure can be facilitated by having the outermost bag slightly larger than the other two. Place the object into the innermost bag, along with some of the mud surrounding it or a little water to which some fungicide has been added. The mud and water will help to maintain the burial conditions to which the object is accustomed and prevent it from drying out. Seal the bag containing the object before sealing the two remaining bags together. If the outermost bag is larger than the other two, it may be better to seal the two inside bags together, then the outside bag separately. The bags should then be placed in a sealed, plastic container with a tight-fitting lid.

An alternate method for keeping bagged waterlogged material wet is to use only one polyethylene bag to hold the object. Then place the filled bag in a sealed, plastic basin half filled with water to which a small amount of fungicide has been added. Cover the container with a snap-on lid and keep it in as cool a place as possible (fig. 4.26). In this way, many bags of waterlogged material can be stored together with a minimum of maintenance. The containers should be

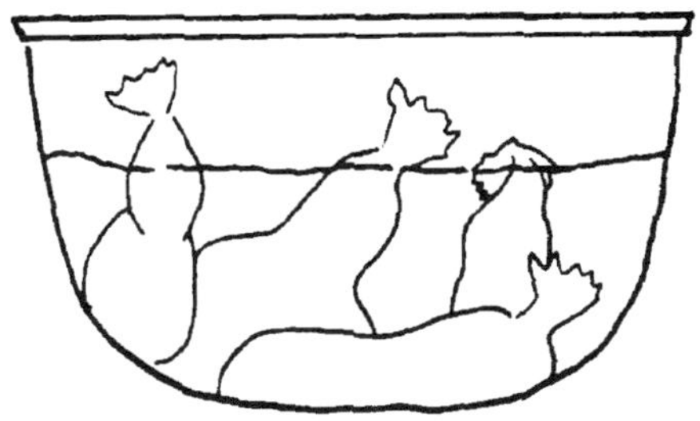

Figure 4.26 Bags of waterlogged material in sealed plastic container

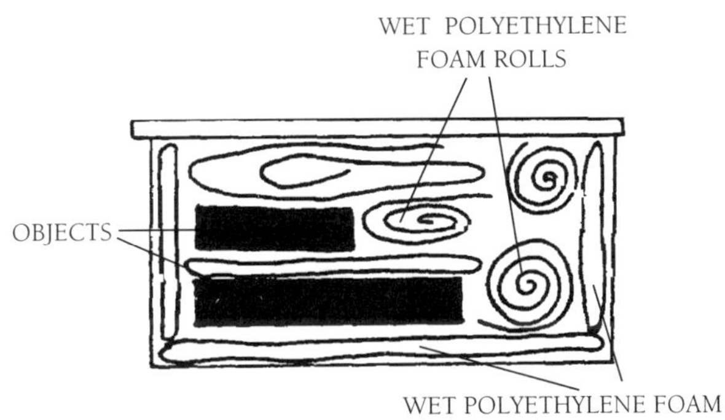

Figure 4.27 Waterlogged material packed in a plastic box with a snap-on lid

checked at regular intervals to make sure the water level is maintained and the objects are not drying out.

Many small objects, such as pieces of leather, can be placed directly into two or three polyethylene bags; fragile objects, however, require more support. Such objects should be placed in a plastic container which is well padded with damp polyethylene foam and capped with a tight-fitting lid. If necessary, use rolls of damp foam to hold the object gently in place (fig.4.27). Add a little fungicide before sealing the container. If the container is small and conditions warrant further protection, it can be placed inside a larger sealed container. Any material packed with fungicide should be labeled meticulously to that effect to ensure that people take the necessary precautions when handling it.

Large waterlogged objects, such as building timbers, pose a more difficult packing problem. Wrap them carefully in several layers of damp polyethylene foam to cushion them and keep them damp. If wood is involved, do not secure the foam with string that can cut through the soft surface of the waterlogged wood; use strips of polyethylene sheeting instead. When the foam is securely fastened, carefully wrap the object in several layers of polyethylene sheeting, followed by a final layer of thick gauge, heavy-duty polyethylene. Make sure that the polyethylene is securely fastened around the object.

Wrapped objects should be covered with damp, water-

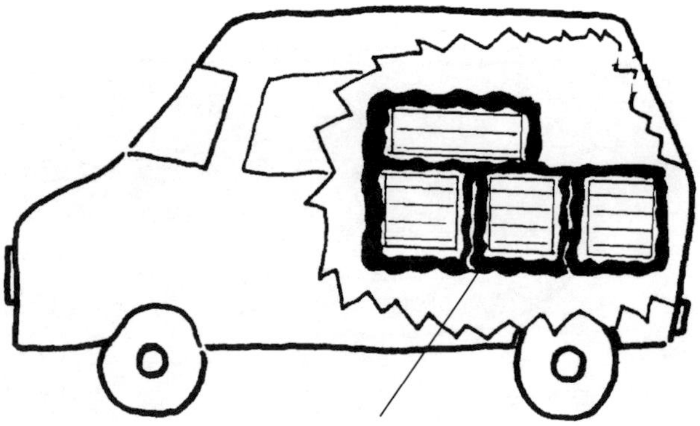

FIGURE 4.28 Method for packing a vehicle

absorbent material and kept in as cool a place as possible. If they must remain outdoors, keep them in a well-shaded spot and wet them down, when necessary, to prevent them from drying out. Transfer them to more permanent storage as soon as possible.

If large pieces of waterlogged material do not go to a conservation laboratory almost immediately after lifting, some form of tank will be needed to store them temporarily. A simple rectangular tank can be built using a wooden or metal frame. The sides can be made of plywood lined with heavy-duty polyvinyl chloride pool lining. Pre-existing tanks can be adapted for use as well. The tank water should have enough fungicide added to it to make up a 0.2% solution.

Place the wrapped objects in the tank. If they are on wooden pallets for support, it may be necessary to weight the pallets to submerge them. To keep out dirt and light, the tank should be covered with a sheet of black heavy-duty plastic stretched taut across the top. Storage of such large pieces of waterlogged material should be attempted only with the advice and close cooperation of a trained conservator who is experienced in handling waterlogged material.

All waterlogged material should be stored in as cool a place as possible to discourage microbiological growth. If possible, refrigerate the material. If this is done, do not allow the material to become cold enough to freeze because serious damage could result. At the end of the digging season, the material should be taken to an experienced conservator; no waterlogged material should remain on site during the nondigging season.

Transportation

Transportation of objects is always a difficult problem. Unfortunately, it is impossible to be specific because every site and the conditions pertaining to it are different. By their very nature, excavations are generally in out-of-the-way places, and transportation can involve anything from backpacking, pack animals, and boats to cars, trucks, and airplanes, or any combination of these. Each has its own particular set of problems regarding fragile objects, and these problems are compounded when two or more modes of transport are involved. For example, there are tremendous vibrations inside the hold of an airplane during flight. If not well packed with extensive amounts of shock-absorbent materials, objects can literally be shaken to pieces. Baggage cars on trains also undergo steady vibrations as well as bumps from uneven roadbeds and shunting. Rough handling can present problems for any form of transport not undertaken or directly supervised by the archaeologist. Use of staff members to transport objects by car or truck is generally the safest means. These people know the nature of the cargo and can make special allowances when necessary. Even so, this form of transportation is not without its problems. Frequently, excavation vehicles are unsprung, and roads to and from the site are bumpy and unpaved, if they exist at all.

Since you cannot change the fact that objects must be transported under less than ideal conditions, be very sure to pack them properly with copious amounts of good shock-absorbent materials. Always err on the side of using more, rather than less, packing material.

Common sense plays a major role here. Before packing the boxes of objects, consider the nature and amount of material being transported, its condition and degree of fragility; also consider the rigors of the journey, its duration, and possible mishaps. Then adjust the extra amount of packing materials to fit the requirements of the trip. Obviously, five to ten small objects packed in small polystyrene boxes traveling by parcel post will require less packing material than ten large boxes of complete pots traveling overland in an unsprung truck, followed by an airplane trip. Those same boxes of whole pots, however, will require much less packing material if the trip involves only a two-hour ride in an air-cushioned truck over smooth highways. Even so, the same packing principles are used in all three instances; what differs is the amount of packing material needed. If a journey involves several different methods of transportation, it may be possible to take advantage of a transfer point to adjust the packing or even repack certain objects to better prepare them for the next stage of the trip.

If a rigorous journey is expected, a double box system is by far the safest packing arrangement; the more layers that shocks are forced to pass through, the more they are dispersed. Any extremely fragile object should automatically be packed using a double- or triple-boxing system (fig. 4.23).

Extremely fragile materials going by air should be hand carried on board by a staff member and not placed in the cargo hold where they could be badly damaged by rough handling and strong vibrations. Vibration in the passenger cabin is only a fraction of that found in the hold.

If you are transporting the objects yourself, certain additional precautions can be taken to protect them. When loading the conveyance—whether a vehicle, canoe, or pack mule—think of it as just another packing box. Pack it by applying the same principles and procedures as when packing boxes with objects. For example, do not put the boxes directly onto the floor of a vehicle or bottom of a boat. A layer of rubber pads, crumpled blankets, or sacking placed directly under the boxes will further protect them and their contents by absorbing shocks (fig. 4.28). This cushioning should extend to the sides of the boxes as well, to prevent them from coming in direct contact with the conveyance or other boxes.

Put boxes with extremely fragile objects in the area of the conveyance which will be subject to the least amount of shock and vibration. Avoid putting them over the wheels or in the very back of a vehicle. Take the smoothest, safest route to your destination, although it may be a longer route. If driving, avoid ruts, potholes, and rough terrain that will cause the load to bounce and jostle. If this is not possible, drive very slowly to minimize the bumps.

If a boat or canoe is used, make sure that all boxes containing objects are carefully sealed in plastic bags. Do this also for all site notebooks, plans, film, and negatives. If it seems appropriate, pack objects in containers that are watertight or that will float. Boxes can also be wrapped in or attached to life preservers to keep them afloat should an accident occur.

Soluble Salt Removal

The presence of soluble salts in objects is one of the biggest conservation problems, not only for freshly excavated materials but also for objects that have been cleaned and are in storage or on display in museums. These salts should not be confused with insoluble salts, which do not harm the objects on which they are found but will obscure detail and decoration (fig. 4.29). Certain salts, mainly chlorides, nitrates, and sulfates, are readily soluble in water and are absorbed by any porous material buried in the ground. Pottery, stone, bone, and ivory are generally contaminated with soluble salts.

Upon excavation, the moisture in the object begins to evaporate; the salts dissolved in it begin to crystallize out, at or just below the object's surface. In the solid, crystalline form, these salts have a larger volume than when in solution, and crystallization exerts a great physical pressure against the underside surface of the object. If the object is re-wet or the relative humidity level becomes high enough, these salts will revert into solution and then recrystallize out when the moisture is again removed. This cycle of wetting and drying,

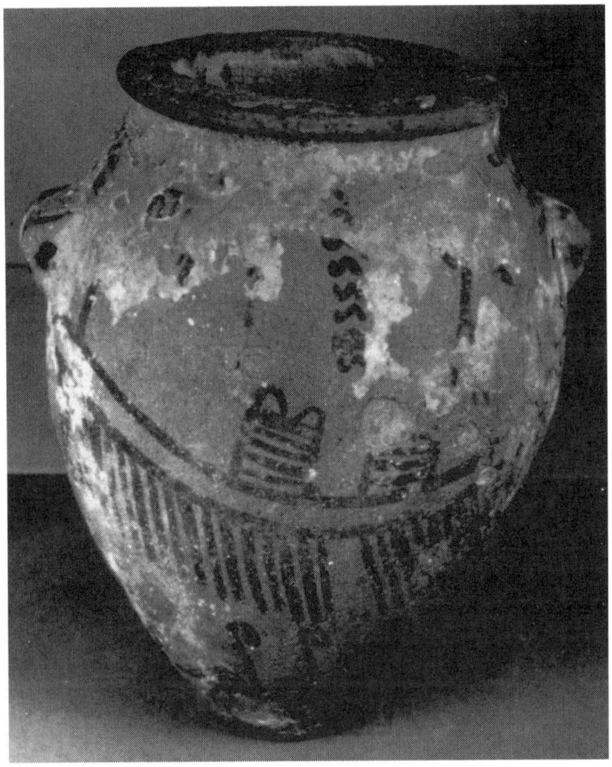

FIGURE 4.29 Insoluble salt encrustation on an Egyptian pot

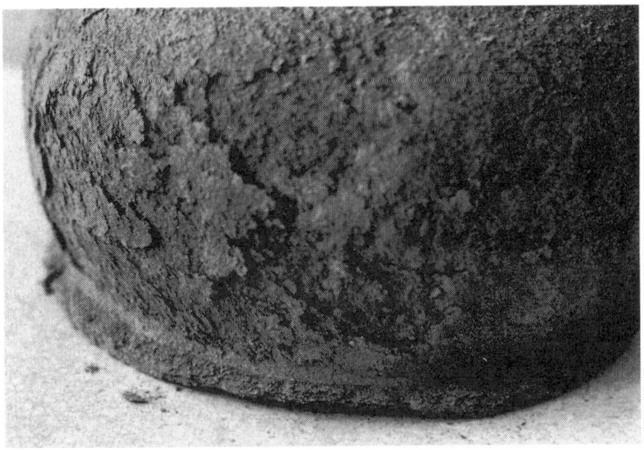

FIGURE 4.30 Soluble salts in a Greek pot cause the surface to exfoliate.

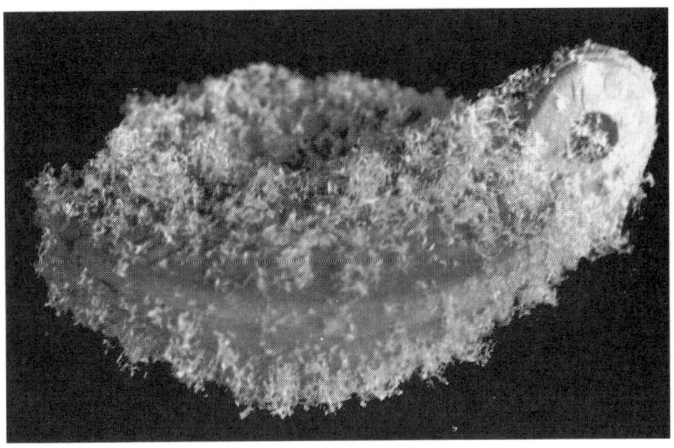

FIGURE 4.31 Soluble salt crystals growing on a Greek ceramic lamp

with its attendant crystallizing and recrystallizing out of salts, will eventually result in the surface of the object literally being pushed off (fig. 4.30). A white efflorescence or bloom on the surface of an object indicates that salts are present, and, in extreme cases, large white salt crystals will grow out of such contaminated material (fig. 4.31).

The presence of soluble salts in pottery can also be caused by inadequate rinsing after a pot has been cleaned with acid. An insoluble salt encrustation, when dissolved by an acid, produces a soluble salt that, if not thoroughly rinsed out, will remain in the fabric of the pot and behave exactly like soluble salts absorbed through burial. If kept in a place where there are drastic fluctuations in relative humidity, pots will undergo the solution/crystallization cycle with the same resulting loss of surface. The final, thorough rinsing of pottery cleaned with acid, therefore, is an essential step that should never be omitted or shortened to speed up the washing process. Untold damage will result later unless extremely dry storage conditions can be guaranteed.

For these reasons, it is important to remove soluble salts from excavated material before they cause any damage. This procedure is not generally undertaken in the field unless a conservator is present as it requires numerous containers, a plentiful supply of uncontaminated or, better still, distilled water, and someone to monitor the process. Even for a trained conservator, this process is difficult to monitor in the field because it is not easy to determine which soluble salts are present or when they have been removed. It is also necessary to have a conductivity meter (an extremely expensive piece of equipment) to read the salt levels in the wash water.

If a material is known to contain soluble salts, it is best to keep it in as dry a place as possible and take it to a conservator at the earliest opportunity. If the soluble salt problem is particularly acute or if large quantities of material contain soluble salts, it may be necessary to set up a soaking system under the supervision of a conservator. No soaking should be undertaken, however, without the advice of a conservator familiar with the site and its material. Frequently, the salts are all that bind the material together; their removal without prior treatment could result in the total disintegration of the object.

Chapter Five

Specific Materials and Treatments

Amber

Amber is the fossilized resin of certain coniferous trees. It has long been thought to come from the extinct *Pinus succinifera*, but recent studies suggest a species of *Agathis* as the source. Although referred to as fossilized, amber is not petrified in the geological sense. How resin is transformed into amber is not completely understood. The process involves the presence of heat, pressure, and sea water, among other things, and takes place over millions of years.

Amber is not a homogeneous substance given that it consists generally of several resinous bodies and often contains inclusions such as air bubbles, bits of wood, leaves, and insects. Slightly heavier than water, it does not float. Slightly harder than gypsum, amber cannot be scratched with a fingernail. It is amorphous and breaks conchoidally, as do glass and obsidian. Amber is not brittle; it can easily be carved, worked on a lathe, and bored. It can take a high polish. When rubbed against wool, fur, or similar materials, however, it becomes strongly charged with static electricity. This electrical property gave it a reputation in the ancient world for having magical and medicinal properties. Because it is a natural resin, amber is soluble in most solvents and in acids.

The chief sources of amber are the Baltic coasts of Germany, Lithuania, and Latvia, but varieties, differing in color and composition, are known from other parts of the world—in particular, England, Canada, Sicily, Rumania, Burma, and the Dominican Republic. All material from archaeological sites that has been called amber is not necessarily true Baltic amber but rather other kinds of resins which are common locally, especially in Egypt.

Amber is uniform in color, although it can range from translucent to cloudy to opaque. The cloudiness in amber, especially Baltic amber, is caused by masses of tiny air bubbles. The natural color of Baltic amber ranges from pale yellow to deep orange-brown; amber that has undergone surface alteration is often red. Amber that is almost white is very rare. A greater range of colors can be found in local, amberlike resins.

Amber was highly prized and used extensively in the Bronze and Iron Ages of Europe. By the late Bronze Age, it had spread as far east as Assyria, thanks to the extensive trade routes developed by the Classical World.

Atmospheric oxygen is the principal cause of deterioration of amber. Exposure to light and heat accelerates the oxidation process, causing amber to darken and lose its polish. It also leads to the development of deep cracks that will eventually render the surface of the amber opaque and brittle. The opaque surface shown in figure 5.1 has crumbled off in places, revealing the shiny unaltered amber underneath. When in situ, amber is often so badly deteriorated that it is difficult to distinguish from its surrounding dirt. If sufficiently deteriorated, amber objects can crumble as soon as they are removed from the ground and allowed to dry out. It is wise to assume that all amber found is extremely fragile. It should be handled very carefully at all times and as little as possible.

If amber is found wet or waterlogged, it should be kept as wet as when found. If it cannot be removed from the ground immediately upon discovery, cover it at once with mud or with layers of damp polyethylene foam or other absorbent material, followed by plastic sheeting.

To lift wet amber, carefully isolate it on a pedestal of dirt, but do not remove all the surrounding mud. Gently loosen the object, lift it off the pedestal, and place it immediately into three well-sealed polyethylene bags along with some of the surrounding mud. Place the bags in a plastic container with a snap-on lid. The amber should be taken to a conservator as soon as possible. If much time will elapse before this happens, keep the amber in a cool place and check it regularly to make sure that it does not dry out.

An alternate method of packing wet amber, especially if it is quite fragile and requires more support, is to place it directly into a plastic container with damp polyethylene

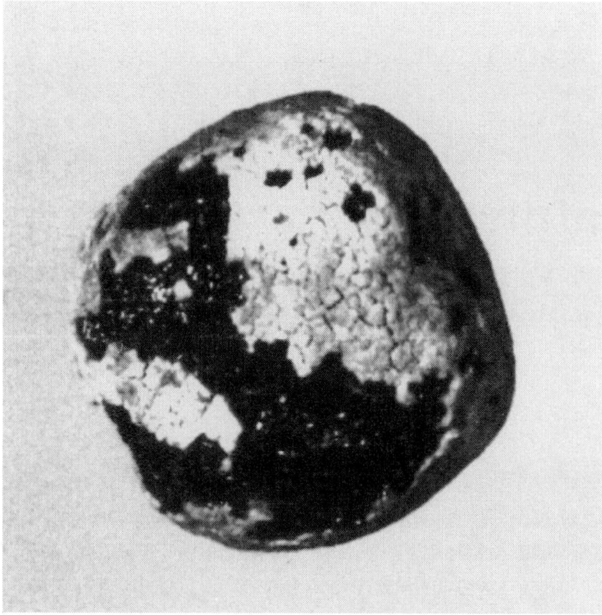

FIGURE 5.1 Amber bead excavated in England. The thick opaque surface of the amber has crumbled off in many places.

foam to cushion it and prevent it from moving inside the box. Cover the container with a tight-fitting lid.

If amber is found in good condition, it should be a straightforward process to remove it from the ground by following general lifting procedures. First, carefully remove all dirt surrounding the object, being sure to use only wooden tools or brushes (metal tools can easily scratch the surface of the amber). Carefully undercut the object and, when it is completely free, gently lift it out of the ground. Place it in a well-padded, rigid container until it can be properly packed.

If the amber is badly deteriorated but still can be lifted, do so very carefully following the method described above, and place the object directly into a rigid container. If necessary, wrap the object in polyethylene foam for support and protection. If the amber is severely deteriorated and extremely fragile, it should be lifted in a block following one of the block lifting procedures set forth in chapter 4. It is not wise to try to consolidate amber while it is still in the ground because it is frequently difficult to distinguish between the amber and the surrounding dirt. Solvent must be chosen carefully because amber is soluble in many solvents. Amber should be consolidated only after it has been properly cleaned.

Once out of the ground, sound amber should not need much more than a gentle cleaning with a soft brush. Hard lumps of dirt can be softened first by being touched with a damp brush and then removed with a wooden toothpick or a soft brush. Do not pry or flick off any lumps of dirt because part of the surface of the object may come off with them. Do not use metal tools, and be careful not to scratch the surface of the amber while cleaning it.

Any remaining dirt can be removed with damp swabs of distilled water. Only water should be used as a cleaning agent. Swabs should be moist but not dripping wet. Do not rub the surface of the amber with the swab because this action can scratch the amber. Rather, gently roll the swab over a small portion of the surface until it is clean. As soon as a swab becomes dirty, discard it for a clean one because a dirty swab can be extremely abrasive.

True amber is slightly soluble in alcohol and organic solvents, wheras amberlike resins are more readily soluble. Since it is virtually impossible to distinguish between true amber and amberlike resins—especially when they have come straight from the ground, avoid the use of all solvents.

If the surface of the amber is crizzled—that is, riddled with a network of minute cracks—and small pieces are flaking or crumbling off, do not attempt to clean it. Instead, pack it carefully as described below and take it to a trained conservator for treatment.

Since amber is sensitive to solvents, no attempt should be made to join broken fragments; the solvent in the adhesive could dissolve the amber. For the same reason, only a trained conservator should attempt to consolidate amber in the field.

Amber objects should be individually packed in rigid polystyrene boxes that are well padded with acid-free tissue or polyethylene foam. Place the object in a depression in the wadded tissue or foam and cover it with another flat wad of padding to keep it firmly in place. Make sure, however, that undue pressure is not exerted on the amber when the lid is closed or the object could break.

Amber objects should be stored away from direct sources of heat and light, which accelerate the deterioration processes. The storage area should not be excessively damp or dry, nor should the amber be subjected to drastic fluctuations in relative humidity.

Antler

Antler, an outgrowth of the skull bones of cervids (a group that includes deer, elk, moose, and caribou), can be treated as bone. Unlike horns of other animals, antlers consist of solid bone, are generally branched, and are shed annually. Structurally they are very similar to long bones in that they consist of a hard outer layer surrounding a spongy central area. Unlike long bones, however, antlers have no central marrow cavity. The outer surface of antler is characteristically rough and channeled to accommodate the numerous blood vessels necessary to supply such a rapidly growing structure. At the base of the antler is a burr where the antler attaches to the skull;

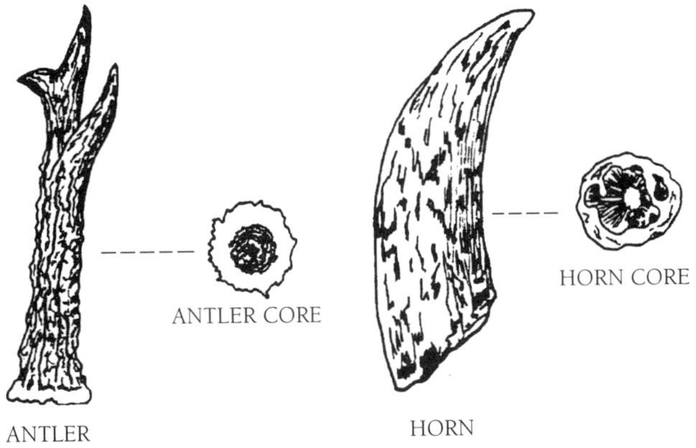

FIGURE 5.2 Differences between antler and horn cores. The antler is hard with a spongy central area, but it does not have a central cavity as do horn cores.

this is a diagnostic feature of antler. Antler, a very hard material tougher than skeletal bone, was used to make tools and was carved into a wide variety of objects. The differences between antler and horn cores are detailed in figure 5.2.

Basketry

Baskets are handmade containers formed by interlacing two or more strands of fibers. These fibers are generally vegetal; the leaves of various palms, twigs, vines, grasses, and roots are the most commonly used materials. Basketry differs from weaving in that no preparation of the fiber (other than cutting it) is necessary. In many instances, however, material was further prepared by stripping off the outer layer or bark and splitting it into suitable widths. These same materials and techniques were used to make things other than containers. Wickerwork, for example, was used to fashion walls and fences, and a wide variety of mats and matting was made and used in antiquity. For the purposes of this book, these materials and objects are all treated as basketry.

Since these natural fibers are perishable, baskets survive archaeologically only under either very wet or very dry stable conditions. Dry, sandy desert sites, as found in Egypt and coastal Peru, are very good for preservation. Numerous good examples have been recovered from the peat bogs of Scandinavia and from waterlogged sites in northern Europe, Britain, the United States, and Canada.

If found dry, a basket should not pose too great a problem. Always keep in mind, however, that the fibers have dried out and are probably extremely brittle. Although they may look sound and robust, they are not. A minimum of very gentle handling is best.

To lift a basket from the ground, carefully clean around it, using only a soft brush or wooden tool to remove all surrounding dirt. Metal tools should not be used because they can damage the fibers and surface of the basket. After freeing it, examine the basket to determine whether or not the dirt inside it should be removed. If the basket is very fragile, the weight of the dirt might be too much for the fibers to bear and the basket will break when lifted. It is possible, however, for this same dirt to provide support for the basket. If the dirt is adhering tightly to the basket, it should probably be left inside. If the dirt has pulled away from the basket and is loose and free to shift, it should be taken out. Remove the dirt gently with a spoon, being careful not to scrape or abrade the inside of the basket. Then carefully undercut the basket and, when free, gently lift it out of the ground, cradling it in both hands. Never pick up a basket by its rim; always support it gently, but firmly, with both hands underneath. Place the basket in a well-padded, rigid container until it can be properly packed.

Do not attempt to clean the basket; even the gentlest of brushing can break the fibers. Even flicking off bits of dirt can exert sufficient pressure to snap brittle fibers. No attempt should be made to join any broken pieces; instead, wrap them in acid-free tissue and keep them with the basket.

The basket should be packed in a rigid box, well padded with acid-free tissue in the following manner. Fill the bottom and corners of the box with crumpled acid-free tissue to make a depression, or well, in the center of the box that is the approximate size and shape of the basket. To prevent the crumpled tissue from snagging and catching on the basket, line the well with pieces of flat tissue to provide a smooth surface. Place the basket in the well. Cover the top of the basket with a smooth wad of tissue, followed by crumpled tissue to fill out the box. When the lid is closed, there should be slight resistance from the packing material to prevent the basket from moving inside the box.

If acid-free tissue is not available, newspaper can be used to pad the container and support the basket as long as a separator, such as a flat sheet of thin gauge polyethylene, is used to prevent the basket from coming in direct contact with the newspaper. The basket can, alternatively, be placed inside a polyethylene bag that has been perforated all over. Do not seal the bag, but rather leave it loosely open to allow the circulation of air.

Keep the basket in an area that is neither too damp nor too dry and away from any sources of heat and light. Take it to a conservator for proper treatment as soon as possible.

A damp or waterlogged basket will pose a lifting problem; its fibers will be very fragile, having lost many of their structural components. Often only the water within the cellular structure has allowed the fibers to keep their shape. If the fibers dry out, the high surface tension of the water will

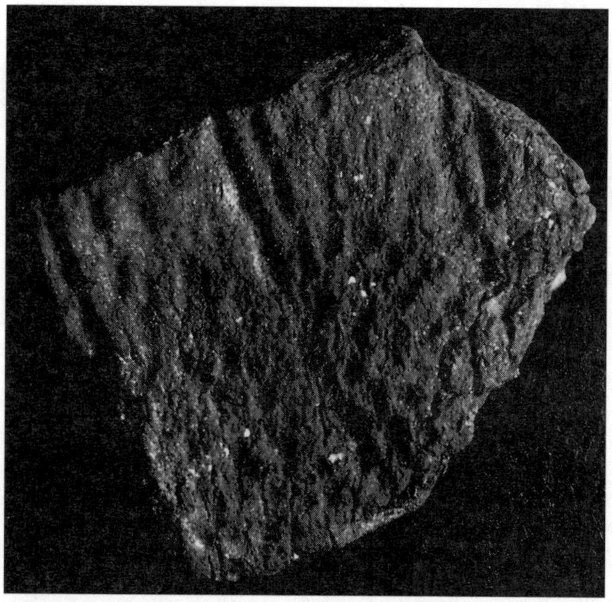

FIGURE 5.3 Minoan potsherd with basketry impressions

force weakened cell walls to collapse; the fibers will shrink, distort, split, and possibly disintegrate altogether. It is essential, therefore, to keep the basket damp from the moment it is uncovered until it is treated in a conservation laboratory. Drying out for even a few minutes can cause irreparable damage. If the basket cannot be taken out of the ground immediately upon discovery, it must be covered at once with layers of damp polyethylene foam or other absorbent material, followed by plastic sheeting. If necessary, spray water frequently on the basket to prevent its drying out. Once a basket is covered in this manner, it is important to keep it covered. Even if it is an extremely important find and visitors want to see it, do not uncover it or it will be subjected to unnecessary risk of irreparable damage.

To lift the wet basket, carefully clean around it to isolate it on a pedestal of mud, but do not remove all the surrounding mud. Being quite cohesive, this mud helps support the basket and will maintain it, while it is packed and stored, in the conditions to which it became accustomed during burial. Carefully lift the basket, along with its surrounding mud, out of the ground, cradling it in both hands. Place it immediately into three polyethylene bags. Before sealing the bags, add 20 to 25 ml of 0.2% fungicide to the bag containing the basket. Seal the bags and then place them, in turn, in a container half filled with water to which more fungicide has been added. Keep the sealed container in as cool a place as possible and take the basket to a conservator for treatment.

If the basket is small enough, it can be put directly into a plastic container with a tight-fitting lid. Pad the container first with damp polyethylene foam to support the basket and keep it from moving. Add a little fungicide to the box before sealing it. Store the container in as cool a place as possible and check the basket regularly to make sure it does not dry out. To ensure safe handling, it is important that any basket packed with fungicide be labeled meticulously.

If possible, refrigerate the wet basket, but make very sure that it does not get cold enough to freeze. Refrigeration may obviate the need for fungicide. Consult a conservator before adding the fungicide.

If the basket is extremely fragile, a block lifting technique may be necessary to remove the basket safely from the ground. Use whichever block lifting technique is suitable for the site. Usually, the first block lifting method described in chapter 4 is best. Remember that because the object and the soil are wet, they will be heavy and unmanageable if too large a block is taken. Once the block is out of the ground, fully support and securely wrap it in several sheets of wet polyethylene foam, then in several layers of polyethylene sheeting. If the block is small enough, it can be placed in three well-sealed polyethylene bags to which 20 to 50 ml of 0.2% fungicide have been added. It can also be put into a plastic basin that is tightly covered with plastic sheeting. Keep the block in a cool place, and take it to a conservator as soon as possible. If it must sit for some time before , check it frequently to make sure it does not dry out. Spray it with a fine mist of water, if necessary, to keep it moist.

It is possible to find evidence of basketry on a site when the basket itself has long since disappeared. Frequently, impressions of basketry or matting are found on pottery sherds (fig. 5.3). These impressions can provide surprisingly detailed information about basketry. Any sherds with such impressions should be carefully cleaned to prevent them from being blurred or obliterated. (See the section on pottery). Simple plaster impressions can be made from such impressions. (See appendix I.)

Bitumen

Bitumen refers to a group of naturally occurring hydrocarbons, that is, compounds consisting primarily of hydrogen and carbon that are derivatives of petroleum. This group includes asphalt, rock asphalt, petroleum asphalt, wood tar, and wood tar pitch. These substances vary considerably in color, hardness, and volatility. The proportion of carbon to other elements also varies considerably. In general, the higher the carbon content, the blacker and more viscous the bitumen.

Bitumen, a dark brown or black substance, is extremely viscous and sticky. It melts with low heat and sets on cooling; the exact temperature at which it softens depends on its composition. The main sources of bitumen in antiq-

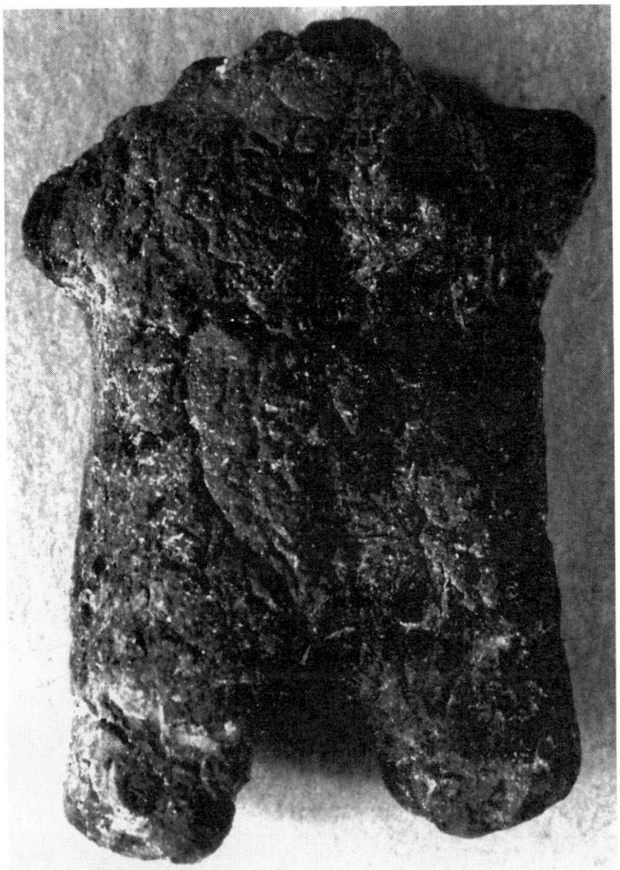

FIGURE 5.4 Mesopotamian figurine made of bitumen

uity were large surface deposits in Mesopotamia where there was once a flourishing industry. This industry died out when the Greeks and Romans introduced a change in building techniques. Bitumen was also found along the Red Sea, in Palestine, and in California.

Bitumen was used mainly in Mesopotamia, but has been found as far east as the Indus Valley and was also known in Neolithic Europe. In California, it was used by Indians. Bitumen was used primarily as a building mortar and waterproofing agent, but it also served as a paint, a core for modeling metal, and a mastic. When used as a mortar or mastic, it was necessary to add a filler of sand, gravel, or some kind of vegetal material, such as straw, to render the bitumen more viscous and prevent it from flowing when it became too hot. In the Middle East and parts of Europe, it was used to secure flints in sickles and for hafting arrowheads. Small objects have been fashioned out of lumps of bitumen, as shown in figure 5.4. In this instance, the bitumen was bulked out with a filler, such as sand or chopped straw, to make it easier to model.

When found on a site, bitumen is generally dark brown or black in color and is hard and brittle. Frequently, the surface is covered with tiny holes which have become filled with dirt, giving the bitumen a spotty appearance. Bitumen is insoluble in water, but will dissolve in petroleum distillates such as toluene. It also dissolves slightly in chloroform and turns brown. It will melt on heating and burns with a smoky flame.

For the most part, bitumen requires little in the way of treatment in the field. Although a stable material, it is generally very brittle so that it must be handled carefully and gently at all times. When lifting and carrying it, try to protect it from any unnecessary shocks.

If found in good condition, bitumen can be easily removed from the ground following general lifting procedures. Carefully clean all around the bitumen to remove the surrounding dirt and define the shape of the object. Be sure to use only wooden tools or a brush because metal tools can scratch and abrade the bitumen. When free of surrounding dirt, carefully undercut the bitumen and lift it out of the ground. Place it in a rigid, well-padded container filled with tissue or polyethylene foam until it can be properly packed.

Once out of the ground, sound bitumen can be cleaned with a soft brush and barely-moistened swabs. Avoid getting water into any cracks on the surface; never immerse bitumen in water. If dirt does not remove easily, leave it for a conservator.

Since bitumen was used as a building mortar and mastic, it is common to find bits of wood, reeds, basketry, and other materials mixed in with it. These materials can be identified botanically, providing important information about the site. When cleaning bitumen, therefore, watch for such organic material and be careful not to damage or remove it. It is also common to find impressions of these materials in the bitumen. Although the organic matter has long since disappeared, the impressions left by it contain structural details that permit botanical identifications to be made. When cleaning pieces of bitumen, be careful not to damage such impressions. If it is not possible for an expert to see them, it is an easy matter to photograph and draw them; it is also possible to make a cast or impression.(See appendix I.) If an impression is to be made with rubber latex, first test the latex on a small, insignificant piece of bitumen to ensure that the ammonia in the latex does not dissolve or affect the bitumen in any way.

Lifting can be a problem if the bitumen is not in good condition. It can be found with deep cracks and, occasionally, be completely shattered. Since bitumen is an impermeable material, it is pointless to attempt consolidation. Also, the solvent of the consolidant could dissolve or otherwise adversely affect the bitumen. If a very friable piece is found, probably the safest course of action is to use one of the block lifting techniques set forth in chapter 4, although simple backing could be used as long as the solvent needed to remove the backing does not dissolve the bitumen. For this reason,avoid using toluene. Test a small fragment by placing it in a small amount of acetone in a covered jar. Watch it carefully for 10 to 15 minutes. If the bitumen does not dissolve, then PVA or Acryloid B72 could be used to back it.

Because it is a stable material, bitumen does not require special packing or storage treatment. Pack the object in a polystyrene, metal, or cardboard box; the rigidity of the box will protect the brittle specimen. Pad the box first with acid-free tissue or polyethylene foam. Place the object in a depression in the tissue or foam, and cover it with another flat wad of packing to hold it firmly in place. Exert no undue pressure on the bitumen when the lid is closed or the specimen could break.

Store the bitumen in a reasonably dry area that does not become extremely hot during the summer months. It should also be kept away from direct sources of heat.

Bone and Bone Objects

All bone, whether animal or human, is made up of components both mineral (mainly calcium phosphate) and organic (largely proteins and fats). These components combine to form different types of bone structure, depending on the part or function of the bone. The long bones of any skeleton consist of an external shell of dense, compact material called lamellar bone, which surrounds an inner spongy material called cancellous bone which, in turn, surrounds a central marrow cavity (fig. 5.5). Lamellar bone is hard and solid,and cancellous bone is composed of large, irregular spaces creating a spongy appearance. Even though lamellar bone may seem solid, it contains minute canals throughout for the passage of blood vessels and nerves. These holes—called *canaliculi*—are a diagnostic feature of bone and serve to distinguish worked bone from ivory (fig.5.6). It was lamellar bone, generally from long bones, that was carved into tools and objects. Worked bone can be distinguished easily from ivory if all traces of cancellous bone have not been removed (fig. 5.7).

Archaeological bone undergoes complex chemical and physical deterioration, depending on the structure and type of bone, what was done to the bone before burial, and soil and environmental conditions to which it was exposed during burial. Acidic soils attack the mineral components which give bone its rigidity and strength. Extremely alkaline soils attack the organic components of bone, rendering it brittle and friable. Neutral or slightly alkaline soils provide the best conditions for preservation. If subjected to heat, the results will be fracturing, shrinking, warping, and white calcination—eventually causing embrittlement.

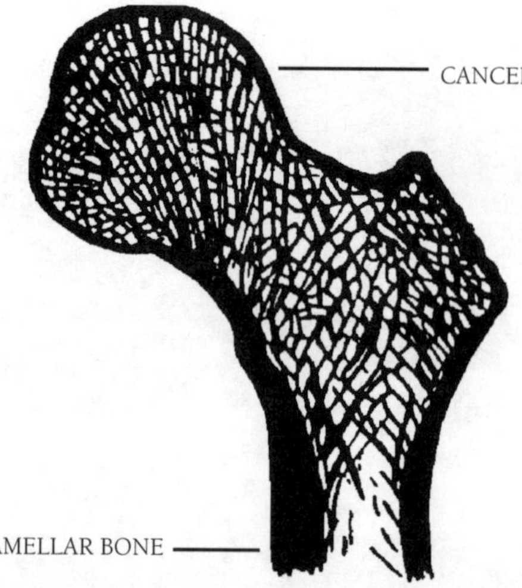

FIGURE 5.5. Structure of bone

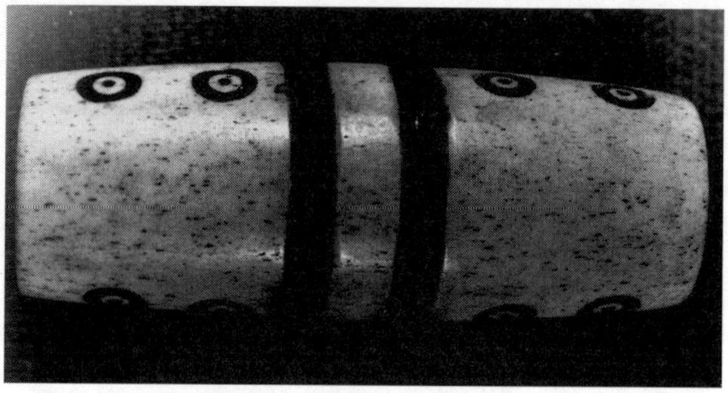

FIGURE 5.6. Canaliculi, the small dark spots, are clearly visible on this worked bone object from the northwest coast of Canada.

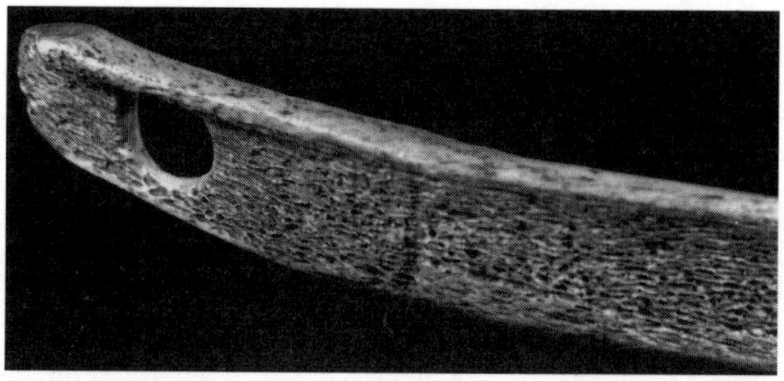

FIGURE 5.7 Eskimo worked-bone object with traces of cancellous bone.

UNMODIFIED ANIMAL BONE: When excavating animal bone, it is important to save all material found. No selection whatsoever should be made of bones or bone fragments unless an expert is present: otherwise, the information provided by the bones can be drastically skewed. The most important animal bones are horn cores, mandibles, pelves, metapodials, and skulls; they provide detailed information on age, sex, and species (fig. 5.8).

If a bone is to be used for radiocarbon dating, it must be collected using the procedure in the section on radiocarbon sampling. Bone to be used for radiocarbon dating must not be consolidated or in any way treated with chemicals because it will become contaminated.

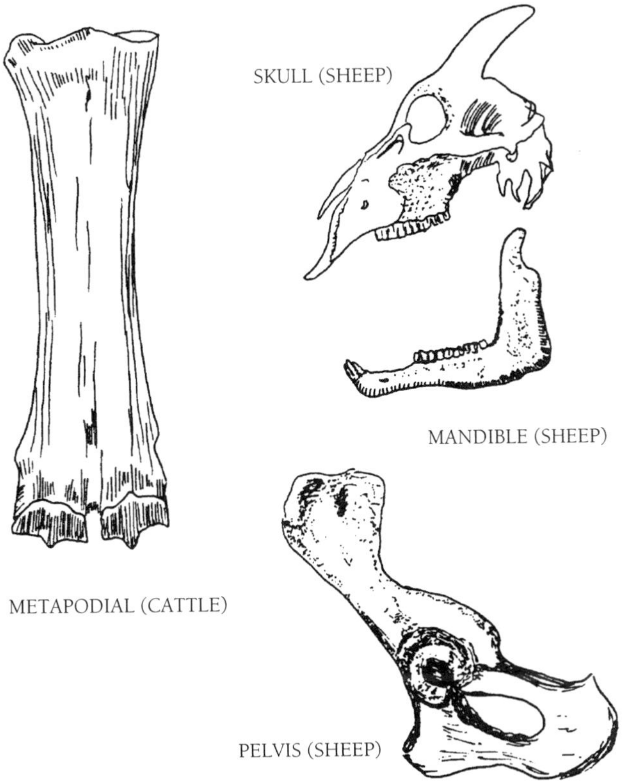

FIGURE 5.8. Animal bones particularly useful for identification.

If bone is sound, it can be lifted easily following general lifting procedures. First, using a stiff paintbrush, carefully clean around the bone to remove all surrounding dirt. Avoid using metal tools because they can scratch and abrade the bone. The bone must be completely free of its surrounding dirt before lifting is attempted or breakage can easily occur; protruding pieces of the bone are particularly vulnerable. After fully exposing the bone, allow it to dry out slowly, shaded from direct sun. This will help harden and strengthen it before lifting. When the bone is dry, slowly undermine it, being careful not to damage any protruding pieces that might be underneath, and lift it out of the ground. Place it in a polyethylene bag or, if there is any question about the condition of the bone, put it directly into a well-padded, rigid container. If a bone breaks during lifting, keep the broken pieces together and make sure they are eventually packed together.

Always handle bone carefully. Although it may look robust and sound, much of its strengthening material may be gone. Also, there may be cracks or breaks—hidden by dirt—which structurally weaken the bone.

If the bone is weak and/or friable, consolidation may be necessary to remove it safely from the ground. Acryloid B72 or PVA in a 3% to 5% solution are suitable consolidants for dry bone; PVA emulsion diluted 1 to 4 with water (or 2% to 4% Acrysol WS24) should be used for wet bone. Acryloid B72 has a tendency to make bone brittle; PVA, being much more flexible, may not provide enough support for the bone. The choice of consolidant can depend not only on the condition of the bone but on its subsequent storage environment as well. If the storage/display conditions for bone will be very hot, avoid PVA because it softens and flows when hot; packing material could become stuck to the object, creating a nasty mess.

Before consolidating a bone, use a stiff paintbrush carefully to clean the surface to which the consolidant will be applied, making sure not to scratch or abrade the surface. Remove as much of the surrounding dirt as possible to prevent large lumps of dirt from being consolidated to the sides of the object. Apply the consolidant to the bone with a brush, allowing it to soak in between applications. Continue applying consolidant until it is no longer absorbed. Allow the consolidant to dry thoroughly before attempting to lift the bone. Remember that any material still wet with a consolidant is more fragile than it was before the consolidant was applied.

Backing provides an excellent means of strengthening animal bone before lifting, especially if the bone has been crushed or shattered in the ground. Follow the backing procedure set forth in chapter 4. Acryloid B72 in a 7% to 10% solution should be used as the adhesive for dry bone, and Acrysol WS24 (also in a 7% to 10% solution) for damp bones. An undiluted PVA emulsion or 7% to 10% PVA can also be used, but these form a more flexible film than Acryloid and Acrysol; in this instance, their use is not desirable because the backing may not provide enough rigidity to support the bone. Any of the block lifting techniques set forth in chapter 4 can be used as well if the bone is badly crushed.

Any collection of animal bones lying together in a deposit should be kept together after lifting. Also, bones that appear to be articulated—that is, lying as though they were joined together at burial —should be kept together. Before lifting, sketch and/or photograph the bones to show their relationships to one another.

If a whole, articulated skeleton is found, it is best to involve a faunal expert in the lifting procedure. If it is necessary to wait for the faunal analyst to arrive on site, cover the skeleton to prevent the bones from drying out, cracking, or warping. If it is not possible for the expert to be present, carefully draw and photograph the skeleton in situ before lifting is begun. The drawings should be as accurate as possible and to scale. Such drawings and photographs can be very helpful to the faunal analyst studying the bones later. When lifting the skeleton, be careful to collect all the bones, including the epiphyses, which are the ends of long bones that are separate from the shaft in immature animals (fig. 5.9). After lifting the skeleton, keep all the bones together. It is helpful to the expert to lift and keep separate the bones from the left and right fore and back legs, if it is possible to distinguish them sufficiently. Wash, pack, and store the bones as set forth below.

If possible, a sample should be taken of the soil from the abdominal and chest cavities of the skeleton. Analysis and study of this soil can yield evidence on diet. Collect, pack, and store the sample following the procedure set forth in the section on soil samples.

Although animal bone should be cleaned for the faunal analyst, it is not necessary for them to be scrupulously clean and scrubbed. All loosely adhering dirt should be removed. If sound, the bone can be washed superficially; otherwise, pack it and leave any further cleaning to the analyst.

Not all bone needs to be washed. If the adhering dirt comes from a sandy site, for example, it can often be easily removed by dry brushing with a toothbrush or stiff paintbrush. Make sure, however, that the brush does not scratch or abrade the surface of the bone.

Animal bone, if sound, can be safely washed in water using a soft brush to help dislodge dirt. Be careful not to brush too vigorously; this can scratch the bone and blur information regarding butchery and wear. Use as little water as possible, although generally the use of more water is preferable if it means less brushing. Keep in mind that wet bone is easily broken and abraded, especially delicate skull bones. Do not add detergent to the water because it can contaminate the bone, making it useless for various chemical and analytical investigations.

After washing, spread the bones out and allow them to dry slowly and uniformly away from direct sources of heat, including sunlight. If possible, place them on a rack of mesh or screening so that air can circulate underneath to facilitate even drying. If the bones are placed on a solid surface, turn them frequently to ensure even drying.

Frequently, animal bones are found in large quantities, making it impossible to treat each bone individually. Quantities of sound animal bones can be washed together by being immersed in water, but do not soak them. Leave them in water only long enough to soften and remove the dirt. An easy method is to place the bones in the middle of a piece of fine netting. Pull the corners of the netting together to form a bundle and immerse the bundle in a bucket of water using the corners as a handle. Gently swirl the bundle in the water, pushing up and pulling down on the bottom of the bundle to facilitate the washing process. A soft brush can be used, if necessary, to help remove dirt. Once clean, spread the bones out to dry away from direct sunlight; turn them occasionally to facilitate uniform drying.

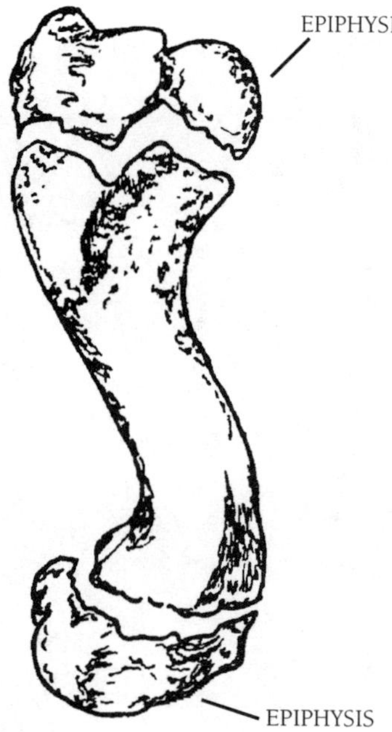

FIGURE 5.9 Pig humerus showing unfused epiphyses

Do not attempt to clean fragile bone or bones that have been consolidated. If there is any doubt as to the condition of a bone, assume that it is too fragile to be cleaned. The dirt can be removed later by the analyst or a conservator.

To prevent the loss of small, broken fragments of bone, reattach them using any of the adhesives recommended in chapter 3. Any major repairs, however, should be left to a conservator.

Before packing up bone, make sure it is thoroughly dry, especially if it is to be packed in polyethylene bags. Cloth bags are also good for packing bone. If plastic bags are used, take care to keep them out of the sun after they have been filled. Although the bone may seem dry, moisture remaining in it will collect on the inside of the bags as they heat up and rewet the bone. If bone is stored wet, it can become moldy and even disintegrate.

It is important to make sure the bags in which bone is packed are not too heavy when filled. If necessary, use several smaller bags; bone can be crushed by its own weight if the bags are too heavy. Also, larger bones will crush smaller, more delicate bones. If plastic or paper bags are used, use double bags to prevent sharp bones from ripping holes in them. When packing bags of bone in boxes, make sure that heavy bags are not put on top of lighter ones. Do not fill the boxes too full or make them too heavy. It will help distribute the weight of the upper layers of bags if a rigid piece of cardboard or expanded foam is placed on top of each layer before adding the next one.

Any special bones, such as skulls, should be packed individually in a rigid container which is well padded with

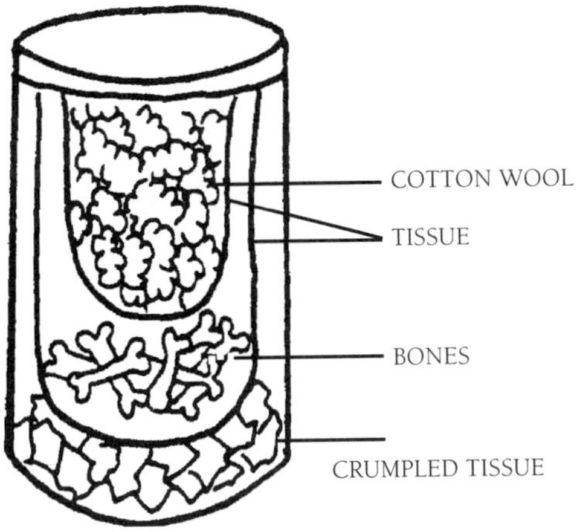

FIGURE 5.10 Plastic film canister used to pack small rodent bones

acid-free tissue or polyethylene foam. Place the bone in a depression in the padding and cover it with a flat wad of tissue or foam. Fill the remainder of the box with crumpled padding to hold the bone firmly in place.

Small, delicate bones (from rodents, birds, or fish, for example) should be packed in polystyrene boxes, pill bottles, or plastic film canisters. These containers should first be padded with acid-free tissue. Avoid using cotton wool because its fibers can easily become entangled in the small bones and cause breakage. If cotton wool must be used, wrap it in a piece of tissue first. After putting the bones in the container, fill the remainder of the space with padding to prevent them from rattling. If a film canister or pill bottle is used, fill the remaining space with a plug of padding to immobilize the bones (fig. 5.10). Small bones can also be placed in small zip-lock plastic bags, which can then be packed in boxes.

If the surface of a bone is breaking off or a white efflorescence appears on the surfaces of drying bone, it probably contains soluble salts. Sometimes the salt crystals are clearly visible. Bone from sites on the sea where there is poor drainage or from saline desert areas is most susceptible to this problem. These salts have been absorbed by the bone from groundwater during burial and will cause considerable damage if not removed. Removal of soluble salts, however, is not generally undertaken in the field unless a conservator is present. For more detailed information, see the section on soluble salt removal in chapter 4.

Bone known to contain soluble salts should be stored in as dry a place as possible and protected from drastic fluctuations in relative humidity. If the bone is very important and an expert cannot study it right away, pack it in sealed containers with silica gel. Or, work out a method with a trained conservator to remove the salts.

If bone is found waterlogged and appears to be sound, it can be dried out safely. Spread the bones out and allow them to dry slowly and uniformly away from direct sources of heat, including direct sunlight. It may help to cover them loosely with a sheet of polyethylene to slow down the drying.

If there is any question about the condition of waterlogged bone, do not attempt to dry it. Rather, keep it wet and pack it in well-sealed polyethylene bags. Before sealing the bags, add 20 ml to 25 ml of 0.2% fungicide. The bags can then be placed in a sealed container half filled with water to which more fungicide has been added. Keep the container in as cool a place as possible, and take the bone to a conservator for treatment. Any bone packed with fungicide must be labeled to ensure safe handling.

If possible, refrigerate wet bone, but make very sure that it does not freeze. Refrigeration may obviate the need for fungicide. Consult with a conservator before adding fungicide.

On some prehistoric sites, bone and fossilized bones are sometimes found cemented together with calcium carbonates. To remove such bones from this matrix and separate them, acid must be used. This is a slow, tedious procedure that is generally best left to a conservator. There are times, however, when this procedure—which should be applied only to sound, robust bones—must be done in the field by the archaeologist.

Remove as much of the soft, loose encrustation as possible with a scalpel or knife, being careful not to damage the surface of the bone. Apply 15% acetic acid locally with a brush or medicine dropper. Make sure that the brush has nylon, not natural, bristles; acid will attack natural bristles as well as the metal ferule securing them. When the fizzing stops, rinse off the acid and dirt with distilled water and remove the softened carbonate matrix with a scalpel or knife. Then apply more acid in the same manner. As the surface of the bone is exposed, coat it with 10% polystyrene in toluene to protect it from subsequent applications of acid. Be sure the bone is dry before applying the polystyrene; allow the polystyrene, in turn, to dry thoroughly before applying more acid. If polystyrene is not available, a 10% to 15% solution of Acryloid B72 can be used. Alternate the acid treatment with mechanical cleaning, applying more polystyrene as the bone surface is uncovered, until the bone is clean or separated. After the final application of acid, thoroughly soak the bone in several changes of distilled water until a neutral pH is verified by pH indicator strips.

Be sure to follow the safety precautions for using acid as outlined in chapter 2 and in the section on pottery.

HUMAN BONE: In general, human bone can be treated in much the same way as animal bone. When lifting a skull, carefully undermine the underside of the cranial vault and face before lifting it. There are many protruding pieces of bone that can easily be snapped off if an attempt is made to lift the skull when it is only half exposed. If possible, remove the mandible, or jaw, before the cranium. This will facilitate lifting the cranium and will also protect the mandible, which generally is loose.

Skulls lend themselves to being lifted in a block or within a pedestal of dirt reinforced with plaster bandage. This procedure can be done relatively quickly and has the advantage of allowing the delicate cleaning and excavation of the skull to be undertaken away from the trench, where it does not impede the excavation progress.

If a complete skeleton needs to be lifted, first photograph it in situ with a scale and make accurate scale drawings. When lifting it, be sure to collect all the bones, including the epiphyses (fig. 5.9). The bones of each part of the body—the skull, vertebral column, ribs, arms, and legs—should be kept separate to facilitate their study later. It is also helpful to the expert to keep the right and left arm and leg bones separate. This step is especially important with a child's skeleton because the bones are incompletely formed and less easy to distinguish after lifting.

Human bone can be cleaned in the same way as animal bone. If sound, it can be washed in water using a soft toothbrush to help remove dirt. Extreme caution should be exercised in washing the skull, however, as there are numerous small, paper-thin bones that can easily be damaged. If at all possible, avoid immersing the skull in water because the combined weight of water and dirt can cause breakage.

Human bone should be packed with acid-free tissue in rigid, well-padded boxes. It is not necessary to wrap each bone individually, but they should be well padded so that they do not rub against one another. The ribs or vertebrae, for example, can be packed together if the box is well padded with tissue and a thick, flat wad of tissue is placed on top of the bones to prevent them from moving inside the box. The more delicate bones—the skull, the mandible, and the pelvis—should be packed individually in well-padded containers. Fill all the corners and the bottom of the container with crumpled tissue to form a well, or depression, in the center. Line the well with a flat sheet of tissue to prevent the crumpled paper from snagging on the bone. Place the bone in the well, making sure that it is fully supported all around and that no one portion of the bone is carrying all the weight. Cover the bone with a smooth sheet of tissue and fill the remaining space in the box with more crumpled tissue to hold the bone firmly in place. The mandible should be packed separately from the skull. The skull itself should be empty of all dirt and be well supported on all sides. Generally, it is best to place it in the container upside down, that is, with the top of the cranium down

WORKED-BONE OBJECTS: Objects made of worked bone can be lifted and consolidated in the same manner as unmodified bone. When removing the dirt surrounding the object, use only a brush or a wooden tool. Metal tools can scratch and abrade the surface of the bone, blurring ancient tool marks and disfiguring the object.

It is always best to avoid washing worked bone objects. Frequently, they can be cleaned extremely well by dry brushing with a soft toothbrush or paintbrush. Be careful, however, not to scratch or abrade the surface. Do not flick or pry off any stubborn lumps of dirt because they can pull off some of the bone surface with them. These lumps can be softened with a drop of water or alcohol, applied locally with a brush, to facilitate their removal. When doing this, try not to get any water or alcohol on the surface of the bone. If this procedure does not suffice to soften the lumps, make no further attempt to remove them and leave them for a conservator.

If sound, a bone object can generally be cleaned safely with swabs dipped in distilled water. Never immerse the object in water. Use as little water as possible; the swab should be moist, but not dripping wet. It should not be so dr that it will abrade the bone surface. Never rub the surface of the bone with the swab; rather, roll it gently back and forth across the surface to remove dirt. Replace the swab as soon as it becomes dirty to prevent it from abrading the surface. After cleaning, allow the object to dry slowly and evenly, out of the sun and away from direct sources of heat.

If a bone object is friable, do not attempt even superficial cleaning unless it is obvious that lumps of adhering dirt will jeopardize the safety of the object. If this is the case, using extreme caution, remove only enough dirt to ensure the safety of the object. Very carefully pack the object with acid-free tissue in a rigid, well-padded container and take it to a conservator.

If a bone object is found waterlogged, it can be dried out if it is very sound. Allow it to dry out slowly and evenly, away from direct sources of heat, including sunlight. Loosely cover the object with a piece of polyethylene sheeting to slow down the drying process.

If there is any question about the condition of the bone, do not allow it to dry out. Pack it in the same manner as that used for damp unmodified bone with soluble salts, as described above. The bone can also be placed in a plastic container with a tight-fitting lid. Pad the container first with damp polyethylene foam to support the object and keep it from moving. Add a little fungicide to the box before sealing it and store the container in as cool a place as possible.

If possible, refrigerate the wet bone, but make very sure that it does not freeze. Refrigeration may obviate the need for fungicide. Consult with a conservator before adding fungicide.

If a white efflorescence appears on a bone object, it probably contains soluble salts. It should be dealt with in the same manner as unmodified animal bone with soluble salts, as mentioned above. Allow the bone to dry out slowly; keep it as dry as possible and take it to a conservator. If storage conditions are very damp, bone can be packed in a sealed container along with silica gel. Follow the procedure used for packing metal objects with silica gel, as described in chapter 4. If damp bone is known to contain soluble salts and no silica gel is available, it is probably best to keep it damp. Place the bone in three polyethylene bags to which 20 ml of 0.2% fungicide have been added and seal well. Keep the bag in a cool, dark place and take it to a conservator for treatment as soon as possible. Check the bone frequently to make sure it does not dry out. Any bone packed with fungicide must be meticulously labeled so that people will take the necessary precautions when handling it.

Sound bone objects can be pieced together with any of the adhesives recommended in chapter 3. Follow the joining procedure set forth in chapter 4. Always make sure that edges to be joined have been thoroughly cleaned. It is possible that separate pieces of bone may have warped slightly during burial and will no longer fit together tightly. If this is the case, do not force pieces together because stresses can be set up, causing the bone to crack and break. It is generally best to leave such pieces unadhered. If the bone is friable, powdery, or known to contain soluble salts, leave any joining to a conservator because other treatment will be necessary first.

Bone objects can be packed and stored in polyethylene bags; however, be absolutely certain that they are thoroughly dry. The plastic bags should be placed in a rigid container. Delicate objects should be packed individually in rigid polystyrene or metal boxes that have been well padded with acid-free tissue or polyethylene foam. Place the object in a depression in the tissue or foam and cover it with a flat wad of tissue or foam to hold it firmly in place. Make sure not to exert undue pressure on the object when closing the lid or the object could break.

Bone should be stored in a room that is not too damp, too hot, or too dry. The relative humidity should fall within 45% to 55%, with the temperature between 5° and 30° C. Drastic fluctuations in both humidity and temperature should be avoided. Bone should be kept away from direct sources of heat and light, including sunlight.

Charcoal and Other Carbonized Material

Frequently, wood, nuts, seeds, and other plant remains are found on archaeological sites. Under normal conditions, these materials will decay through the action of bacteria in the soil and will not be preserved. They will survive, however, if they are carbonized before burial as a result of being burned in an inadequate supply of oxygen.

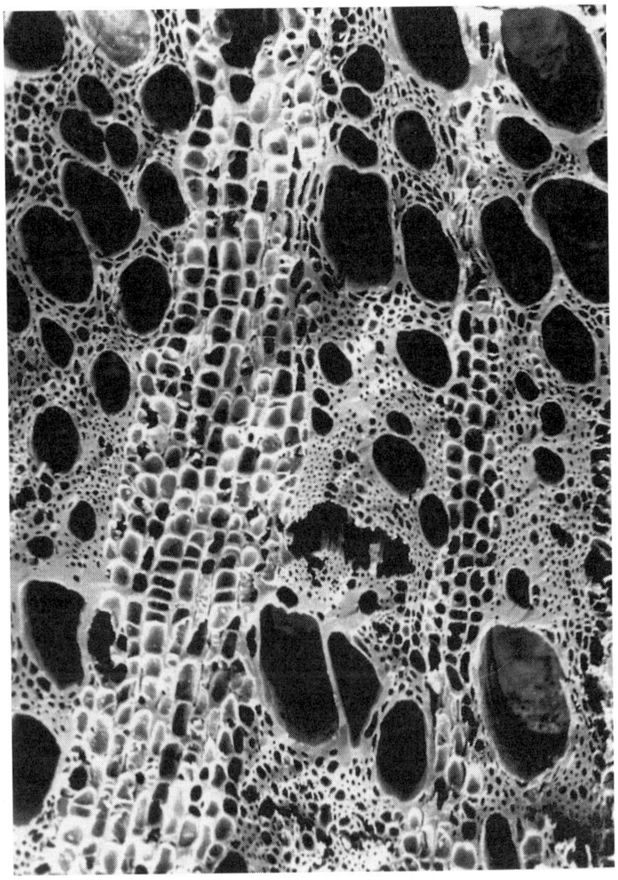

FIGURE 5.11 Cross section of almond (*Prunus dulcis*) wood charcoal (enlarged by scanning electron microscope 165 times) from the Greek Bronze Age. The two bands of even-sized squarish cells running through the section are rays. On either side are large round vessels in a matrix of very thick-walled fiber cells. Arrangement of cell types is used to identify wood.

Partial carbonization preserves the structural features of wood and other plant remains in astonishing detail so that they can be identified and studied by botanists (fig. 5.11). Complete carbonization, however, will turn the material into an amorphous mass and destroy most structural detail. Even partial carbonization will affect the size, shape, and proportion of structural detail, with the amount of change being proportional to the degree of carbonization.

Charcoal is the name given to carbonized wood. When buried, charcoal is almost completely resistant to chemical and biological activity but is susceptible to physical actions. For example, mechanical wear brought on by the action of frost and thaw can abrade charcoal and, in so doing, destroy structural detail. As a result, there is a tendency for it not to survive as well in northern, temperate climates as in warm, dry climates.

Charcoal and, to a lesser extent, charred plant remains are common finds on archaeological sites because of their resistance to decay. Large pieces of charcoal are readily visible and are easily collected by hand. Seeds, pits, and other smaller remains, however, may not be seen so easily. In fact, it may not be known that they are present unless dry sieving, wet sieving, or flotation is used on site. If collected in a systematic manner, much charred material can be identified, providing important information about a site. If the charred material is to be used for radiocarbon dating, the sampling procedure set forth in the section on radiocarbon samples should be followed to avoid contaminating the sample.

Before lifting charred material, carefully remove the dirt surrounding it with a soft brush or wooden tool. Do not use a metal tool because it can easily abrade or damage the edges of the material. When free, gently pick up the charred material and remove as much of the dirt adhering to it as is safe and possible. Always handle charred material very carefully because it fragments easily, especially when damp. Gently wrap it in a piece of absorbent, soft paper toweling or tissue; these need not be acid-free. Place the wrapped material in a paper envelope so that it can dry out thoroughly. Plastic bags or airtight containers should be avoided unless the charred material is thoroughly dry. Store the envelope in as dry a place as possible, away from direct sources of heat.

If charred material is found in discrete groups, collect each group separately, even if the groups are found near one another. Also, collect and keep together fragments known to be from the same piece of charred material. It is very helpful to the expert studying the material to know whether a sample originally consisted of several small pieces or one larger piece that subsequently fragmented. For this reason, indicate on the label the number of pieces originally in the sample.

It is helpful, but not essential, for the expert who will study the charred material to have a sample of the surrounding soil for comparison. If many charred samples come from one area, only one soil sample measuring 25 to 55 cc is necessary. This sample can be the adhering dirt that was removed from the charred material prior to packing. The soil sample should be dried thoroughly before being packed in a clean plastic bag. See the section on soil samples for details of handling, drying, packing, and storing. Do not pack the soil sample together with the charred material.

If large timbers are found, it is not necessary or practical to take the whole piece for identification. Photograph and measure the size and orientation of the timber and then remove a small piece, approximately 2 x 2 x 4 cm, for identification. Since diagnostic structural features are visible in all dimensions and the different sections are used in identifying different types of wood, it is important to take a sample that includes the transverse, radial longitudinal, and tangential longitudinal sections (fig. 5.12). If possible, snap off a long piece from the end of the timber or, using a sharp knife, cut a piece from the timber that will give all three sections (fig. 5.13).

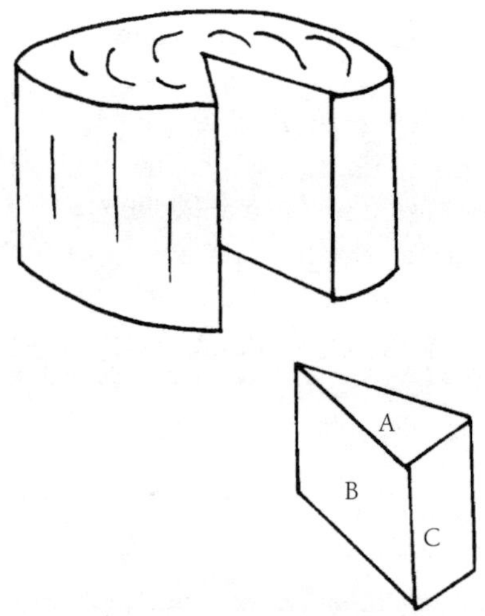

FIGURE 5.12 Significant sections of a wood or charcoal sample: A, transverse; B, radial longitudinal; C, tangential longitudinal.

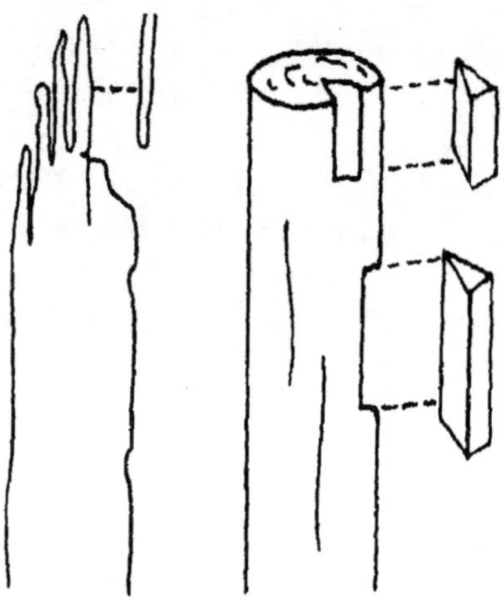

FIGURE 5.13 Ways to obtain samples containing all significant sections from a charred timber.

Coins

The earliest known coins, made of the gold-silver alloy electrum, came from Asia Minor about 650 BC. Coinage seems to have spread westward, with copper, bronze, iron, lead, gold, silver, and electrum being employed. Although a wide range of alloys were used, the coins most commonly found on excavations are made of bronze and silver. The condition of excavated coins varies tremendously, depending on the type of metal and the burial conditions. Coins can be found in very fine condition, but more frequently they are corroded, often quite heavily, with deep cracks and a blistered or warty surface.

Since the archaeologist is interested in coins primarily because they provide valuable chronological information for interpreting strata and levels, the temptation is strong to clean coins on site to identify them. This temptation must be resisted. The cleaning of coins is a delicate job requiring a trained conservator and, unless a conservator is present, the appropriate tools are not usually on hand in the field. Injudicious rubbing, scraping, or cleaning by an inexperienced person can easily result in irreparable damage to the detail of the coin. Often a seemingly sound surface is really only a thin layer of hard corrosion products on top of badly deteriorated, powdery, or mineralized silver or bronze. This delicate layer can crumble or be flaked off with the least amount of pressure. As well, the detail of a coin often remains only in the corrosion layers; an inexperienced person will not be able to recognize this condition. Attempts to remove the corrosion will result in the destruction and loss of this detail.

For these reasons, never immerse coins in chemicals to clean them. None of the many home remedies used on excavations in the past to chemically clean coins are recommended. While a few coins may have been cleaned nicely, the majority will have suffered, not only from the harsh treatment itself, but also from not being thoroughly rinsed afterward.

Coins should never be immersed in water to clean them, either in the field or in the dig house. Water, in the presence of oxygen, can initiate corrosion processes or exacerbate them if active corrosion is present. This situation is especially true in areas where the natural water supply contains large amounts of salts or where the water has been chlorinated.

If a good, sound, original surface can be seen, some superficial cleaning can be attempted with a stiff, but soft, brush. Never use a metal tool because it will scratch the surface of the coin. Be very sure to remove only the dirt adhering to the coin. No attempt should be made to remove any corrosion. Its removal is a delicate process that should be left to a conservator.

Frequently, numismatists want to have casts of coins made to take with them for further study. Casts are desirable, also, if the numismatist cannot visit the site to see the coins. Such casts can easily be made from coins with a good-to-excellent surface. (See appendix I.)

Coins should be packed in small, acid-free envelopes, made specifically for this purpose, or in perforated polyethylene bags. The coins should be placed, along with silica gel, in a metal or plastic container with a tight-fitting lid. If plastic bags are used, stapling each bag to a file card will help to keep the coins in order (fig. 4.20). The container can be further sealed with tape if the storeroom has a tendency to be damp. Take the coins to a conservator for cleaning and further treatment.

Composite Objects

Frequently, objects are found which are composed of two or more materials: an iron knife with a bone or wooden handle, a gilded bronze brooch with enamel insets, or sections of stained glass with lead surrounds. At the best of times, these objects are problematic because of the differing treatment and storage procedures appropriate for each material (especially if they are found wet). For example, iron should be kept as dry as possible, while bone and wood should be kept under more humid conditions because they will crack and split if kept too dry. Often, a decision has to be made as to which component of the object is more important before the object can be treated. If, for example, a piece of waterlogged timber has an iron nail in it and such nails are very common to the site—while structural timbers are not—the wood is obviously the more important component, and the object should be packed with the well-being of the wood in mind.

Under no circumstances should the object be taken apart; valuable technological information can be lost if this happens. If, upon lifting, the object comes apart of its own accord, keep the components separate, packing them in the manner suitable for each material. Clearly indicate that they belong together and take them to a conservator as soon as possible.

It is almost impossible to give explicit treatment details for composite objects because the variables involved are numerous. The best advice that can be given is to exercise common sense and to take all composite objects to a conservator as soon as possible to ensure the optimum care for all the components.

If it is known ahead of time that a site will produce large numbers of composite objects, a conservator should be a member of the excavation team. At the very least, discuss with a conservator the relative merits of the materials involved. A conservator can frequently give an idea of the kind of information that might be forthcoming from each component material. Such advice can help determine a suitable method of handling composite materials as well as help elicit the optimum amount of information from the objects.

On the whole, the less work done to a composite object the better; this includes cleaning. Generally, it is wise not to attempt to clean the object. The dirt in and around the object may be the only thing holding the various parts together. If the object should inadvertently fall apart, valuable technological information may be irretrievably lost.

Most combinations of materials can safely be kept dry.

Pack them carefully in polystyrene boxes that are well padded with acid-free tissue or polyethylene foam. Place the object in a depression in the padding and cover it with another flat wad of tissue or foam to hold it firmly in place. Make sure, however, that no undue pressure is exerted on the object when the lid is closed. Store the object in an area that is as dry as possible.

If the object consists only of metals (or if the important component is metal), silica gel should be put in the bottom of the box before padding it with tissue or foam. Make sure several layers of padding separate the object from the silica gel, or first place the silica gel in a perforated packet. Tape the crack between the halves of the box to make it airtight.

If plastic boxes are not available for packing metal objects, place the objects in unsealed, perforated polyethylene bags. Place the bags, along with silica gel, in a metal or plastic container with a tight-fitting lid and seal the top with tape.

If the object is found waterlogged and the important component is made of organic material, the object should be kept wet. Lift it directly from the ground into three polyethylene bags. If necessary, wrap the object first in wet polyethylene foam for support. Add 20 ml of 0.2% fungicide to the innermost bag (containing the object) before sealing the bags. Place the bags, in turn, into a sealed container half filled with water to which 0.2% fungicide has been added. Keep the container in a cool, dark place and take it to a conservator as soon as possible. It is important that any object packed with fungicide be meticulously labeled to this effect to ensure that people will take the proper precautions when handling the object.

If the object consists only of metals and is found wet, it should be allowed to dry out slowly and evenly and then be packed with silica gel, as described above, in a rigid, well-padded, sealed container. There are differing opinions, however, on how metals should be packed. Thus it is best to consult with a conservator for advice on specific composite objects.

Copper and Copper Alloys

Copper, a reddish-yellow metal that is malleable, ductile, and has a brilliant luster when polished, was first used in antiquity in its native, or uncombined, form. The greatest proportion of copper used in antiquity, however, was obtained from smelting the many minerals containing this element. Although easily worked, it is too soft to be suitable for tools, weapons, or implements. It is possible, however, to harden copper by hammering it while it is cold. As the copper takes on the desired shape, it hardens and becomes more brittle. In this way, usable cutting and working edges can be fashioned. Cold-working of copper was known and practiced in antiquity.

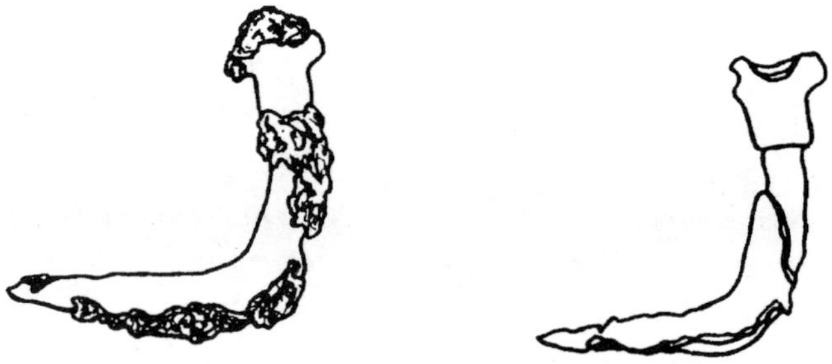

FIGURE 5.14 Damage from bronze corrosion on a bronze pin. A, fluffy growth on the metal is bronze disease; B, bronze disease removed to reveal the degree of metal loss.

Copper can also be hardened by alloying it with various other metals, a procedure that was practiced in antiquity as well. Addition of 1% to 10% tin to copper produces an alloy known as *bronze*. If the tin content is raised to approximately 30%, the alloy becomes whiter and is called *speculum*. Speculum is a hard, tough metal that takes a high polish; it was used primarily for making mirrors and coins. The addition of up to 40% zinc to copper produces *brass*, which becomes yellower the higher the proportion of zinc. Properties of these alloys vary with the percentages of copper to tin and zinc. Other alloys contain antimony, arsenic, and lead.

Numerous copper-gold alloys called *tumbaga* were developed and used extensively in antiquity by many different groups in Central and South America. They are generally regarded as being gold alloys and will be discussed, therefore, in the section on gold and gold alloys.

Excavated copper alloy objects can exhibit a variety of colors of corrosion products. Green is by far the most common one, but blue, black, red, and reddish brown are found as well as mottled combinations of all of them. Copper alloys frequently are found well preserved but will suffer drastically if buried in saline soils. Chlorides will form an unstable corrosion product which, in the presence of moisture and oxygen, will set into motion a self-perpetuating system of corrosion. Within only a few hours of excavation, this corrosion can lead to what is called *bronze disease,* a form of corrosion producing a fluffy, powdery material varying in color from emerald to pale green. Bronze disease can cause considerable damage to copper alloys, resulting in deep pitting and disintegration of the metal (fig. 5.14).

Preservation of copper alloy objects is further complicated by the presence of decoration composed of other metals. It was common in many parts of the ancient world to apply a thin layer of gold, silver, or tin to the copper alloy object to enhance it. On freshly excavated objects, it may be difficult, if not impossible, to distinguish such coatings, especially if the object is heavily corroded. When the copper underneath corrodes, corrosion products form on top of the gilded, silvered, or tinned surface. Because the object is covered with these products, it is easily assumed to be made exclusively of copper. The layer of gold, silver, or tin may have been disrupted if the corrosion of the copper alloy substrate is particularly extensive; as a result, it may be lost within the corrosion.

Do not pull copper alloy objects out of the ground because they snap and break easily. Sound objects can be removed from the ground following general lifting procedures. First, carefully remove all dirt surrounding the object, being sure not to scratch the surface in the process. Gently undercut the object and, when it is completely free, carefully pick it up, supporting it in the palm of the hand. Place it in a paper envelope until it can be properly packed in the dig house. The paper envelope is only a temporary measure, but it will allow the object to dry out. A copper alloy object should not be placed directly into a polyethylene bag when it is still damp from the ground. Moisture will collect on the inside of the bag and keep the object wet, which can easily initiate or exacerbate the corrosion process. If the plastic bag sits in the sun, as it is more than likely to do before being taken to the dig house, this wetting process will be speeded up.

Always handle copper alloy objects carefully. There may be little metal left, and dirt and corrosion can easily hide cracks and splits in the object. Unnecessary handling can cause considerable damage; so, handle the object as little as possible. All copper alloy objects, especially long, thin ones, should be carefully supported at all times.

If the metal is shattered or badly corroded with deep cracks, the object may need to be backed to remove it from the ground. Follow the backing procedure in chapter 4, using a 10% solution of Acryloid B72. Do not use an emulsion because the water in it could initiate or exacerbate the corrosion process. Any of the block lifting methods can be used to lift fragile copper alloy objects.

Corrosion products of copper alloy can be extremely tricky and difficult to remove. Their removal, therefore, should be undertaken only by a trained conservator. If little or no metal remains, the entire object can disintegrate if cleaning is attempted by an inexperienced person. Injudicious cleaning can irreparably damage an object and destroy not only surfaces and decorative detail but also organic and environmental evidence preserved by the corrosion. Small textile fragments can be found adhering to copper alloy objects, the biological deterioration processes of the fibers having been stopped by the toxic metallic ions of the copper (fig. 5.15). Textiles can be replaced by corrosion products, as well, with these products forming an exact replica of the textile fragment. Often this is the only way in which such evidence is preserved (fig. 5.16).

Only superficial cleaning, therefore, should be undertaken in the field. If the object is wet, allow it to dry out slowly and uniformly away from any direct sources of heat, including sunlight. Gently brush off any adhering dirt with a soft, stiff brush. Never scrape dirt off with a metal tool because it will scratch the surface of the object. If a copper object is found dry, do not wash it in water; washing can initiate the corrosion process. This is especially true in areas where the water naturally contains large amounts of salts or where the water supply has been chlorinated. Do not attempt to join any broken pieces of a copper alloy object in the field. The condition of corroded metal is never easy to determine. Although an object may seem sound, an adhesive can, in fact, be stronger than the metal. If the object is subjected to

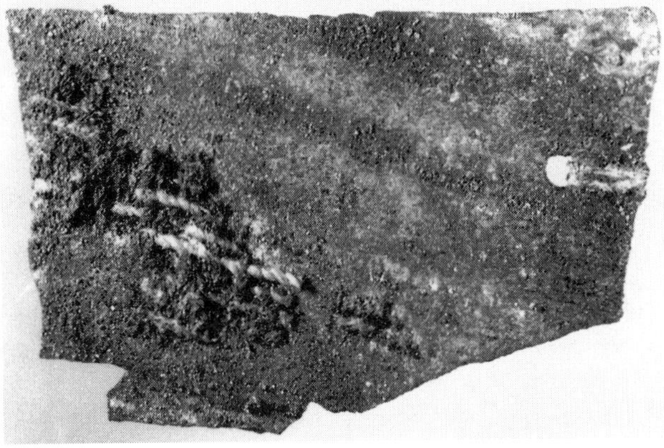

FIGURE 5.15 Wool threads preserved on a pre-Columbian *tumbaga* object

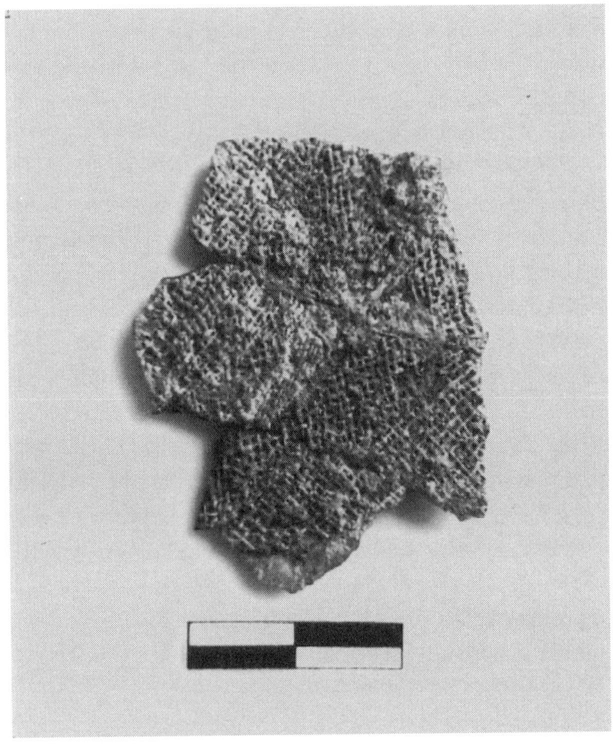

FIGURE 5.16 Mineral replacement of a Minoan textile on a piece of bronze

considerable handling, especially rough handling, the adhesive will hold, but the object can break in new places, usually on either side of the join. Once the mended object gets to a conservator, the adhesive must be removed before any further treatment can be carried out. This process can result in the loss of edges, making for more difficult, if not impossible, joining later on.

Copper alloy objects should be packed individually in polystyrene boxes which are well padded with acid-free tissue or polyethylene foam. Fill the bottom of the box with a layer of silica gel before padding it, and make sure that several layers of padding separate the object from the gel. The gel can also be packed in perforated packets, as described below, to ensure that it will not come in direct contact with the object. Place the object in a depression in the padding and cover it with another flat wad of tissue or foam to hold it firmly in place. Be careful, however, that no undue pressure is exerted on the object when the lid is closed or the object may break. Then tape the crack between the halves of the box to make it airtight.

If plastic boxes are not available, copper alloy objects can be packed in sealed polyethylene bags with silica gel. Do not store these objects without gel. Since silica gel must not come in contact with the object, place it in a sealed polyethylene bag to form a small packet. The packet must be thin and flat to provide as much surface area of the gel as possible. Then perforate the packet all over with a needle or other small, sharp object.

An alternate method of packing copper alloy objects is to place them in unsealed, perforated polyethylene bags. Put the bags, along with a large packet of silica gel, into a metal or plastic container with a tight-fitting lid. Further seal the container with tape. For very unstable objects, an ideal repository is a glass Mason jar containing silica gel. The rubber seal makes the jar airtight and will keep the objects safe in a very damp storeroom (fig. 4.21).

If the objects do not go directly to a conservator, check them frequently for the appearance of the bright green powdery spots of bronze disease. Any objects with bronze disease should be packed carefully with silica gel and taken to a conservator as soon as possible. Check the silica gel, as well, from time to time and regenerate it as necessary. Copper alloy objects should be stored in as dry a place as possible.

Egyptian Faience (Frit)

Technically, *faience* is a term reserved for certain tin glazed earthenware. What is known as Egyptian faience is not a true faience, but rather a glazed siliceous material very similar to both clay and glass. Although *frit* is the correct term for this material, it is also used to denote certain types of colorants. To avoid confusion, the term *faience* is used here.

Faience is made by mixing sand with natron (a naturally occurring combination of sodium salts) and a small amount of clay and water to form a paste that is modeled like clay. As it dries, salts migrate to the surface; on firing, they act as fluxes, allowing the surface to form a glaze. The result is a porous, granular material with a consistency varying from a chalky to sandstone-like texture; this is covered with a hard, thin, brightly colored glaze. Although the glaze is most frequently blue, green, or turquoise, it can also be violet, white, or yellow. The core is generally white, although it can be brown, gray, or yellow, depending on the source of the sand used to make the paste. The Egyptians used faience extensively to make a wide variety of objects, almost all of which were relatively small in size. It was also used for a great range of vase types on Crete and Cyprus and in mainland Greece, northern Syria, and Mesopotamia.

Faience objects can be lifted from the ground following general lifting procedures. Carefully clean around the object or sherd to remove all surrounding dirt. Use a soft brush or wooden tool rather than metal tools which will easily scratch and abrade the faience. Faience, especially when it has lost its outer glazed surface, can be extremely soft and friable. Carefully undercut the object and, when it is completely loose, lift it gently out of the ground. Place it directly into a rigid, well-padded container.

If found in good condition with its glaze intact, faience can be cleaned with little trouble. It should never be immersed in water or cleaned with acid. Instead, remove all loosely adhering dirt with a soft brush and clean the surface with swabs dipped in distilled water. The swab should be moist but not dripping wet. Do not rub the faience with the swab as this process can abrade the surface. Rather, roll the swab gently back and forth over a small section of the surface until it is clean. As soon as the swab is dirty, discard it for a new one; a dirty swab can be extremely abrasive. If the glazed surface is cracked or crizzled, avoid letting water seep down into the cracks.

Sometimes, faience objects are found with the glaze still intact but in poor condition. Often water, soluble salts, and/or dirt have worked into cracks on the surface and under the vitreous layer. A buildup of dirt or the action of soluble salts crystallizing out at the glaze/core interface can cause the glaze to flake off. The core, too, may have deteriorated, becoming soft and powdery; this can drastically weaken the attachment of the glaze. Flaking can also result if the object was exposed to drastic temperature fluctuations or to a freezing and thawing cycle during burial. The glaze, being a different material, will expand and contract at a different rate than the core and can easily pop off as a result. Rather than crumble, the glaze usually flakes off in large pieces. A sherd with the glaze still intact is shown in figure 5.17.

Where the glaze is missing reveals the powdery white core underneath.

Do not attempt to clean detached flakes of glaze because they will easily break under even the slightest pressure. Carefully wrap loose pieces individually in acid-free tissue and pack them, with the object, in a well-padded, rigid container as described below.

Glaze that is still in place but so loose that it will not survive until it gets to a conservator should be consolidated with a 3% to 5% solution of Acryloid B72. Touch the edge of the glaze flake with a fine brush full of acetone (if the consolidant is made with toluene, use toluene instead) and allow it to be pulled into the crack and under the flake. Continue adding acetone as it is absorbed. The acetone should be pulled off the brush by merely touching it to the crack. When this happens easily, fill the brush with the consolidant and touch it to the crack. The consolidant should be pulled off the brush just as the acetone was. Continue applying consolidant in this manner until it is no longer absorbed. Make sure, however, that it is indeed going under the flake rather than running out elsewhere. Apply gentle pressure to the flake until the consolidant has dried and the flake is secure.

Frequently with excavated faience, the outer vitreous layer is completely gone, leaving only the porous inner core (fig 5.18). This is especially likely to occur when natron is used in making the paste. Natron produces a sodium glaze that is not terribly stable because the sodium salts can be leached out slowly during burial, leaving the surface porous and fragile. The remaining core can be quite granular and friable. If found in this condition, faience should not be immersed in or cleaned with water. If the surface is strong enough, it can be cleaned with a soft brush. Make very sure, however, that brushing does not abrade the soft faience surface. Any lumps of adhering dirt should be softened by touching them with a brush filled with water or alcohol. They can then be removed with a brush or a wooden tool. Do not pry or flick off these lumps because bits of the surface can be removed along with them. If the object does not appear strong enough to withstand any cleaning, pack it as described below and take it to a trained conservator.

No attempt should be made to join broken fragments of faience. Even if they seem sound, the edges of the core will be soft and powdery, making it difficult to obtain a good bond. If the bond gives way, bits of the edges will be pulled away with the adhesive, causing difficult joins later on. If joined pieces have to be taken apart and readhered—as is so often the case with objects joined in the field—some of the edges will be lost, making subsequent joining more difficult and unsightly. It is best to leave the joining of faience objects to a conservator.

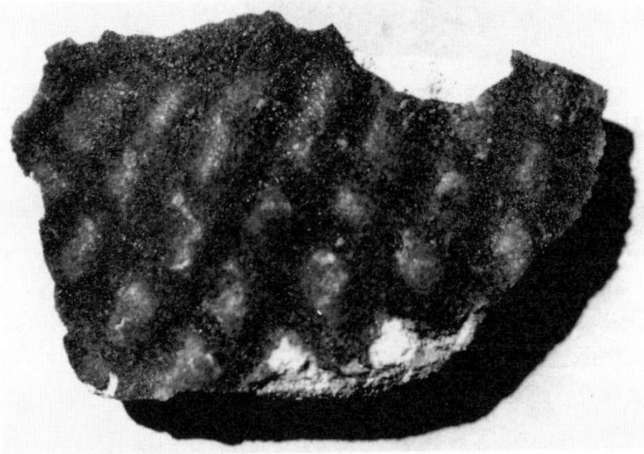

FIGURE 5.17 Sherd with glaze

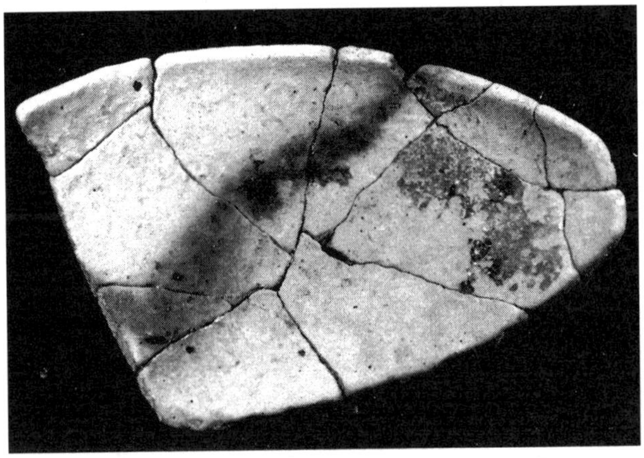

FIGURE 5.18 Faience bowl fragment. The glazed surface is completely gone, leaving the soft, powdery inner core.

Faience objects should be packed individually in rigid polystyrene boxes which are well padded with acid-free tissue or polyethylene foam. Place the object in a depression in the padding and then cover it with another flat wad of tissue or foam to keep it from moving. Make sure, however, that no undue pressure is exerted on the object when the lid is closed or the object can break.

Sherds of faience can be packed in polyethylene bags. Make sure the sherds are thoroughly dry before bagging them, and then place the bags in a rigid container for protection. Faience should be stored in a dry place.

Feathers

Feathers have served a decorative and spiritual function throughout the history of man. Birds and, hence, feathers are universal, and it is to be assumed that feathers were used extensively in antiquity all over the world. Unfortunately, burial conditions are generally such that feathers have survived archaeologically in only a few areas of the world. For example, ostrich feathers have been found in Egypt, and in South America many objects—generally textiles—have been found richly adorned with feathers.

All parts of feathers are composed of the protein keratin. A feather consists of a central shaft ending in a quill that was originally embedded in the skin of the bird. The shaft provides support for the vane of the feather, which is made up of hundreds of barbs. These barbs are actually an outgrowth of the shaft and appear as lateral branches off the shaft. Finer branches, called *barbules*, project off the barbs. Many of these barbules have tiny hooks that slide and hook over the barbs, keeping the feather's shape.

Although keratin is quite resistant to both alkaline and acidic conditions, it is rare for feathers to survive burial. Generally, they will survive only under very dry, desert conditions. More often than not, they will be found in association with a textile or even be part of a textile. If this is the case, everything said about the lifting, cleaning, and handling of textiles applies to feathers.

Feathers found not associated with textiles can be lifted following general lifting procedures. Carefully remove the dirt surrounding the feather with a soft brush. Gently loosen the feather, lift it carefully, and place it in a padded, rigid container. Keep the feather out of the sun and take it to the dig house at the earliest opportunity.

Always handle feathers extremely carefully and as little as possible. By their very nature, they are quite delicate and will have been weakened by being buried in the ground. It is a good idea to place the feather on a sheet of paper or cardboard so that it can be picked up and moved without actually being handled.

Never wash a feather. Water can cause the barbules to lose their grip, allowing the barbs to separate. The vane will then be disrupted, and the feather will lose its shape. Since feathers are very delicate, it is best to leave any cleaning to a trained conservator. If absolutely necessary, some superficial cleaning can be undertaken if the feather appears to be sound. With a soft brush, lightly remove loose surface dirt, being careful to work in the direction of the barbs. Start at the shaft and work outward, following the direction or grain of the barbs. Do not attempt to remove any hard lumps of dirt. Do not pry or flick them off because they will most certainly pull off part of the barbs.

Feathers should be packed flat in a rigid container which is well padded with acid-free tissue or polyethylene foam. Cover the feathers with a flat wad of padding to prevent them from moving inside the container. Be very sure, though, that no undue pressure is exerted on the feathers when the lid is closed or the feathers could be crushed. It is best to avoid putting feathers in plastic bags because static electricity in the bags can exert a force strong enough to pull off barbs and barbules.

Feathers should be stored in an area which is neither too dry nor too damp. They should be kept away from any direct sources of heat and light and be taken to a conservator for treatment.

Glass

Glass was manufactured in antiquity in Egypt, Mesopotamia, and Phoenicia and later throughout the Mediterranean and Europe by the Greeks and Romans. The Arab world also produced glass objects in great quantities. Glass is an amorphous solid made by fusing silica with an alkali. It is noted for its transparency, hardness, and rigidity at ordinary temperatures, but plasticity at elevated temperatures. The source of silica in antiquity was generally quartz sand, but where pure sand was not available, crushed flint was used. The main alkalis used were sodium (or soda), potassium (or potash), lead, and calcium. These alkalis act as fluxes, lowering the melting point of the silica and allowing it to fuse. Fluxes also influence the properties of the resulting glass. For example, potash lowers the melting point of the glass more than soda, giving it a wider temperature range in which it is plastic. Soda glass, however, is clearer and more lustrous. At first, the choice of flux depended in large part on the natural resources at hand, but certainly by Roman times, fluxes were deliberately chosen for the specific properties they imparted to the glass. Color was produced by adding small amounts of the salts of certain metals.

Besides affecting the properties of glass, the amount and proportions of the fluxes used influence its stability. Too much soda renders the glass soluble in water. The addition of lime will prevent this from happening, but too much lime will cause the glass to devitrify, that is, become crystalline. Egyptian and most Near Eastern glass is soda-lime glass. Roman glass is also soda-lime, but it is extremely stable, most likely because the ideal proportions of the fluxes were used. The composition of Roman glass is amazingly uniform no matter where in the Empire it was made. Medieval European glass, on the other hand, contains higher proportions of potash and lime and is thus less stable.

The condition of excavated glass, therefore, will vary considerably depending on its composition, date and place of manufacture, and burial conditions. On the whole, glass will be reasonably well preserved in acidic soils. Burial in alkaline soils, however, will result in severe deterioration. Under these conditions, the flux is leached out preferentially to the silica, although it too will be removed to a lesser extent. This leaching renders the glass porous, pitted, and covered with a layer of carbonates (fig. 5.19). If this process continues indefi-

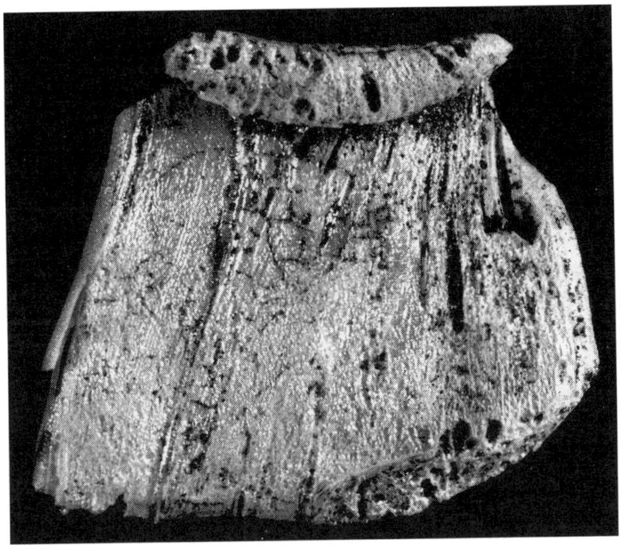

FIGURE 5.19 Badly deteriorated glass fragment. The vitreous quality of the glass is gone, leaving a pitted, opaque surface.

nitely, no structure will be left.

Weathering of soda glass results in the formation of many thin, transparent layers of almost amorphous silica, one on top of the other. Eventually these layers separate slightly and, being of different and irregular thicknesses, refract light differently, giving a colored effect known as *iridescence*. If this process goes too far, the layers become extremely fragile and peel off in very thin, onion skin-like pieces. Unfortunately, there is no way to restore such deteriorated glass. Glass can also become devitrified; in this condition, the surface has become crystalline with patchy areas of iridescence.

Because glass undergoes subtle physical changes during the normal aging process, it is extremely difficult to predict how ancient glass will behave. It is always best, therefore, to treat it very carefully, never subjecting it to undue handling or physical or thermal shocks.

Before lifting a piece of glass, clean around it carefully with a wooden spatula or soft brush to remove all surrounding dirt. Do not use metal tools because they will scratch the surface of the glass. Be careful not to inadvertently detach any iridescent layers from the surface. If necessary, leave some of the dirt adhering to the glass to protect these thin layers. Carefully undercut the object and, when it is completely free, gently pick it up and place it in a rigid, padded container. Keep the glass in a cool place, away from direct sunlight, and take it to the dig house at the earliest opportunity.

Glass found dry should be kept dry. Gentle dry brushing with a soft brush should be sufficient to remove adhering dirt. Do not pry or flick off adhering lumps of dirt because they can take some of the surface of the glass along with them. Soften them first by touching them with a brush filled with alcohol or water, trying not to get any moisture on the glass itself. Gently brush or scrape the lumps off with a wooden tool. If this procedure does not suffice, make no further attempt to remove the lumps of dirt. Leave them for a conservator.

Never immerse any glass in water. Extremely sound pieces of glass can be cleaned with swabs dipped in distilled water, but loose dirt should be removed first with a brush. The swab should be moist but not dripping wet. Do not rub the surface of the glass with the swab because this action will abrade the surface. Rather, gently roll the swab over the surface until it is clean. As soon as a swab becomes dirty, discard it for a new one because a dirty swab can be extremely abrasive.

If the glass is covered with thin iridescent layers, do not attempt to clean it, as these layers are extremely fragile and can easily be dislodged. No attempt should be made to consolidate these layers, either; this step should be left to a conservator. This is also true for any glass that has been painted or enameled.

Because springing is frequently a problem, the joining of glass pieces is best done by a conservator. When a glass vessel is made, the glass is put under a certain amount of tension. If the vessel is broken, this tension will be released and distortion can occur in one or more of the pieces. This condition is called *springing*. Although it can happen to any glass, it is more likely to occur on very thin-walled vessels. When springing occurs, the pieces will not fit back together properly. Even without springing, it is difficult to obtain good alignment of joins because the pieces have a tendency to slip while the adhesive is setting. Another consideration is that partially pieced glass objects can pose difficult packing problems. If joining in the field is absolutely necessary for profiling or photography, any of the adhesives recommended in chapter 3 can be used.

Dry pieces of glass should be packed in a rigid container which is well padded with acid-free tissue or polyethylene foam. The glass should be laid out flat in layers separated by acid-free tissue or foam. Be careful to put as little pressure as possible on pieces with fragile iridescent layers. If it seems necessary, wrap individual fragile pieces in acid-free tissue before packing them. When necessary, shaped pieces of glass should be padded and supported with additional wads of tissue or foam. Empty spaces in the container should be filled with crumpled tissue to prevent the pieces from moving, but

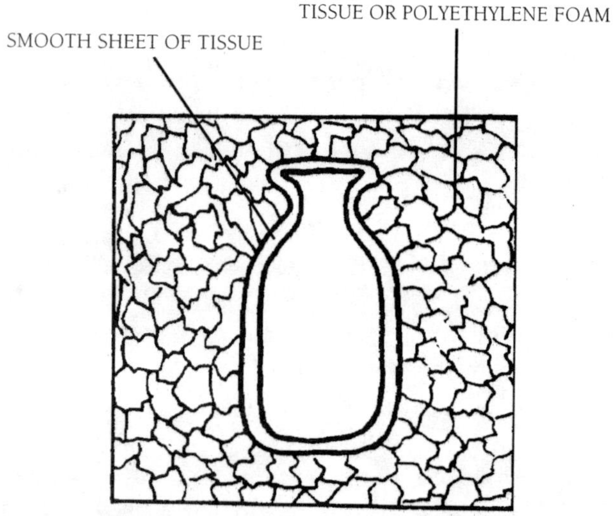

FIGURE 5.20 Method for packing a glass vessel

make sure that no undue pressure is exerted on the glass when the lid is closed or the glass may break.

Sound sherds of glass can be packed individually in perforated polyethylene bags. The bags should then be placed in a rigid container to protect the sherds. If they are small, the bags can be stapled individually to file cards; these can then be filed in a box (fig. 4.20).

An intact glass vessel should be carefully wrapped in acid-free tissue and placed in a rigid container which is well padded with acid-free tissue or polyethylene foam. Fill the bottom and corners of the box with crumpled or wadded-up tissue or foam to form a depression in the center in which the vessel will be placed (fig. 5.20). Make sure the vessel is firmly supported all around and that no one area bears the entire weight of the vessel. Put a flat wad of tissue or foam on top of the vessel, followed by crumpled tissue to fill the box. If wrapping will be too harsh on the vessel, place it directly into the depression, but first line the depression with pieces of smooth tissue to prevent the crumpled tissue or foam from snagging on the glass.

Glass should be stored in as stable an environment as possible. Ideally, the relative humidity should be 40% or less. Many pieces of glass are sensitive to moisture. Sodium and potassium are slightly soluble in some glass compositions. In the presence of high relative humidity, these components can be leached out to the surface of the glass where they are converted to carbonates. These carbonates attract moisture, and small droplets of water begin to appear on the surface of the glass; hence, the name *weeping glass*.

The leaching process causes tiny cracks to appear in the glass, and eventually the glass can become opaque with small surface flaking. Further leaching and droplet formation will be stopped if the glass is kept at a relative humidity below 40%. If the storeroom is very damp, it may be necessary to pack glass in airtight containers with silica gel. Follow the procedure set forth in chapter 4 for packing metal objects with silica gel.

If glass is found wet, it should not be allowed to dry out because it may delaminate. Also, any adhering dirt will harden on the surface and become very difficult to remove. Therefore, keep the glass as wet as when found. Carefully clean around it to remove some, but not all, of the surrounding dirt or mud. Undercut the object, gently lift it out of the ground, and place it directly into three polyethylene bags along with its surrounding dirt and seal well. The mud will help to keep the glass damp and maintain the conditions to which it has become accustomed. Place the sealed bags in a rigid plastic container with a tight-fitting lid.

An alternate method for packing wet glass is to place it directly into a rigid plastic container with a snap-on lid. Pad the container first with damp polyethylene foam. Do not use tissue or cloth to pack wet glass because they will almost certainly rot before the glass can be unpacked and treated. Place the pieces of glass flat in layers on the foam. Separate each layer with damp foam and fill in empty areas of the container with rolls of damp foam to keep the glass from moving.

Containers of wet glass should be kept in as cool a place as possible and taken to a trained conservator for treatment as soon as practicable. If available, refrigeration can help prevent microbial growth. The glass should not be allowed to freeze. If the glass must wait some time before going to a conservator, check it frequently to make sure it does not dry out.

Gold and Gold Alloys

Gold is a rich yellow metal that occurs more commonly in the native, or uncombined, form than as an ore. Native gold is widely distributed in nature and was probably the only source of gold used in antiquity. It was one of the first metals to be exploited by man. Gold is a very soft, malleable, and ductile metal that is easily worked. It can be beaten into very thin foil without being annealed (heated) and is capable of being delicately shaped. Pure gold is far too soft and rare to have been used for most practical purposes, but it was highly prized for ornamental and decorative uses. It was alloyed with other metals, usually copper or silver, to strengthen and harden it. Not all gold, however, was purposely alloyed since native gold is generally a natural alloy of gold with copper and/or silver. When alloyed with silver, a pale-colored metal is produced. If the amount of silver approaches 30%, the alloy is almost white in color and is called *electrum*. In antiquity, electrum was used primarily for coinage and for decorating vessels. The addition of copper produced a reddish gold. Small amounts of other impurities were purposely added, as well, to produce different colors of gold.

In Central and South America, an alloy of gold and copper called *tumbaga* was used extensively. Tumbaga composition varies tremendously, ranging from 30% to 65% copper. With the addition of copper, tumbaga objects could be cold-worked to obtain a hardness approaching that of bronze. This alloy, however, was easier to cast than bronze and was capable of reproducing finer detail. By further treating the surface with acid, the copper on the surface of the tumbaga was removed, leaving a thin, porous film of pure gold which was then polished or heated to create an even gold surface. In such a way, objects made of a base alloy were given a surface that was originally indistinguishable from pure gold. This process of surface enrichment—sometimes referred to as *depletion gilding*—also afforded a means by which large surfaces could be made of gold and served effectively to stretch a short supply of the valuable material. Frequently, the soft gold surface wore away through use; if the object is not badly corroded, the reddish base alloy can be seen underneath.

Pure gold is durable and resistant to corrosion, but other metals present in the alloy will corrode. If this corrosion is extensive, it can be difficult to recognize some excavated gold. Copper corrosion products, for example, can completely cover a gold object, making it green like a corroded piece of bronze. Conversely, what at first may seem to be gold may be only a fragile layer of gilding sitting on top of bronze or another copper alloy.

Even apparently sound gold and gold alloy objects may be quite weak structurally, and will crack or break with careless or excessive handling. Tumbaga objects—especially those with a high copper content—are very fragile, and the gold layer on the surface can crack and flake off easily. The outer surface of a very badly corroded piece may be only a fragile shell, the metal core underneath having corroded away. Therefore, always handle gold and gold alloy objects as little as possible and very carefully, supporting them fully at all times.

Sound gold and gold alloy objects can be removed from the ground after first carefully removing all surrounding dirt. Carefully undercut the object and, when it is completely loose, gently lift it out of the ground. Place it directly into a padded, rigid container. Never transfer a gold or gold alloy object directly from the ground into a plastic bag because it will still be damp. Moisture will collect on the inside of the bag and wet the object; this can easily initiate or exacerbate the corrosion process. If the bag sits in the sun, as it is more than likely to do before being taken to the dig house, this wetting process will be accelerated.

Sometimes the gold alloy object is shattered or so badly corroded with cracks that the object needs to be backed to remove it from the ground. Follow the backing procedure set forth in chapter 4, using a 10% solution of Acryloid B72. Do not use an emulsion as the water in the emulsion could start or exacerbate corrosion. Any of the block lifting methods given in chapter 4 can also be used.

Any gilt, suspected gilt, or tumbaga object should be packed immediately, with no attempt to clean it other than carefully removing superficial dirt with a soft brush so as not to scratch the gilded surface. The layer of gilding and the gold-enriched layer on tumbaga can be extremely thin; consequently, injudicious rubbing or cleaning can damage or remove these layers. Do not flick off any adhering lumps of dirt because they can take off areas of gilding with them. Soften the lumps first by touching them with a brush filled with alcohol and then carefully scrape them off with a wooden tool or soft brush.

Gilded and tumbaga objects should be packed individually in rigid polystyrene boxes which are well padded with acid-free tissue or polyethylene foam. Before padding the box, put a layer of silica gel in the bottom or insert a packet of silica gel. Then put the object in a depression in the padding and cover it with a flat wad of tissue or foam to keep it from moving. Make certain that no undue pressure is exerted on the object when the lid is closed or the object might break. Tape the crack between the halves of the box to make it airtight. Then take the object to a trained conservator for cleaning.

Gold and gold alloy objects generally need little treatment. A gentle dry brushing is usually sufficient to clean them, but make sure that brushing does not abrade or scratch the surface. More persistent dirt can be removed with swabs dipped in distilled water. Do not rub the surface with the swab as this process can scratch it. Instead, roll the swab gently over the surface until it is clean. As soon as a swab is dirty, discard it for a new one; a dirty swab can be very abrasive.

Any further cleaning or removal of corrosion products should be left to a trained conservator. While dilute acid can be used to clean relatively pure gold, this treatment should not be attempted in the field unless a conservator is present. It is extremely difficult to determine in the field the nature and composition of the alloy and the techniques used to make it. This information must be known before any object can be treated with acid; acid cannot be applied indiscriminately to just any object made of gold. Gilded surfaces can be very thin and delicate. The outer surfaces of tumbaga objects can be mere shells, with little or no metal core remaining. Such surfaces, formed by depletion gilding, can be badly cracked and fragile. In all of these instances, contact with acid could severely damage, if not destroy, the gold surface. Moreover, if the object is likely to be used for metallographic analysis, the use of acid may invalidate any results. The cleaning of even sound gold objects can be a tricky procedure and must be done cautiously. For example, it is possible to deposit a layer of copper over the surface of a gold alloy object as a result of cleaning it with acid. This layer of copper is extremely difficult to remove and subjects the object to considerable (and unnecessary) further treatment.

Due to the softness of the metal, gold objects are frequently found crushed, bent, or folded over. Pieces of gold foil are invariably crushed or crumpled. Although the temptation is strong to try to unbend them or push the gold back into shape, resist doing so. Gold, when alloyed, becomes brittle upon aging; any attempt by an inexperienced person to manipulate it will result in cracking and breaking.

No attempt should be made to join broken fragments of gold. Although the metal may seem sound, the adhesive can be stronger than the metal. If the object is roughly or excessively handled, adhered joins will hold, but the metal may break in a new place (generally on either side of the join). When the object finally gets to a conservator, any joins will have to be taken apart to fully treat the object. When this is done, parts of the edges will inevitably be lost, making later joining more difficult, if not impossible, especially if the edges are quite thin.

Gold objects should be packed individually in rigid polystyrene boxes which are well padded with acid-free tissue or polyethylene foam in the same manner as described above for gilded objects. Since it is impossible to determine the composition of the freshly excavated metal in the field, it is wise to pack all gold objects with silica gel.

If plastic boxes are not available, gold objects can be packed in unsealed, perforated polyethylene bags. Place the bags, along with silica gel, in a metal or plastic container with a tight-fitting lid and seal the top with tape. Gold objects should be stored in as dry a place as possible.

Horn

Horn is an outgrowth of the skin of cattle, sheep, goats, and antelopes that covers a core of bone. It consists mainly of protein and is fibrous and frequently laminated. Upon drying out, it has a tendency to warp and delaminate. Horn is relatively soft and flexible, appearing slightly translucent when removed from its bone core. It was used to make, among other things, ornaments, jewelry, combs, handles, vessels, and gaming pieces. It was used in ancient Egypt from the earliest periods and extensively throughout Europe, especially in the medieval period. Horn is rarely preserved archaeologically; generally, all that remains is the hollow core which, being bone, can be treated like other bone (fig. 5.2).

In the unlikely event that horn is found dry, it can be lifted carefully following general lifting procedures. Do not touch or scrape the horn with metal tools during the lifting process because the surface can be very soft and easily damaged. Place the object in a perforated polyethylene bag until it can be properly packed. Keep it out of the sun, and take it back to the dig house as soon as possible.

Only superficial cleaning—nothing more than gentle dry brushing with a soft brush—should be attempted in the field. Do not use any water because the horn can crack, warp, and delaminate upon exposure to moisture. Do not flick or pry off any adhering lumps of dirt because portions of the surface can be removed with them. If lumps do not come off easily with gentle brushing, leave them for a conservator to remove.

Objects made of horn should be packed individually in a rigid container that is well padded with acid-free tissue or polyethylene foam. Place the object in a depression in the padding and cover it with a flat wad of tissue or foam to hold it securely in place.

Horn should be stored in an area that is neither too wet nor too dry. Ideally, the relative humidity should be kept between 45% and 50%. Horn should be kept away from direct sources of heat and light.

More frequently, horn is found under waterlogged conditions. Do not allow wet or waterlogged horn to dry out, even for a short period, or it will warp and crack. If it cannot be removed from the ground immediately upon discovery, it should be covered again with mud or with a thick layer of damp polyethylene foam or other absorbent material, followed by several pieces of thick plastic sheeting. If necessary, spray the horn with water to keep it wet.

To lift the horn, carefully clean around it to isolate it, but do not remove all the surrounding mud. Carefully undercut the object, lift it out of the ground, and immediately place it into three polyethylene bags along with some of the surrounding mud. Add 20 ml of 0.2% fungicide to the innermost bag containing the horn and seal well. The bags can then be placed in a plastic container half filled with water to which more fungicide has been added. Seal the container with a tight-fitting lid and keep it in as cool a place as possible until it can be taken to a conservator.

If the horn is very soft and requires support, it can be wrapped in sheets of damp polyethylene foam. Avoid using cloth or paper because they are likely to rot before the object can be treated.

An alternate method of packing waterlogged horn is to place it directly into a plastic container with a tight-fitting lid. The container should be padded first with damp polyethylene foam. Use rolls of damp foam to fill empty spaces in the container to prevent the object from moving. Add 20 ml of 0.2% fungicide to the container before sealing it.

If possible, refrigerate the wet horn, but make very sure that it does not freeze. Refrigeration may obviate the need for fungicide. Consult with a conservator before adding the fungicide. It is important that any horn packed with fungicide be labeled to that effect so that people will take the necessary precautions when handling it.

Iron

Although iron ores are the most widespread ores on earth, iron appeared comparatively late because of the complicated technology needed to extract it. This metal came into use in the early part of the third millennium BC in Mesopotamia and Asia Minor. The first iron produced was soft and no more useful than bronze. A true Iron Age did not develop until considerably later when smelting technology was developed. Once smelting was known, use of iron slowly spread westward until it became extensive throughout the Middle East, the Mediterranean, and Europe. Extracted iron was not known in the Americas until the advent of Europeans; however, meteoric iron was used in North America prior to European contact.

Ancient iron is not pure iron, but rather wrought iron, an alloy of iron and carbon. A very heterogeneous metal, with an average carbon content of approximately 0.1%, it has been hammered and worked into the desired shape. It was an accidental—although not surprising—product because the extraction process involved heating ores with large quantities of charcoal, which is pure carbon. Strictly speaking, all archaeological iron should be called *steel*, the name given to an alloy of iron and carbon. To prevent confusion with modern steel, which requires further, more complicated treatment, the convention is to use the term *iron*. Cast iron, which contains a minimum of 2% carbon and requires a more advanced technology, is not produced until much later. Some bog iron was worked in England and northern

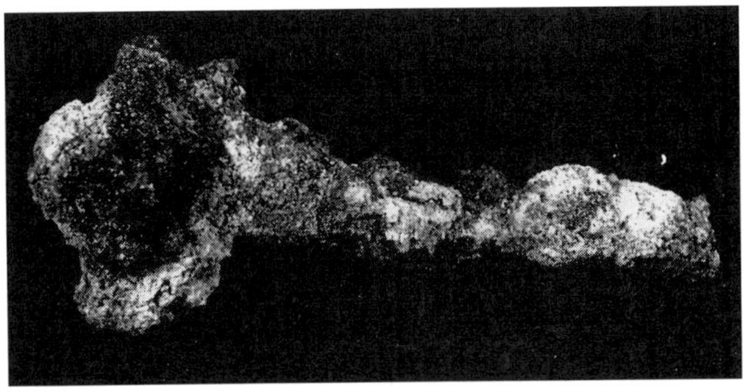

FIGURE 5.21 Corroded iron nail or bolt showing uneven, warty surface.

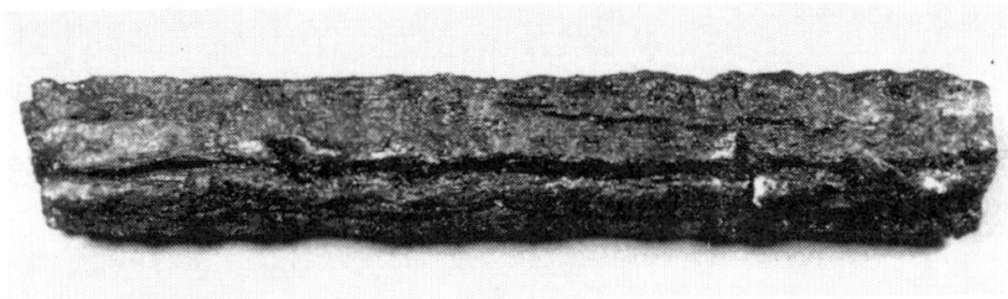

FIGURE 5.22 Corroded iron bar showing deep cracks caused by the increase in volume of the corrosion products.

Europe, but it produced a soft iron that was inferior to bronze.

Iron is a silver-white, lustrous, malleable, ductile, and very hard metal. Perhaps the most characteristic property of iron is its magnetism. In the field, testing with a magnet is the best way to determine whether an object is made of iron. As most corrosion products of iron are not magnetic, a magnet is also useful in determining how much iron remains in an excavated object.

Iron corrodes easily in the presence of moisture and oxygen, rust being its most familiar and easily identifiable corrosion product. Iron does not corrode uniformly in layers over the object as copper does, but rather unevenly, forming an irregular, warty crust of corrosion products (fig. 5.21). These products, often mixed with dirt and grains of sand, are generally porous in nature. As they form, they expand in volume so that badly corroded iron usually exhibits deep cracks and fissures and deformation of the original shape (fig. 5.22).

The condition of excavated iron can be very difficult to determine because its appearance can be extremely deceptive. What may seemingly be a sound object will in fact be structurally weak, its deep pits and cracks hidden by corrosion products and dirt. In addition, there may be microscopic cracks— not visible even on a clean piece of iron—which gravely weaken the structure of the metal. Often, there is little sound metal left, and the corrosion products themselves, although they may look sound, can be very porous and fragile. Iron objects, therefore, should always be handled extremely carefully and as little as possible. All iron objects, especially long, thin ones, should be supported at all times.

Do not pull iron objects out of the ground because they can easily snap and break. They can be removed following general lifting techniques. First, clean around the object to remove all surrounding dirt. Carefully undercut the object. When it is completely loose, pick it up gently, supporting it fully, and place it in a padded, rigid container until it can be properly packed in the dig house. The iron can also be placed in a paper envelope, which is then put in a rigid container. The paper envelope will allow the iron to dry out, but it should be regarded only as a temporary storage measure. Iron should never be put directly into a plastic bag because the object will still be damp from the ground. Moisture will subsequently collect on the inside of the bag and wet the iron, which can easily initiate or exacerbate the corrosion process. If the bag sits in the sun, as it more than likely will before being taken to the dig house, this wetting process will be accelerated.

If iron objects are found dry, keep them dry. Do not wash them with water because this procedure can initiate the corrosion process. At most, gently brush the iron with a soft, but stiff brush to remove superficial dirt. Do not pry or flick off hard lumps of adhering dirt or pebbles because the pressure necessary to remove them can break the object. Loosen such lumps of dirt by touching them with a brush filled with alcohol and then scrape them off with a wooden tool or brush. If the lumps do not come off easily, leave them for a conservator to remove. No further cleaning should be attempted in the field. Organic material can be preserved in iron corrosion (fig. 4.11), and injudicious cleaning of dirt and corrosion can destroy such evidence.

Do not attempt to join broken iron objects in the field. Any adhesive applied will have to be removed before further treatment can be carried out. This process can result in the loss of edges and small chips, making for more difficult, if not impossible, joining later.

Conservators differ in their opinions on how to store iron objects that are found wet. Some feel it is preferable to dry them out rather than to store them wet, even though some damage may result. If this method is followed, allow the object to dry out slowly and evenly away from direct sources of heat, including sunlight. Other conservators recommend that wet iron be kept wet. Considerable research is being done to assess methods of dealing with wet iron by packing it in solutions of corrosion inhibitors (frequently a 2% solution of sodium hydroxide). If quantities of wet iron are likely to be found, it is best to consult with a conservator who is experienced in its handling.

Dry iron objects should be packed individually in rigid, sealed containers with silica gel. Put a layer of the gel in the bottom of a polystyrene box. Pad the box with acid-free tissue or polyethylene foam, using this material as a separator between the iron and the silica gel as well as for padding. Place the object in a depression in the padding and cover it with a flat wad of tissue or foam to keep it from moving. Be careful, however, that undue pressure is not exerted on the object when the lid is closed or the object may break.

To ensure that the box is as airtight as possible, tape over the join between the halves of the box. Silica gel is effective only when used in an airtight container. Gel also can be packed in perforated packets, as described below, to ensure that it will not shift and come in direct contact with the iron.

If plastic boxes are not available, iron can be packed in sealed polyethylene bags together with silica gel. Because gel must not come in contact with the iron, place it in a polyethylene bag sealed to form a small packet. The packet should be thin and flat to expose as much of the gel's surface area as possible. Perforate the packet all over with a needle or other small, sharp object. Do not pack iron in sealed polyethylene bags without silica gel. The bags should then be placed in a rigid container to protect the iron.

An alternate packing method is to place the iron in unsealed, perforated polyethylene bags. Put the bags, along with a packet of silica gel, into a metal or plastic container with a tight-fitting lid. Further seal the container with tape.

If only a few objects are involved, a glass Mason jar containing silica gel is an ideal repository. The rubber seal makes the jar airtight, ensuring the safety of the objects even in a very damp storeroom. This storage procedure is described in chapter 4.

Active corrosion of iron usually takes the form of wet droplets or pustules surrounded by the orange color associated with rust. This condition, known as *weeping iron*, indicates extremely unstable iron that requires the immediate attention of a conservator. Any iron in this condition should be packed in airtight containers with silica gel and taken to a conservator as soon as possible.

Iron objects should be stored in as dry a place as possible.

Ivory

Strictly speaking, the word *ivory* should only refer to elephant tusk, but it is frequently used to describe other materials with very similar properties, including hippopotamus and walrus teeth. All were used in antiquity. Ivory comes from the upper incisors of the elephant; they are not covered with enamel like other teeth, but instead consist almost entirely of dentine. They have a small pulp cavity at the root end. Growth is achieved by laying down successive layers of dentine, normally on a seasonal basis. This layered structure is not always noticeable until the ivory has begun to decay. It will then crack and delaminate in concentric circles along these layers (fig 5.23).

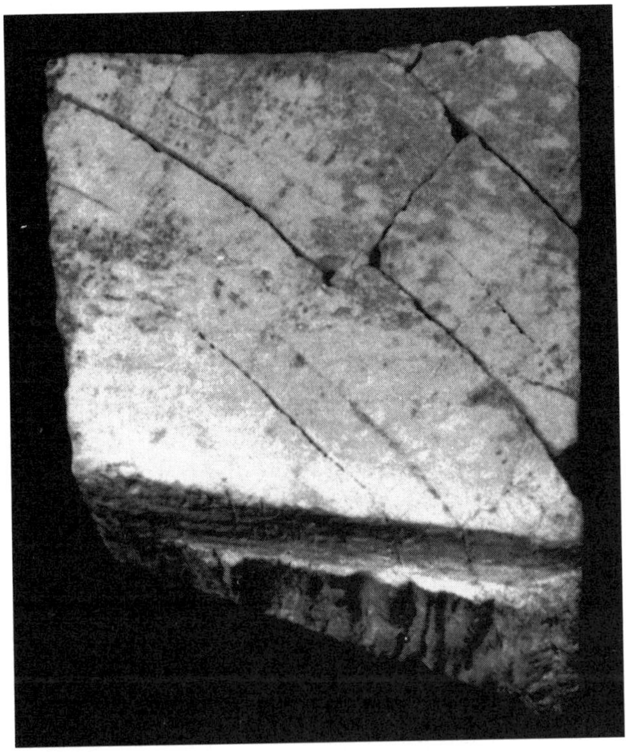

FIGURE 5.23. Piece of Late Bronze Age elephant ivory partially worked showing curved cracks along the grain of the tusk

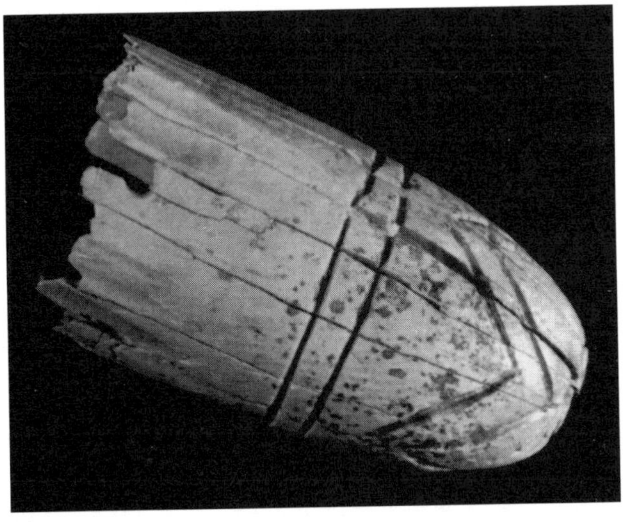

FIGURE 5.24 Egyptian cup made from a hippopotamus incisor showing longitudinal cracks along the bands of the dentine

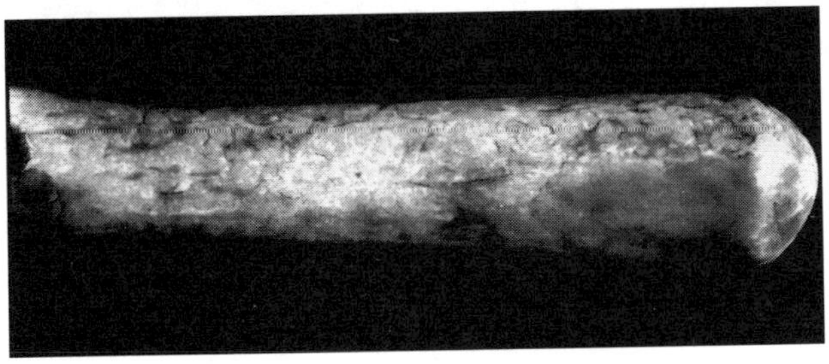

FIGURE 5.25 Detail of an Eskimo handle made of walrus ivory. The mottled effect in the center is characteristic of walrus ivory.

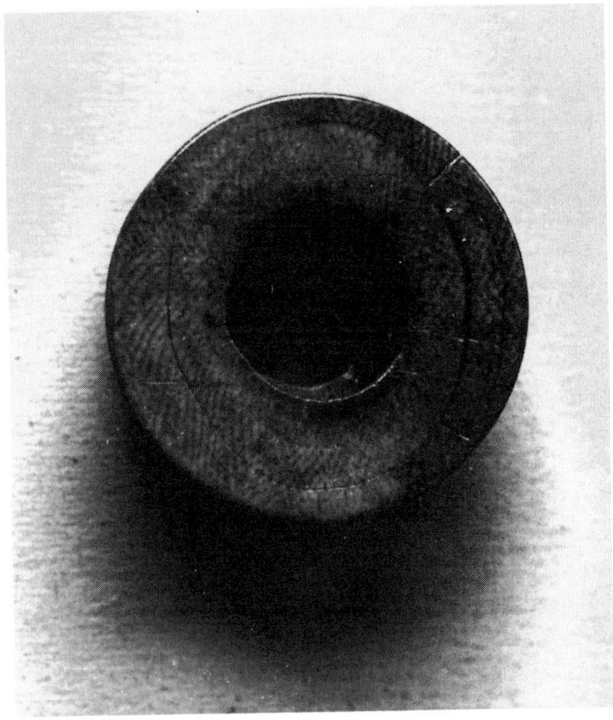

FIGURE 5.26 Worked elephant ivory showing characteristic intersecting arcs and concentric cracks

Hippopotamus canines and incisors were used, especially in Egypt, as a substitute for ivory. Unlike elephant tusk, these teeth have large pulp cavities, and the dentine is banded. These bands run the length of the tooth; when the tooth decays, it will split longitudinally along these bands (fig. 5.24) rather than concentrically as does elephant tusk.

The upper canines of the walrus also lack enamel. The dentine grows in two distinct layers: an outer, more homogeneous layer and an inner layer with a marbled, mottled nature which is characteristic of walrus ivory (fig. 5.25).

Ivory is a very dense and homogeneous material that is well suited to being carved. Its hardness and fine grain allow intricate and detailed work to be executed. In antiquity, ivory was frequently painted, gilded, and inlaid with metals and precious stones. In Egypt, it was sometimes artificially stained, usually red, but other colors were used as well.

Worked and decorated ivory may be very difficult to distinguish from worked bone. Ivory found during excavation can be even more difficult to identify. In general, it is more compact, denser, and heavier than bone and frequently, although not always, has a translucent quality. Because of its laminated structure, intersecting arcs of light and dark areas often can be seen on a cross section of a sound piece (fig 5.26); this characteristic is not true of bone.

Because of its laminated structure, ivory should be handled extremely carefully at all times. Try to avoid any unnecessary handling. Ivory objects can be removed from the ground following general lifting procedures. Carefully clean around the object to remove all surrounding dirt. Do not use a metal tool because it can scratch and abrade the ivory. Undercut the object and, when it is completely free, gently lift it out of the ground. Place it in a rigid container that is well padded with acid-free tissue. Take it to the dig house as soon as possible. Until then, keep it in a cool place. Do not let it sit in direct sunlight or it will dry out too quickly and may crack or warp.

When ivory is found in a fragile condition, it may need to be consolidated before it can be safely lifted out of the ground. To consolidate damp ivory, use a PVA emulsion diluted 1 to 4 with water or use Acryloid WS24 in a 2% to 4% solution. If the ivory is dry, use a 3% to 5% solution of Acryloid B72.

To consolidate a piece of ivory, carefully clean the surface to which the consolidant will be applied. Use a soft brush, making sure not to scratch or abrade the ivory. Remove as much of the surrounding dirt as possible to prevent large lumps of dirt from being consolidated to the sides of the object. Apply the consolidant with a brush, allowing it to soak in a little between applications. Continue applying the consolidant until it is no longer absorbed. Allow the consolidant to dry thoroughly before attempting to lift the ivory. Any material still wet with a consolidant is more fragile than it was before the consolidant was applied.

If the ivory object is shattered in the ground, it is best to back it rather than to try to lift all the pieces individually since some small pieces will inevitably be left behind. Follow the backing procedure described in chapter 4. Acryloid B72 in a 3% to 5% solution should be used as adhesive for dry ivory; undiluted PVA emulsion should be used for damp ivory. Any one of the block lifting techniques given in chapter 4 also can be used if the ivory is badly crushed.

Although very similar to bone in many ways, ivory is much more sensitive to moisture and must be treated accordingly. If ivory is found dry, do not wash it, even if it appears to be in good condition. Clean it with gentle dry brushing; make very sure that the brushing does not abrade the surface. If the ivory is in very good condition, surface dirt can be removed with swabs dipped in water. The swabs should be moist but not dripping wet. Do not rub the ivory with the swab because this motion can abrade the surface; instead, gently roll the swab back and forth over a portion of the surface until it is clean. As soon as a swab becomes dirty, replace it with a new one; a dirty swab can be extremely abrasive. Do not allow water to seep into cracks in the ivory. Be careful to work in small areas and dry each area quickly and thoroughly before moving on to the next. If the ivory shows any signs of cracking or warping—which can happen before your eyes—stop work immediately and leave any further cleaning to a trained conservator.

No attempt should be made in the field to join broken pieces of ivory. Since it is most likely that further treatment will be necessary in the conservation laboratory, any joins done at the site must be taken apart later. The ivory could suffer considerable damage from exposure to the solvents necessary to do this. Instead, keep the pieces together and take them to a conservator.

Ivory objects should be packed individually in rigid polystyrene boxes that are well padded with acid-free tissue or polyethylene foam. Place the object in a depression in the padding and cover it with another flat wad of tissue or foam to hold it firmly in place.

Dry ivory should be stored in an area that is neither too damp nor too dry. Over the course of a year, the room should maintain a relative humidity between 45% and 55%. Ivory should be kept away from direct sources of heat and light.

If ivory is found wet, it should be kept as wet as when found. Place it with some of its surrounding mud into three polyethylene bags. The object can be wrapped in damp polyethylene foam if it requires additional support. Do not wrap it in either paper or cloth, both of which will certainly rot before the object can be treated. Add 20 ml of 0.2% fungicide to the innermost bag containing the object and seal the bags well. Ivory packed with fungicide must be meticulously labeled to that effect so that the necessary precautions will be taken when handling it. The bags can then be placed in a rigid plastic container with a tight-fitting lid to further protect the ivory from drying out. The ivory should be taken to a conservator as soon as possible.

In the meantime, make sure the object does not dry out. Check it frequently and moisten it with a spray of water, if necessary. The container should be stored in a cool area. If possible, refrigerate the wet ivory, but make very sure that it does not freeze. Refrigeration may obviate the need for a fungicide. Consult with a conservator before adding fungicide.

Ivory, especially from sites on the sea where there is poor drainage or from saline desert areas, frequently contains soluble salts absorbed from groundwater during burial. These salts will cause extreme damage if they are not removed. Removal is a tricky procedure that can easily result in the destruction of the object if attempted by inexperienced people. Therefore, only a conservator should undertake the process in the field. Any ivory known to contain soluble salts should be kept as dry as possible and be taken to a conservator as soon as possible.

Jet

Jet is an unusual material that is classified between peat and coal. Essentially, it is fossilized vegetal material that has been altered by heat and pressure much the same as coal but to a lesser degree. It is generally regarded as a variety of lignite. The main source of jet is in Yorkshire, England, but analogous materials occur in the rest of the world. Jet was used extensively in Britain from prehistoric times onward. It was also used in Europe, and worked jet has been found in the Mediterranean and the Middle East.

Jet is hard, compact, and homogeneous in texture. Frequently it is possible to see the grain of wood in jet. It is a uniform black in color with a slight resinous luster. It breaks conchoidally like obsidian or glass and will burn. It is easily carved and turned and takes a very high polish. It was prized in antiquity, as today, for making beads, buttons, and other such ornaments.

If jet is found wet or waterlogged, it should be kept as wet as when found. Do not allow it to dry out, even for a short period, because it will warp and crack. If the jet cannot be removed from the ground immediately upon discovery, cover it at once with mud, layers of damp polyethylene foam, or other absorbent material, followed by plastic sheeting. Spray it with water, if necessary, to keep it wet.

To lift the jet, carefully clean around it but do not remove all the surrounding mud. Gently lift the object out of the ground and place it immediately, along with some of the surrounding mud, in three polyethylene bags and seal well. The bags can then be placed in a plastic container with a tight-fitting lid. Keep the container in a cool place, and take it to a conservator as soon as possible.

An alternate method of packing wet jet is to place it directly into a plastic container padded with damp polyethylene foam and closed with a tight-fitting lid. After placing the object in the container, add rolls of damp foam around it to prevent it from moving.

If jet is found dry, it can be removed from the ground following general lifting procedures. Although water can be used for cleaning, do not immerse the object in it; rather, clean it with swabs dipped in distilled water. The swab should be moist, but not dripping wet. Do not rub the jet with the swab because this motion can scratch the surface; instead, gently clean the surface by rolling the swab over it. As soon as the swab becomes dirty, discard it for a new one; a dirty swab can be very abrasive.

Minor repairs can be made to broken jet objects by using any of the adhesives recommended in chapter 3. Major repairs, however, should be left to the conservator.

Dry jet objects should be packed in rigid polystyrene boxes which are well padded with tissue or polyethylene foam. Using acid-free tissue is recommended but not necessary. Place the object in a depression in the tissue or foam and cover it with a flat wad of padding to hold it securely in place.

Dry jet objects should be stored in a dry, cool place.

Lead

Lead appears late in the history of metals because smelting lead ore is an intricate process. Lead smelting seems to have started sometime in the third millennium BC in Asia Minor and then spread both east and west. By the beginning of the first millennium BC, lead was common all over the Middle East, with the exception of Egypt. Although it was used throughout the Aegean, it was not extremely common until Roman times. In prehistoric Europe, lead was not common before the La Tène period (circa 300 BC).

Lead is a bright, bluish-gray, heavy metal. As corrosion takes place, it changes color, tarnishing first to a dull, then a light, gray and finally to a grayish white. Fresh lead leaves a black streak when rubbed on a piece of white paper or unglazed porcelain. Being soft, malleable, and ductile, it is easily worked. Because lead has a very low melting point, it can be easily cast.

Excavated lead is generally covered with grayish white corrosion products. This corrosion is accompanied by a decrease in the metal's cohesiveness, causing the surface to become powdery and the lead to lose its characteristic ductility. If corrosion is advanced, deep cracks will have formed all over the surface, as well as in the underlying metal. The object will be covered with powdery corrosion products and will crack and fragment easily (fig. 5.27). Although these corrosion products are generally stable, the lead itself can be extremely weak and malleable. Therefore, handle all lead objects carefully and as little as possible.

For the most part, lifting lead objects out of the ground should not be a problem. Carefully clean around the object to remove all surrounding dirt. Undercut the object and, when it is completely free, gently lift it out. If the object is small, place it in a plastic bag; do not seal the bag because the lead will still be damp from the ground. Keep the bag out of the sun to prevent moisture from condensing on the inside of the bag and rewetting the lead. If the piece of lead is large, place it directly into a rigid, well padded container with acid-free tissue or polyethylene foam. Take it to the dig house for proper packing.

If the object is very fragile or shattered, it may be necessary to back it to remove it safely from the ground. Follow the backing procedure described in chapter 4, using a 3% to 5% solution of Acryloid B72 as the adhesive. PVA or PVA emulsion should not be used because PVA breaks down to form organic vapors that will attack the lead. Any of the block lifting techniques described in chapter 4 can also be used to lift fragile lead objects.

Because lead is a soft, easily scratched metal, and its corrosion products are generally harder than the metal

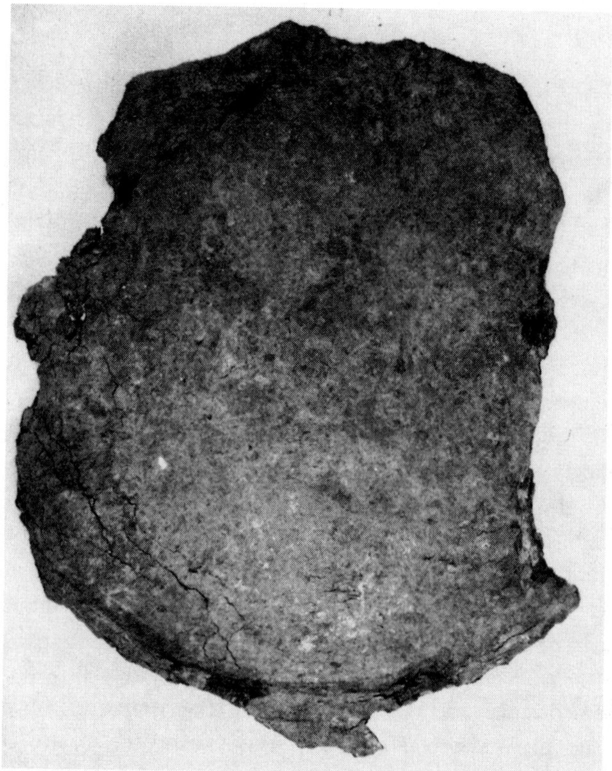

FIGURE 5.27 Medieval English corroded lead plate showing deep cracks and crumbly left edge.

itself, no attempt should be made to clean the object other than to remove superficial dirt with a soft brush. Otherwise, any inscription or decoration present on the surface can be inadvertently damaged. It is possible for inscribed lead to be so badly corroded that the inscription is retained only in the corrosion products.

Frequently, lead objects are found crushed, folded, or bent. In the Classical world, pieces of lead containing inscriptions were purposely rolled up. Do not attempt to unroll or unbend lead because it will only break and the corrosion products on the surface will crumble. In this way, an inscription can be lost very easily. Unfolding should only be undertaken by a trained conservator.

Do not attempt to join broken pieces of lead. Any joins made in the field will have to be taken apart later in the laboratory before any treatment can take place. Small bits of the edges will then be lost, making subsequent joining more difficult and unsightly. Also, only certain adhesives can be used with lead; leave this task to a conservator.

Vapors from organic materials cause lead to corrode; therefore, paper, cardboard, and wood (especially freshly cut wood) should be avoided when packing and storing lead objects. Acid-free tissue, polyethylene bags and foam, and polystyrene boxes can be used.

Lead objects should be packed individually in rigid polystyrene boxeswith silica gel. Put a layer of the gel in the bottom of the box. Pad the box with acid-free tissue or polyethylene foam, using this material as a separator between the lead and the silica gel as well as for padding. Place the object in a depression in the padding and cover it with a flat wad of padding to keep it from moving. If the object is a vessel, make sure that it is well supported all around and that no one portion bears all the weight of the object.

Lead should be stored in a dry area. Ideally, it should be kept on metal rather than wooden shelving.

Leather

Leather is an animal skin or hide that has been tanned, tawed (had an alum dressing applied), or in some other way chemically treated. With this treatment, the leather is rendered soft, flexible, resistant to putrefaction, and reasonably impervious to wetting. Leather is made up of many layers of collagen fibers which give skin its characteristic flexibility and elasticity.

There are many ways to make leather, several of which were used in antiquity. Smoking, oiling, salting, and tawing were employed, but produced no permanent chemical effect because the chemicals were only absorbed into the skin and could subsequently be washed out during use. Tanning, however, is an irreversible process because tannins combine chemically with the components of the skin.

In general, leather does not survive unless unusual burial conditions exist. A very stable environment, either very wet or very dry, is necessary. In dry, arid climates, such as in Egypt, leather can be found dry. Through desiccation it has generally become rigid and brittle and thus must be handled extremely carefully.

Before lifting a dry piece of leather, carefully remove all surrounding dirt with a soft brush or wooden tool. Do not use a metal tool because it can scratch and abrade the leather. Carefully undercut the leather and, when it is completely free, gently pick it up while supporting it from underneath. Place it directly into an unsealed polyethylene bag or well-padded, rigid container until it can be properly packed. Keep the leather out of the sun and take it to the dig house at the earliest opportunity.

Never wash dry leather. Water will stain the leather, and, if the leather is soaked in water, it will become sticky and lose cohesion. On drying out, it will crack and warp irreversibly. Dry leather should be cleaned only by gentle dry brushing with a soft brush, with care being taken not to abrade the surface of the leather. Do not pry or flick off adhering lumps of dirt because they can pull off areas of the leather surface with them. They can be softened by being touched with a brush filled with alcohol and then scraped off with a wooden tool or soft brush. Try not to let the alcohol touch the leather.

Do not attempt to relax or flatten pieces of leather that are folded over or bent. Because the fibers of the leather are brittle and desiccated, any attempts to unbend them will result in cracking and tearing. Water will not restore flexibility to the desiccated leather. Any unfolding attempts must be left to a conservator.

It is best not to join any broken pieces of leather because further cleaning and treatment may be necessary. Adhesives can easily stain the porous material, as will any later attempts to separate these joins with solvents.

Flat pieces of dry leather should be packed in a rigid plastic or metal container that is well padded with acid-free tissue or polyethylene foam. The leather should be laid flat in layers separated by more acid-free tissue or foam. If a piece is bent or shaped in any way, it may be necessary to further support vulnerable areas with small rolls or wads of padding.

Dry leather should be stored in an area that is neither too damp nor too dry. The relative humidity should fall between 40% and 50%. If the storeroom has a tendency to be damp, check the stored leather periodically to make sure there is no mold, mildew, or fungal growth on it.

It is more common for leather to be found in a wet or waterlogged state. Under these conditions, as long as no oxygen is present and the mud is acidic, leather will generally be preserved quite well. Such leather, however, has more than likely lost much of its internal strength. All dressings and most tannins will have been gradually leached out during burial, rendering it once more vulnerable to bacterial attack and decay. If too much moisture is present, the collagen fibers themselves will break down into smaller units, leading to a loss of form. If the process progresses far enough, the leather will become an amorphous gel.

Although waterlogged leather may appear sound, it is almost certainly greatly weakened and should always be handled very carefully and as little as possible. It should never be allowed to dry out, even under controlled conditions. If it does dry out, it will lose up to 90% of its weight and 50% of its volume in a very short time, becoming shriveled up, distorted, and cracked. It can even disintegrate altogether. Waterlogged leather should be kept wet from the moment it is uncovered. If it cannot be removed from the ground immediately, keep it carefully covered with mud, wet polyethylene foam, or other absorbent material followed by thick polyethylene sheeting, until it can be lifted. If necessary, spray it frequently with water. This step will certainly be necessary while the leather is exposed for in situ drawing and photographing.

Waterlogged leather can be lifted easily following general lifting procedures. Carefully clean around the leather to remove some, but not all, of the surrounding mud. Undercut the leather and carefully lift it out of the ground together with the mud immediately surrounding it. Place it directly into three polyethylene bags with the mud and 20ml of 0.2% fungicide and seal well. The mud will help to support the leather while keeping it moist and will maintain as closely as possible the burial conditions to which the leather became accustomed. Place the bags, in turn, into a plastic container half filled with water to which additional fungicide has been added. Seal the container with a tight-fitting lid, and keep it in as cool a place as possible.

Not all fungicides are suitable for use with waterlogged leather. The proper fungicide will maintain the leather on the acidic side of the pH scale. If a fungicide is too alkaline, it will actually contribute to the deterioration of the leather. Orthophenyl phenol, available as Topane WS, Dowicide 1, and nonfoaming Lysol spray, is a suitable fungicide. It is important that any leather packed with fungicide be meticulously labeled to that effect so that the necessary precautions can be taken when handling it.

An alternate method of packing wet leather is to put it into a rigid plastic container with a tight-fitting lid. Pad the container first with damp polyethylene foam to cushion the leather and prevent it from moving.

If possible, refrigerate wet leather to help prevent bacterial growth. Make sure, however, that the leather does not freeze. Refrigeration may obviate the need for a fungicide. Consult with a conservator before adding any fungicide.

Mosaics

Mosaics are pictures or decorative surfaces produced by cementing together small pieces of colored stone, glass, or tiles. One generally thinks of floor decoration but, in fact, walls and pillars have also been adorned with this technique. In Mesopotamia, walls and pillars were elaborately decorated with terracotta cones embedded in bitumen or mud plaster. In Greece and the Mediterranean, early floor mosaics were made with colored pebbles before the use of cut cubes of stone or glass (*tesserae*) became common. Tesserae were usually embedded in a lime mortar.

Mosaics present a difficult conservation problem because they are an integral part of an immovable architectural whole. To transfer or remove them is to destroy the unity of these architectural remains. Ideally, mosaics should be left in situ, but to do so poses other difficult problems. It presupposes the careful preservation of the building, and the construction of protective enclosures (for example, roofs) all of which are expensive and not always included in the original excavation schedule or budget. What is done to a mosaic, therefore, depends on a number of factors, including the long-term future of the site, the preservation and protection of the building, its geographical position, the

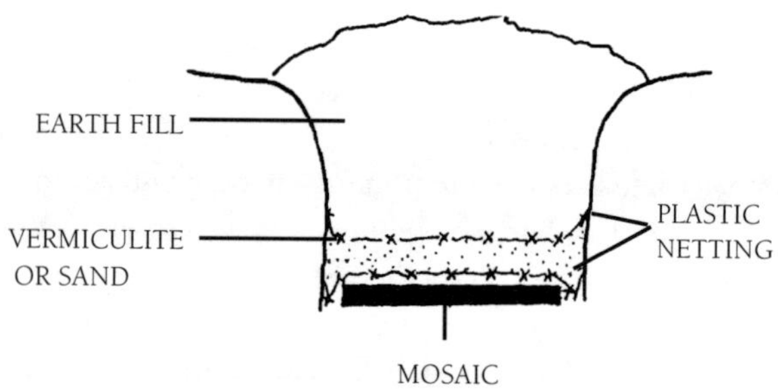

FIGURE 5.28 Method for backfilling a mosaic. *After Mora 1984*

climate, and guardianship of the site—not to mention the time and money available.

Removal of a mosaic can be justified only when the structure (and therefore the mosaic) is threatened with destruction if left in situ. The transfer of mosaics is a difficult and time-consuming job, and only the first part takes place in the field. The actual lifting must be followed by backing, cleaning, and mounting by trained conservators in a conservation laboratory. Removal, therefore, should not be attempted unless there is a museum nearby where the mosaic can be taken immediately upon removal from the ground.

There are instances in which mosaics are removed even though the structure will not be destroyed and the mosaic will ultimately be left in situ. For example, if there has been considerable subsidence and the surface of the mosaic is, as a result, very uneven, it is possible to lift the mosaic, lay a new foundation, and reset the mosaic.

If mosaics are likely to be found and, they will have to be lifted, an experienced conservator should be a member of the excavation team. If a mosaic is found unexpectedly and no conservator is present, it can be cleaned and left exposed for planning, drawing, and photographing, but it should be carefully covered up before the end of the digging season in the following manner:

1. Remove as much of the overlying dirt as possible by dry brushing. Clean the mosaic carefully with water and brushes. Be sure to remove all vegetation and roots. Watch out for loose or misplaced tesserae, being careful not to disturb them. When washing a mosaic, it is important to make sure the wash water is thoroughly drained off the surface. It may be necessary to make drainage channels first to ensure proper runoff. These channels will also help to ensure good drainage after the mosaic has been covered up.
2. Cover the mosaic with a sheet of plastic netting, not a solid sheet of plastic. A solid sheet of plastic will cause considerable damage by impeding the natural seepage and drainage of groundwater. Where it lies horizontally, it will collect pools of groundwater. It will also encourage condensation underneath that will in turn promote microbial activity.
   The netting should be a tight mesh (0.5 mm) but still be easily permeable to water. The netting helps keep the dirt and fill in place as well as facilitating its removal at a later date. If the mosaic is to be covered up forever, the netting can be omitted.
3. On top of the netting, cover the mosaic with a 15 cm to 20 cm layer of vermiculite (fig. 5.28). If vermiculite is not available, clay, salt-free sand, or dirt from the site can be used. Never use sea sand because it is contaminated with soluble salts. The fill material should be put down loose rather than in bags because air pockets between the bags will leave areas of the mosaic unprotected.
4. Place another sheet of plastic netting on top of the fill material; fill in the remainder of the trench or area with earth to a level at least 15 to 20 cm higher than the surrounding ground level to allow for settling (fig. 5.28). If the mosaic remains covered for a long period, it is important to check it at least annually to make sure erosion is not taking place and to prevent harmful plant and animal life from becoming established.

The following removal techniques are not necessarily those that can be executed competently by inexperienced people. These techniques are tricky and unpredictable in the best of times and should be done by an experienced conservator. There are occasions, however, when inexperienced people must do the job. For this reason, the following removal techniques are given. They are all operations requiring at least two people. When the actual lifting takes place, especially when using the carpet method, it is wise to have the help of additional people.

If it is absolutely necessary to lift a mosaic, one of the following procedures can be used. The first involves cutting the mosaic into sections and then lifting them; in the second, the entire mosaic is removed at once, rolled up like a carpet. Both are destructive processes in that only the tesserae are removed, with most of the mortar being left behind.

The choice of lifting method depends on the size and condition of the mosaic and the time and help available. Taking the mosaic up in sections is a time-consuming process, and great skill is required in the later stages when the mosaic is reassembled. The cut sections can be difficult to realign, resulting in disruptions in the surface of the mosaic and the design. If the design is intricate and does not lend itself to being sectioned, it is better to use the rolling, or carpet, method. If the mosaic is extremely large, the sectional method can be better. Also, if the condition of the mosaic is such that there are many areas of missing tesserae that, in effect, isolate sections of sound mosaic, the sectional method may prove more efficient.

Before any work is done and regardless of which method is used, it is important to make detailed, scale drawings of the mosaic showing the main elements of the design. The condition of the mosaic should also be noted: where there are missing areas, where tesserae are loose or missing, where there are uneven areas, and so forth. These drawings should be augmented with a full photographic record of the whole mosaic before starting the lifting procedure.

SECTIONAL METHOD: Since the sectional method can take considerable time, a cover should be erected over the mosaic if the site is in an area where rain is likely. Then, follow these steps:

1. Carefully study the design of the mosaic to determine where the mosaic will best be sectioned; obviously, the cuts must follow the lines of the tesserae. If possible, divide the sections along pattern lines, especially where sections of different colors meet one another. When reassembled, the joins are less likely to show and disrupt the pattern. For ease of handling and reassembly, do not make the sections too large. The size will be dictated to a certain extent by the mosaic itself. It is not necessary for all the sections to be the same size or shape.
2. Draw a grid on the drawing of the mosaic and indicate boundaries of all sections. It is possible that boundaries may coincide with grid lines.
3. Thoroughly wash the surface of the mosaic, using a brush to clean between the tesserae. Remove all puddles of water and allow the mosaic to dry. If the climate is not conducive to drying, it may be necessary to use a hair dryer or hot-air blower to dry the mosaic.
4. Although animal glue is the traditional adhesive used for lifting mosaics, PVA emulsions are used more frequently now and are recommended, especially if the site is damp. Cover the mosaic with a thin coat of undiluted PVA emulsion, being sure to get it into all the cracks between the tesserae. Allow this coat to dry, then apply a second coat. Leave the mosaic to dry until the resin appears hard; this process can take from one hour to a day or so, depending on climatic conditions.
5. Apply a third coat of undiluted PVA emulsion and then cover the mosaic with a thin cotton cloth that extends at least 10 cm beyond the mosaic on all sides. The cloth should be robust, but thin enough to enable one to see sufficient design detail through it. If one piece of cloth is not large enough to cover the entire mosaic, use several smaller pieces, being sure to overlap all joining edges by at least 5 cm.
6. Using a stiff, broad brush, add more emulsion and carefully tamp down the cloth to ensure it is saturated with adhesive and good contact with the mosaic is achieved. Try to remove all air bubbles trapped under the cloth. Eliminate any creases in the cloth by pulling it gently, but do not pull so tightly as to pull the cloth out of the cracks between the tesserae. Allow the PVA to dry for at least 24 hours. Drying rate will depend on the climate.
7. Mark the grid on the cloth facing with an indelible felt marker. To ensure proper orientation of the sections when lifted, use different colors, one for the horizontal grid lines and another for the vertical. Mark section lines in the same manner.
8. Number each section and note the number in the appropriate place on the grid and drawing. Do not forget to label each section.
9. Using a sharp knife, razor blade, or matboard cutter, cut through the cloth facing and the mortar along the predetermined lines of the sections.
10. Starting at an outer edge, insert the blade of a mason's trowel or a stiff spatula underneath the tesserae. Carefully work the blade in under the mosaic and free it by loosening the mortar just below the tesserae. The mortar is generally soft and friable and should cut quite easily. As the edge of the mosaic section is freed, pull it up gently and work the blade farther under the mosaic. As the freed area becomes larger, it can be gently rolled up out of the way.
    If the mosaic is especially delicate, a piece of hard board can be inserted under its edge. The cutting is then done underneath the board to protect the mosaic. Push the board further under as the mosaic is freed.
    During the cutting process, check frequently to make sure that the cloth is adhering well to the tesserae. Stop the cutting process to investigate any obstructions encountered.
11. When the entire section is free, carefully insert a rigid piece of wood or metal underneath the section. If a hard board was used throughout the cutting process, the section will already be on a board. Lift the section and invert it onto a second board so that it is lying face down (that is, with the cloth facing down).
12. Leave the section on the hard board when packing it to facilitate lifting and handling. Place the section in a shallow, rigid box or tray for storage and transport. If necessary, place wadded paper around the edges and corners to immobilize the section.
13. If any tesserae come loose during the cutting and lifting processes, bag them separately. Label the bag with the number of the section and keep it with the section. If known, make a note of the location on the section from which the tesserae came.

14. Repeat the above steps for each section until the entire mosaic has been lifted.
15. Take the lifted sections to a conservation laboratory as soon as possible. Be sure to include a record of all materials used in the facing and lifting processes, including trade names and grades.

ROLLING OR CARPET METHOD: The advantage of the rolling or carpet method over the sectional is that the mosaic is not cut up which—no matter how well done—will always result in some disruption of the design. The carpet method has been used successfully to lift mosaics of all sizes, but it is an extremely difficult and labor-intensive undertaking and should not be entered into lightly. Be well aware of how large a mosaic you can successfully lift. Mosaics larger than two square meters can be extremely heavy and unieldy, especially if the tesserae are large. If lifting them is attempted without experienced personnel and suitable equipment, there is a serious risk of damage to the crew as well as to the mosaic. Also, bear in mind that once lifted, mosaics will have to be transported, moved through doorways, and taken in and out of a laboratory. Make sure, therefore, that the mosaic will fit these parameters;otherwise, the sectional method should be used.

Many people must be on hand to help with the cutting and rolling. The number of people needed will depend on the size of the mosaic, but it is always a good idea to have several extra people available just in case there is a problem.

A number of facings are needed for the rolling method. The number and type of facings will be dictated by the size of the mosaic and the tesserae. If the mosaic is small enough and the tesserae are small, two facings may be sufficient. The innermost one, that is, the one directly on top of the tesserae should have a loose weave, such as gauze or veterinary bandage, to enable it to be worked deeply into the cracks between the tesserae. The outer facing should have a tighter, stronger weave, such as light linen. If the mosaic is large, two thin facings might be followed by two thicker ones. Heavier facings will also be needed if the tesserae are quite big. For the rolling method, follow step 3 of the sectional method. When cleaning the mosaic, be sure to remove any surplus mortar between the tesserae to ensure a key for the adhesive. Then, proceed with the following steps:

1. Any missing areas, or holes, in the mosaic must be filled to support the tesserae along its edges and prevent the mosaic's edges from fraying. The missing area can be filled with lime plaster filled with enough aggregrate to make it quite dry and crumbly. Plasticineor other modeling clay can also be used. When filling the holes, make very sure that the edges are fully supported
2. Cover the mosaic with a thin coat of undiluted PVA emulsion, being sure to get it into all the cracks between the tesserae. Lay the facing cloth onto the emulsion on the mosaic making sure that it extends beyond the edges of the mosaic a good 10 cm on all sides. This excess is used later in securing the mosaic to a support. If the piece of cloth is not large enough to cover the mosaic, use several pieces being sure to overlap all joining edges by at least 5 cm. If the tesserae are large, it may be neccessary to have a wider overlap to increase the strength of the facing.
   Using a stiff, broad brush, add more emulsion and carefully tamp down the cloth to ensure it is saturated with adhesive. Be sure to work it well down into the cracks between the tesserae. This tamping is extremely important to ensure that excellent adhesion between the facings and the mosaic is achieved. Try to remove all air bubbles trapped under the cloth. Allow the PVA to dry for at least 24 hours. The drying rate will depend on the climate.
3. Repeat the above process for each facing. Make sure to place the new facing with its grain perpendicular to that of the previous facing. This will give the facings maximum strength.
4. Starting at one corner and using a sharp spatula or knife, carefully undercut the mosaic by loosening the mortar just below the entire length or width of the mosaic. When a complete strip has been loosened, place a strong cardboard tube or wooden roller parallel to the strip, making sure that it extends as much as possible beyond the mosaic at both ends. Gently begin to roll the mosaic onto the tube. Slowly and carefully continue to loosen the mosaic while rolling it up as it is freed until the whole mosaic has been rolled up. A sheet of corrugated cardboard should be interleaved in the roll as the mosaic is rolled up to prevent one layer from being crushed against the next.
5. When completely rolled up, securely tie the roll at several points along the length.
6. If any tesserae come loose during the cutting and lifting procedure, bag them, noting from where they came, and keep them with the mosaic.
7. If the mosaic is large, it will have to be transported rolled up. When it reaches the museum or conservation laboratory, however, it should be unrolled immediately and laid flat with the cloth side down on a rigid, flat surface. If the mosaic is small, it should be unrolled at the site right after lifting. Place it cloth side down on a flat, rigid surface and transport it on this support. To prevent the mosaic from sliding off the support, tack it down to the support through the excess facing cloth at the edges.

8. Be sure to include a record of all materials used in the facing and lifting processes, including trade names and grades.

Mummified Remains

The term *mummification* generally brings to mind the particular process used by ancient Egyptians to preserve their dead. There are, however, many instances of natural mummification of human bodies found throughout the world that should also be included here. In fact, mummification is not restricted to humans. The ancient Egyptians mummified a wide range of animal species, and natural preservation of animal bodies also occurs. The definition of the term, therefore, will be expanded here to include all well-preserved bodies, both human and animal.

Mummification, the process by which human or animal bodies are preserved by rapid desiccation, occurs when soft body tissues dry out rapidly, before putrefaction can take place. Mummification can be achieved by either artificial or natural means. Artificial mummification, for example, was practiced and perfected by the ancient Egyptians using natron (a naturally occurring salt) as the main desiccant. The ancient Peruvians also practiced artificial mummification, using evisceration and fire and smoke curing, as well as various resins, herbs, and oils. Natural mummification was common in arid desert areas of the southern and southwestern United States, generally in caves and rock shelters. To a lesser extent, it also occurs in Peru and Chile.

Bodies are occasionally preserved in other ways. In South America (in the high Andes), in Siberia, and in arctic Alaska, well-preserved human bodies, mammoths, and other animals have been found frozen. In these cases, the cold prevented putrefaction, and the extreme dryness of the air succeeded in freeze-drying the body.

In Denmark and some parts of northwestern Europe, remarkably well-preserved bodies have been found in peat bogs. Here, preservation is a result of the exclusion of air, which prevented putrefaction from occurring,and the soil acids and tannins present in the bog water in essence tanned the skin and tissues of the body.

Any mummified material should be handled carefully at all times. Avoid any unnecessary handling because it is possible that bacterial and fungal hazards may be present in the body. Gloves should always be worn when handling mummified material; if any superficial cleaning takes place, it would be wise to wear a dust mask. As an added precaution, make sure that all persons who handle the material wash their hands afterward.

Mummified remains can be removed from the ground following general lifting procedures. First, however, it is necessary to determine the configuration and condition of the mummy. To do this, carefully remove all surrounding dirt to delineate the body. Clean the entire area surrounding the mummy at the same time because, frequently, a body was wrapped in fur, cloth, or deerskin and/or objects were buried with it. The best cleaning tool is a brush. Do not use metal tools that can abrade and cut the delicate tissues of the mummy or damage any fragile objects or materials around it.

Once the mummy has been fully exposed, it should be documented in situ with detailed scale drawings. These drawings should be augmented with a full photographic record before any lifting takes place.

If the body is flexed, small, or well wrapped to form a compact bundle, it should be possible to remove it by careful undercutting. When completely free, gently lift it, making sure it is firmly supported from underneath. Lifting may require more than two hands if it is large or heavy. Place the mummy in a well-padded, rigid container so that it is fully supported. A bucket or box filled with dirt or sand can be ideal for this purpose if it will not be too heavy to lift and move. Take the mummy to the dig house as soon as possible, and, when moving it, try to avoid any shocks to the container.

If the body is extended or there has been sufficient deterioration so that the body, although small, does not form a compact, cohesive unit, it will be more difficult to remove it from the ground. The research potential of the mummy will be greatly lessened if the body is not intact; so, do not break or cut it into sections. It is better to lift the mummy in a block with its surrounding dirt. The size, shape, and weight of the mummy will determine which block lifting procedure is most appropriate. Follow the procedures in chapter 4.

Unfortunately, there will be instances when the mummy's condition would dictate block lifting, but surrounding soil conditions will not allow this. If the body was placed in a stone-lined pit or cist, for example, it may be difficult, if not impossible, to lift the burial out intact. In this case, the mummy will have to be supported in another way. It may be possible to wrap it firmly with gauze bandage or cloth strips. When doing this, try to get as far underneath the mummy as possible with the bandage. This process may entail bandaging a section at a time as the mummy is slowly undercut. Although slow and tedious, this method can be quite successful.

If a more rigid support is needed, plaster or resin-coated bandage can be used. To prevent the plaster or resin from coming in contact with the mummy, make very sure the mummy is completely covered with either foil or plastic film, or both, before applying the bandage. See chapter 4 for this procedure.

If a body is found waterlogged, do not uncover it completely until it is ready to be lifted. The body should not be allowed to dry out, even for a short period, as it will shrivel, warp, and crack. If there are only fragments of a body or the body is very small, it can be lifted by removing some, but not all, of the surrounding dirt. Carefully undercut the piece, lift it, and place it into three polyethylene bags along with some surrounding dirt. Seal the bags well and place them, in turn, into a plastic container with a snap-on lid. Keep the container in as cool a place as possible; take it to a conservator at the earliest opportunity.

If the body is large or if small fragments cannot be lifted immediately, it should be covered with dirt, wet polyethylene foam, or other absorbent material, followed by several thick sheets of polyethylene. If necessary, spray the body to keep it wet. The lifting of such a body requires a great deal of thought and planning. Lifting, therefore, should not take place until all aspects of lifting, housing, and storing have been carefully worked out with a trained conservator.

After lifting any mummy, take samples of the surrounding soil, which can be used for microbiological testing and can provide valuable information about the mummy. See the section on soil samples for sampling, packing, and storing procedures.

If the mummy was not lifted in a block and it appears to be quite robust, a certain amount of superficial cleaning can be done. Use a soft brush, being extremely careful not to abrade the surface of the mummy. No more than superficial cleaning should be undertaken; any lumps of dirt adhering to the mummy should be left for a conservator to remove. If the mummy is wrapped to form a bundle, do not unwrap it.

The mummy should not be treated in any way. The addition of chemicals and materials to the body could affect any pathological testing done at a later date. No consolidation or adhering of broken fragments should be undertaken.

The mummy should be packed in a rigid container which is well padded with acid-free tissue. Fill the bottom and sides of the container with crumpled tissue, leaving a well the size and shape of the mummy in the middle of the container. Line the well with smooth sheets of tissue so that the crumpled tissue will not snag on the mummy. Place the mummy in the well and add smooth wads of tissue, if necessary, to ensure full support. Cover the mummy with one or more smooth sheets of tissue and fill the remainder of the container with crumpled tissue. Seal the box, and keep the mummy in as dry a place as possible until it can be taken to a conservator. If this step occurs almost immediately after lifting and the mummy was initially packed in a bucket or box with sand or dirt, the mummy can remain in the box as long as it is fully supported.

Any grave goods that accompanied the mummy should be kept with it.

Papyrus

Papyrus (*Cyperus papyrus*) is an aquatic plant of the sedge family which grew abundantly along the banks of the Nile in ancient Egypt. Used for a variety of purposes by the Egyptians, its principal value was as a writing material. Stems of the plant were cut into longitudinal strips, which were laid side by side to form the desired width of the sheet. A second layer of strips was laid on top and at right angles to the first layer. The sheet thus formed was soaked in water from the Nile, hammered or pressed, and dried in the sun. Any surface roughness was polished out with a smooth object. Sheets were used individually or pasted together to form rolls. These sheets and rolls were used for writing not only by the Egyptians but by the Greeks and Romans as well.

Papyrus is usually found either rolled up or in a badly crumpled condition. Since it generally owes its survival to hot, dry burial conditions, it is almost invariably desiccated and extremely brittle. Although the temptation is strong to unroll or uncrumple the papyrus, resist doing so; it will split, break, and disintegrate unless the fibers are first humidified. This procedure is tricky and should be undertaken only by a conservator experienced in treating papyrus.

Papyrus should always be handled extremely carefully and gently, because even the gentlest of pressures can cause it to split and break. Always support the entire piece or roll during handling. It is best to keep it in a padded, rigid container so that it can be moved and studied without actually being touched.

To remove papyrus from the ground, carefully clean around it to remove all surrounding dirt. When the piece is loose, pick it up gently and place it directly into a well-padded, rigid container until it can be properly packed. Place further padding around the papyrus, if necessary, to prevent it from moving inside the container. Keep the papyrus out of the sun and take it to the dig house at the earliest opportunity.

Do not attempt to clean papyrus in the field. Remove only those lumps of dirt that might jeopardize the safety of the papyrus before it can be taken to a conservator. Never use water on papyrus. Water will certainly stain it and can cause it to disintegrate, and the ink, which is almost certainly water soluble, will smudge or disappear altogether.

Papyrus should be packed in a rigid, well-padded container with acid-free tissue or polyethylene foam. If the object is a fragment of a sheet, it should be packed flat on a fairly firm support, such as a piece of polyethylene foam. If the support is too soft or flexible, the sheet can split or break when pressure is applied from above. Any wrinkles or folds should be supported with tissue or foam. Place a flat sheet of tissue on top of the papyrus and fill the remainder of the container with padding to keep the papyrus from moving.

A roll of papyrus should be placed in a depression in the padding in the container. Line the depression with a sheet of smooth tissue to prevent the padding from snagging on the roll. Cover the roll with a flat sheet of tissue and fill the remainder of the container with padding to prevent the papyrus from moving. Make very sure, however, that undue pressure is not exerted on the papyrus when the lid is closed or the fibers can break.

Papyrus should be stored in a dry place and taken to a conservator as soon as possible for cleaning and treatment.

Pewter

Pewter is an alloy of lead and tin; tin is the predominant element. Traces of impurities in the form of iron and other elements are generally found as well. In antiquity, the proportions of tin to lead varied considerably, so that no two pieces of pewter have exactly the same composition. Roman pewter, however, was reasonably consistent in composition, being approximately 70% tin and 30% lead. Although pewter was used in Egypt, Greece, Rome, and the Far East in antiquity, its popularity did not peak until medieval European times.

Pewter, a gray metal that can take a high polish, is much harder than lead and more brittle. When polished, it is only slightly duller and grayer than silver. Upon excavation, it is a dull grayish white and looks very much like lead. Excavated pewter can be treated like lead.

Pottery

The hardening of clay by firing to produce a durable, reasonably waterproof material was a process known and used since very early times. The term *pottery* refers to objects that have been manufactured of clay and then baked. Once heated above a certain temperature, clay particles begin to soften and fuse together, forming a durable, hard material. Depending on the temperature to which the clay is subjected, fired pottery can exhibit a wide range of porosity and hardness. The higher the temperature, the harder and less porous the pottery. At just below 1000°C, only slight fusing will take place, producing terracotta. Firing temperatures between 1000° and 1200°C will produce earthenware, and higher temperatures will produce stoneware, china, and porcelain. Archaeological unglazed pottery generally falls within the range of terracotta and earthenware.

The raw clays used to make pottery are basically aluminum silicates, but they do vary in chemical composition and in the nature and quantity of impurities, so that it is only natural to find great diversity in the fired pottery as well. A further difference is introduced by the temper, or filler, which the potter purposely adds to the clay to give it more body and porosity and to minimize shrinkage as the shaped clay dries. In antiquity, quartz sand, pebbles, and calcined flint were common tempers, but chaff and ground-up shell were used as well.

Because of differences in composition and hardness, pottery will react differently to various burial conditions. On the whole, well-fired pottery will survive burial in all kinds of soil quite well. If it contains a calcareous temper, however, and is buried in acidic soil, it may be found in a soft, weakened condition. Inadequate firing will also leave pottery soft and porous, especially when it is damp. If the ground is very saline, pottery can be greatly weakened during burial by the activity of soluble salts.

The term *pottery*, as used here, means any object made of clay, not just vessels and sherds. For example, loom weights, figurines, or sling bullets made of clay can be treated as pottery. Terracotta is dealt with in a separate section in this chapter. Since it is sometimes difficult to distinguish between terracotta and other pottery, read the section on terracotta before treating any pottery.

UNGLAZED POTTERY: Unglazed pottery in good condition can easily be lifted from the ground and should present few problems. Some basic procedures should be observed, however.

Never pry or flick sherds or pots out of the ground. Impatience is the cause of much needlessly broken pottery. Before lifting, carefully loosen the surrounding dirt, especially if it is hard and dry. Always remember that freshly uncovered pottery, especially low-fired pottery, can be very soft and friable while still damp. When cleaning around pottery, use only wooden tools or brushes; metal tools can easily scratch and abrade pottery.

When pottery comes out of the ground, avoid the temptation to clean it by scraping, brushing, rubbing, or immersing in water. It is very easy to remove delicate decoration and paint in this way, and to scratch and/or abrade the surface. Also, the edges of sherds can be easily abraded and chipped, which will make joining more difficult and unsightly.

Do not lift a sherd or pot before ascertaining the condition of its surface. Make sure there is no paint layer or applied decoration that has become, or will become, detached from the sherd when it is lifted. If detachment is a problem, the first bandaging process described in chapter 4 should be used.

All sherds from the same pot, including the smallest, seemingly most insignificant-looking pieces, should be kept together after being removed from the ground. When a large concentration of sherds is found, it is not always possible to determine immediately whether all belong to the same pot. It is safer and much easier in the long run to collect and keep together all sherds found together. Later, after piecing, sherds not belonging to the pot can be returned to the general pottery batch.

If a large piece of pottery or a pot is found badly crushed into a myriad of cracks, breaks, small chips, and pieces, do not attempt to lift all the pieces individually. Inevitably, small fragments will be left behind or lost. Treat the fragments as a whole and lift them together with the help of bandaging. Keeping the numerous small fragments together in their relative positions can greatly aid the conservator later, when restoring the pot. Use the backing procedure outlined in chapter 4. If the pottery is damp, an undiluted PVA emulsion should be used as the backing adhesive; if the pottery is dry, use a 7% to 10% solution of Acryloid B72.

If a pot is found intact, it can usually be lifted out of the ground after the surrounding dirt is carefully removed. Do not pull complete pots out of the ground without first following this procedure or they can crack or break. Undercut the pot and, when it is completely free, gently lift it out of the ground, cradling it in both hands. Place it in a well-padded, rigid container until it can be properly packed. If a box is not available, the pot can be placed in a bucket filled with dirt or sand (fig. 4.4).

If a pot is intact but has major cracks or breaks, it can be lifted out whole if it is first wrapped firmly with strips of gauze bandage. See chapter 4 for the bandaging process. This procedure can also be helpful for lifting a broken pot when the sherds are still held in place by dirt inside the pot. If the pot is large and the sherds are loose, the bandaging may have to be done piecemeal as the dirt is slowly removed from around the pot. If simple bandaging does not afford sufficient support, a more rigid support can be achieved by further wrapping the pot with plaster bandage or bandage impregnated with resin. See chapter 4 for the procedure.

If pottery is found in a fragile condition, it must be consolidated before it can be safely lifted from the ground. A 3% to 5% solution of Acryloid B72 is a suitable consolidant if the pottery is dry. If the pottery is damp, a PVA emulsion diluted 1 to 4 with water should be used.

To consolidate a sherd or pot, carefully use a brush to clean off the surface to which the consolidant will be applied. Make sure the surface of the pottery is not scratched or abraded in the process. Remove as much of the surrounding dirt as possible to prevent large lumps of dirt from being consolidated to the sides of the object. Using a brush, apply the consolidant to the pottery, allowing it to soak in. Continue applying consolidant sparingly until it is no longer absorbed by the pottery. There should never be a thick, glossy layer of consolidant on the pottery surface; excess consolidant will have to be removed in the laboratory, possibly to the detriment of the pot. Allow the consolidant to dry thoroughly before attempting to lift the pottery. Any material still wet with consolidant is more fragile than it was before the consolidant was applied. Do not consolidate any sherds to be used for analysis because the sample will be contaminated.

No attempt should be made to clean, mark, or join consolidated pottery. It should be packed immediately, spread out in layers in rigid, well-padded containers. If the sherds were consolidated with PVA, make sure they do not come in contact with cotton wool. When hot, PVA will soften, causing the cotton fibers to stick to the surface of the pottery. Pottery consolidated with PVA, therefore, should be stored in as cool a place as possible.

Not all pottery needs to be washed in water. Frequently, a gentle dry brushing with a stiff brush is sufficient to remove dirt. The majority of well-fired sherds can be washed in water without difficulty. Before washing them, however, separate out any pieces of painted or unbaked clay objects that might not survive the washing process. If there is any question about the durability of the sherds, first test an insignificant sherd in water. Do not wash a sherd that needs consolidation or has already been consolidated. Friable pottery and pottery with fugitive paint, postfiring paint, or inscriptions should go directly to a trained conservator without being washed or cleaned.

Immerse the sherds or pot in water and use a soft brush to remove the dirt, but do not scrub too vigorously because the surfaces and edges can be easily abraded, making for bad joins later on. Change the wash water frequently, if possible, because the dirty water itself can be very abrasive. If water is not sufficiently plentiful, devise a raised rack made of plastic mesh or screening and place the sherds on it to keep them out of the sludge at the bottom of the wash basin (fig. 4.12).

After washing, spread the sherds out and allow them to dry thoroughly before marking and bagging them. If possible, place them on a raised rack made of mesh or screening to facilitate even drying. If the sherds are placed on a solid surface, turn them frequently to ensure even drying.

Upon drying (following either lifting or washing), a white efflorescence may appear on the surface, indicating that the pottery probably contains soluble salts. Pottery from poorly drained sites on the sea or from saline desert areas is most susceptible to this condition. These salts have been absorbed from the groundwater by the porous pottery during burial and will cause considerable damage if they are not removed (fig. 5.29). The removal of soluble salts, however, is not generally undertaken in the field unless a conservator is present. If pottery is known to contain soluble salts, it should be kept in as dry a place as possible and taken to a conservator at the earliest opportunity.

Frequently, pottery is heavily encrusted with insoluble salts or a mixture of insoluble salts and dirt that will not come off in water. These encrustations obscure detail and decoration and are unsightly, but they do not otherwise harm the pottery (fig. 4.29). Since the only means of removing these encrustations is with acid, it is best to leave cleaning such pottery to a trained conservator. If this is not practical, the pottery can be cleaned using the following procedure. Remember that acid cleaning is a very harsh treatment on even the strongest pottery; use it only when absolutely necessary. Acid can be extremely dangerous when handled by inexperienced people and should not be used carelessly. Strict safety precautions must be observed at all times:

1. Always wear protective clothing, (including chemical splash goggles and thick rubber gloves) when handling acid or sherds in acid. Avoid getting acid on clothing or skin since serious burns can result.
2. When preparing an acid solution, always add the acid to the water; never add water to the concentrated acid. Large amounts of heat can be produced by adding water to acid which can cause the acid to sputter and spit. Add the acid slowly to the water, stirring continuously to dissipate any heat that may be generated.
3. If acid gets on clothing or skin, flush the area immediately with copious amounts of water. Rinse the area with a dilute solution of bicarbonate of soda. For safety reasons, acid should only be used in close proximity to a source of water. For more detailed information on dealing with acid spillage, see the appropriate section in chapter 2.
4. Use acid only in well-ventilated areas. Be careful not to inhale the fumes which can cause serious and irreparable damage to the eyes, nose, throat, and lungs. See chapter 3 for more detailed information on the hazards of acids.
5. Dispose of used acid in a safe place after diluting it thoroughly with water. See the section on acid disposal in chapter 2.

Before subjecting pottery to an acid bath, remove any sherds with painted decoration or friable surfaces. Objects made of unbaked clay should also be removed, as should fragments of stone vessels that might have been confused with potsherds (fig 5.30). Neither pottery with fugitive paint nor

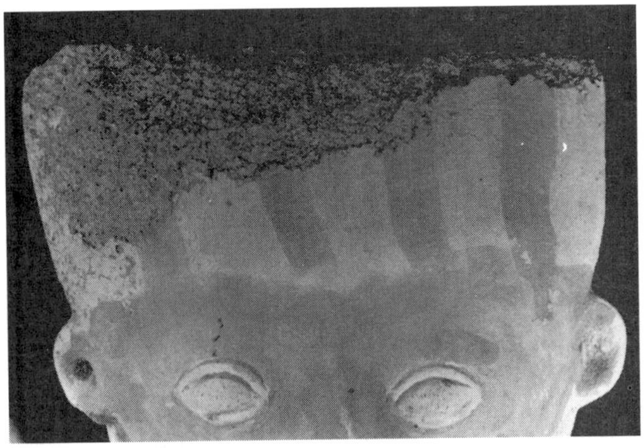

FIGURE 5.29 Damage by soluble salts to head of a Peruvian ceramic figure.

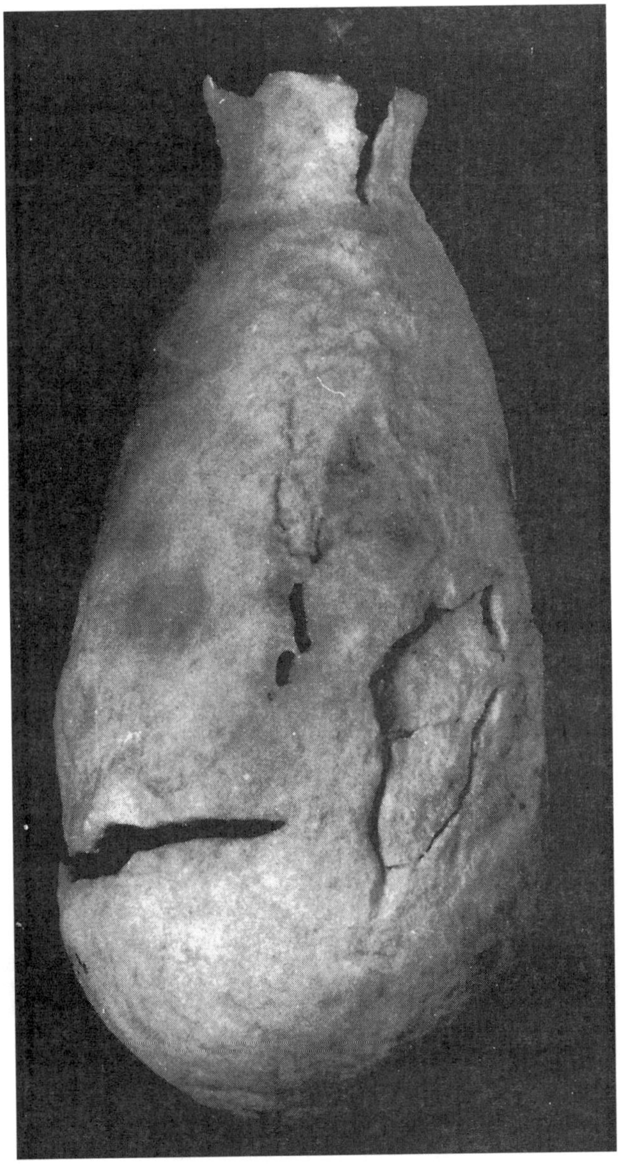

FIGURE 5.30 Near Eastern alabaster juglet that went through an acid bath.

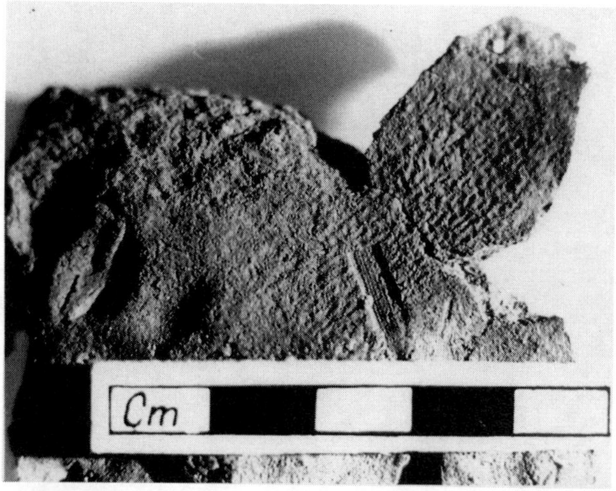

FIGURE 5.31 Textile and grass impressions on a Scottish Dark Age potsherd.

consolidated pottery should be subjected to acid cleaning.

Test an insignificant sherd to make sure the pottery fabric can withstand contact with acid. Certain pottery, such as some earthenware and terracotta, cannot withstand acid. Any pottery with a calcareous temper will be drastically weakened and may even disintegrate because acid will attack and dissolve the temper. Inadequately fired pottery can be extremely soft when wet, and the effervescence of the dissolving salt can literally destroy the sherd.

The acid bath should be dilute, not exceeding 5%. If the concentration is too high, the pottery will either be overcleaned, producing a raw, porous surface, or the surface will be softened so that subsequent cleaning will leave brush marks.

After testing a sherd and finding that acid does not harm the fabric, soak the sherds or pot in water for a minimum of one hour, to wet the fabric thoroughly. Tap or shake the container frequently to release any air bubbles clinging to the pottery to ensure uniform wetting. This soaking prevents the acid from being pulled deep into the fabric of the pottery. It is an extremely important step that should never be omitted, nor should the soaking time be shortened.

When it is thoroughly wet, immerse the pottery in dilute (5% or less) hydrochloric or nitric acid until the encrustation has been dissolved or loosened sufficiently to allow it to be removed mechanically. A good way to immerse the pottery is to place it in a plastic colander or a basket made of plastic-coated wire mesh. Keep in mind that anything made of metal or organic materials will be attacked by the acid.

Check the pottery frequently while it is in the acid. If it shows any sign of deterioration, remove it immediately and rinse it thoroughly in water. Do not leave pottery in acid any longer than is absolutely necessary to remove the encrustation. Generally, five to ten minutes is enough. It is better to immerse the pottery several times for short periods—after mechanically removing loosened dirt and encrustation—than to keep it immersed for one long period.

After being treated with acid, all pottery must be soaked thoroughly in several changes of water, preferably distilled water, until a neutral pH is reached, that is, until all traces of the acid are gone, as verified by pH indicator strips. This rinsing also removes the soluble salts produced when insoluble salts are dissolved by an acid. The importance of this rinsing process cannot be emphasized enough. This step must never be left out or shortened, although it may be tempting to do so. If all traces of acid and the soluble salts produced are not removed from the pottery, they can cause considerable damage later on (figs 4.30, 4.31, 5.29).

If only small patches on individual pots are encrusted with insoluble salts, it is not necessary to use the elaborate procedure described above. After soaking the pot for a minimum of one hour in water, use a medicine dropper to drop acid locally onto the encrustation. This is best done next to a source of running water so the pot can be easily doused with water every minute or so to rinse off the acid and dirt. As with any acid treatment, thorough soaking in water must follow this procedure. When thoroughly rinsed, spread the pottery out to dry as described above for washed pottery.

Frequently, impressions of basketry, matting, textiles, wickerwork, or seeds are found on pottery (fig. 5.31). These impressions can provide valuable information about the site that might not otherwise be obtained. For them to be studied, it may be necessary to make an impression or a cast of the impressions.(See appendix I).

Pottery joining is best done by a conservator. If profiles are needed in the field, join only what is absolutely necessary. Joins made by inexperienced people in the field generally have to be taken apart in the laboratory, to the detriment of the pot. Do not join damp pottery. If the adhesive turns milky, the pottery is still damp. Any of the adhesives recommended in chapter 3 are suitable for joining pottery. Do not use any cyanoacrylate instant adhesives (super glue), rubber cement, or epoxies. Follow the treatment procedure outlined in chapter 4.

No restoration of missing areas should be attempted in the field unless a conservator is present. Before restoration can take place, all joins must be in perfect alignment. If pots have been put together inexpertly in the field, they will need to be rejoined first. Further treatment may also be necessary before a pot can be restored; leave any restoration to the conservator.

Sherds can be packed in polyethylene or cloth bags. If polyethylene bags are used, make sure the sherds are thoroughly dry before bagging them. Do not allow bags of pottery to sit in the sun. Although the sherds may seem dry, some moisture may remain in them. This moisture will collect on the inside of the bags as they heat up and will re-wet the sherds. Use double plastic bags as the sharp edges of sherds will rip holes in a single bag. When filling bags, make sure they are not too heavy; sherds can be crushed by their own weight. If filled bags are placed in a box, do not put heavy bags on top of lighter ones. Do not fill boxes too full or make them too heavy. To help distribute the weight of the upper layers of bags, place a rigid piece of cardboard on top of each layer (fig. 4.25).

Complete pots and partially pieced pots should be packed in rigid containers using crumpled paper or foam to support and cushion them. Delicate pots should be packed individually in boxes commensurate with their size. Fill the bottom and corners of the box with crumpled paper or foam to form a deep well in the center of the box in which the pot is to be placed. Before placing the pot in the well, put it in a polyethylene bag to keep it clean and prevent the wadding from snagging on the pot. Fill the remainder of the container with crumpled paper. A partially pieced pot may need additional support in the form of small wads or rolls of paper or foam. When placing the pot in the container, make sure that no one area—especially a weak one—bears all the weight of the pot.

Pottery should be stored in a dry area. Pottery known or suspected to contain soluble salts should be kept as dry as possible. It may be necessary to pack such pottery in sealed containers with silica gel if the storeroom is too damp.

GLAZED POTTERY: Glazes are vitreous coatings applied to the surfaces of pottery either for decoration or to render it impermeable or both. The composition of glazes is basically the same as that of glass. Slightly higher firing temperatures are required to fuse the glazes so that, in general, glazed pottery tends to be harder and stronger than lower-fired unglazed wares. Although the pottery itself may be stronger and better preserved, the glaze does not always fare as well. Glazes will not be well preserved in alkaline soils, but they will survive better in acidic soils.

Although glazed pottery is covered with a vitreous layer, when it is sound it can generally be treated in the same manner as unglazed ware. It should not, however, be subjected to acid cleaning as some glazes can be irreversibly damaged by acids. Before cleaning any porcelain or china, make very sure there is no overpainting that might lift off in water or be scrubbed off.

Glazed ware is a serious problem only when the glaze is poorly attached to the clay body. The glaze is often imperfect, incomplete, or cracked, allowing water, soluble salts, and dirt to get in under the glaze and into the fabric of the pottery. If the attachment was originally weak, a buildup of dirt or the action of soluble salts crystallizing out between the glaze and the pottery can cause the glaze to flake off. This process can also be caused by thermal forces. If the pottery is subjected to cycles of freezing and thawing, the glaze, being only a thin surface coating, will expand and contract at a different rate than the pottery and can easily pop off as a result. Rather than crumbling, the glaze usually flakes off in large pieces.

Do not attempt to clean any detached pieces of glaze. It is best to leave them dirty as they are thin and fragile and will break under even the slightest pressure. Wrap the loose pieces individually and carefully in acid-free tissue and pack them, along with the pottery, in a well-padded container.

If the glaze is still in place on the pot but is so loose that it will not stay there until it reaches a conservator, it should be consolidated with 3% to 5% Acryloid B72. Touch the edge of the glaze flake with a fine brush full of acetone (if the consolidant is made with toluene, use toluene instead) and allow it to be pulled into the crack and under the flake. Continue adding more acetone as it is absorbed. The acetone should be pulled off the brush by merely touching the brush to the crack. When this happens easily, fill the brush with the consolidant and touch it to the crack. The consolidant should be pulled off the brush just as the acetone was. Continue applying more consolidant in this manner until it is no longer absorbed. Make sure, however, that it is indeed going under the flake rather than running out unnoticed elsewhere. Apply gentle pressure to the flake until the consolidant has dried and the flake is secure.

The glaze can also become detached by the movement of soluble salts within the pottery. If this is the case, small white crystals are generally visible on the clay body, on the surface of the glaze, and in the cracks of the glaze. Reattaching the glaze in this instance can cause problems later on, so it is better not to do so. Rather, pack the flakes of glaze carefully in acid-free tissue, place them in a small, rigid box, and keep them with the pot or sherds. Any glazed sherds or pottery known to contain (or suspected of containing) soluble salts should be kept as dry as possible and be taken to a conservator for treatment as soon as possible.

If there are any doubts as to the safety of cleaning glazed pottery, it is best to leave it dirty. Wrap it carefully in acid-free tissue to prevent any abrasion to the glaze, and place it in a rigid, well-padded container. Take it to a conservator for treatment.

Frequently, pottery found in an archaeological context has badly weathered glaze, resulting in the loss of its characteristic translucency. It appears dull, whitish, and opalescent, and any color or design under the glaze will be obscured. This opalescence is often only superficial, but it can go deeper, rendering the glaze powdery and friable. Thin, small flakes of glaze will come off with adhering dirt, and so no attempt should be made to clean pottery in this condition. Neither should the surface be dampened to discern the design or decoration under the glaze. Pack such pottery carefully in acid-free tissue, place it in a rigid, well-padded container, and take it to a conservator for treatment.

Glazed pottery can be packed and stored in the same manner as unglazed pottery.

Radiocarbon (C^{14}) Dating Samples

A radiocarbon dating sample must consist of a substance that was once part of a living organism. A wide variety of organic materials are potentially suitable for radiocarbon dating; however, unless the carbon content is high, inordinately large amounts of the sample are needed, and the results tend to be less accurate. The following archaeological materials are suitable for radiocarbon dating, in order of preference based on carbon content: charcoal, charred organic material, well-preserved wood, vegetable matter (seeds, nuts, grains, grasses, and basketry materials), cloth, well-preserved antler, shell, charred bones, and uncharred bones.

Samples to be used for radiocarbon dating must be collected and packed carefully to avoid contamination from dirt and modern packing materials. It is unlikely that actually touching the sample will have any measurable effect on the results unless they fall at the far end of the C^{14} range, that is, unless the sample is likely to be 70,000 years old. Nevertheless, it is best to be on the safe side and avoid touching it. If it is necessary to handle the sample, wear clean, disposable plastic gloves. It is also important that all tools and containers that come in contact with the sample be free of all organic matter, greases, oils, lubricants, and preservatives. Only tweezers with flat, smooth blades should be used; those with ridged blades can introduce contaminants.

To collect the sample, use a clean metal spatula or tweezers to lift it out of the ground. Remove as much adhering dirt and rootlets as possible and place it on a clean piece of aluminum foil. Wrap the sample in foil or a thick piece of polyethylene, sealing it securely with tape. A self-sealing polyethylene bag can also be used. Place the sample in a rigid container to protect it. If small enough, it can be placed in a clean, plastic film canister.

Use only clean tools to cut a sample from a larger piece of material and allow the cuttings to fall directly onto a clean piece of foil or polyethylene. Ideally, the sample should contain at least 4 grams of carbon for maximum accuracy, although as little as 1 gram may be sufficient. Since no sample will contain 100% carbon, much larger quantities will be necessary. The recommended sample sizes differ considerably from laboratory to laboratory. The minimum sample size necessary for materials most likely to be collected for dating is given in the following list.

Material	Size of sample (in g dry weight)
Charcoal	10
Charred organic material	10
Well-preserved wood	10
Vegetable matter: seeds, nuts, grasses, fibers,grains	10
Cloth	10
Hide	10
Peat	10
Well-preserved antler	100
Shell	30
Charred bone	100
Ivory	100
Uncharred bone	500

Check with the laboratory that will process your samples beforehand to determine the sample sizes requiredbythat particular laboratory.

Seed Samples

Seeds and pits can be some of the most informative plant remains found on archaeological excavations. Although wood can usually be identified only to genus, seeds can frequently be identified to species if preservation is good. Most often, seeds are found carbonized. Although carbonization involves shrinkage, a great deal of structural detail is preserved. Unfortunately, although plant remains do exist on many sites, they are not generally recognized and recovered during excavation.

If carbonized seeds are to be used for radiocarbon dating, the strict sampling procedure set forth in the section on radiocarbon sampling should be followed to avoid contaminating the sample. If the remains are large—olive pits, for example, they can be seen easily, recognized, and collected by hand (fig 5.32). More frequently, however, seeds are recovered through dry or wet sieving or flotation of soil samples. Depending on the size of the screening used, quantities of small seeds, as well as other plant and faunal remains, can be recovered. If large quantities of seeds are visible in the soil, a sample should be taken for flotation. In such instances, it is best to avoid dry sieving as this will rattle the seeds against one another and against lumps of dirt, causing the seeds to break.

Before taking a sample, loosen the soil carefully with a small pick and take up the soil in chunks. Avoid scraping up the soil with a trowel; this action can destroy much of the

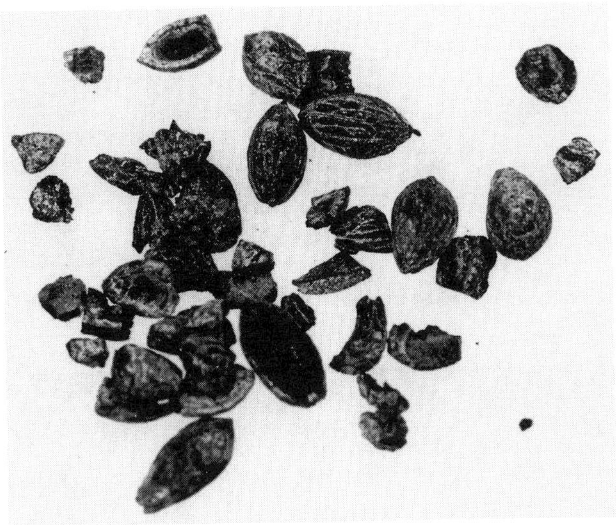

FIGURE 5.32 Carbonized ancient Greek olive pits.

detail on the seeds (and other botanical and faunal remains), and destroy the seeds themselves.

After a sample has been taken for flotation, set it aside following the instructions set forth in the section on soil samples and leave it for an expert to deal with. If this is not possible, a simple wet-sieving procedure can be used. Place the soil sample in the middle of a large piece of plastic screening with a mesh size no greater than 1 mm. Pull the corners of the screening together to form a bag. Holding it firmly at the top, immerse the bag in a bucket of water and gently swirl it around. At the same time, place the other hand on the bottom of the bag, gently push it up to flatten it, then allow it to fall back. Continue this motion until the dirt has been washed out of the bag. Remove the bag from the water and empty the residue onto a clean sheet of plastic by turning over the screen and gently tapping it. Do not scrape or scoop out the seeds or even pick them out with your fingers. They will be very fragile, and this movement could abrade or crush them.

Spread the wet seeds carefully in a plastic tray or box to dry. Allow them to dry slowly and evenly away from the sun or other direct source of heat. It is important that this drying process be slow. If dried too quickly or unevenly, the seeds can explode. While it is possible to spread out drying seeds on a piece of absorbent paper or toweling, the toweling may draw out the moisture in the seeds too quickly, causing them to explode. Be sure to keep drying seeds out of a strong wind so as to not lose the sample as it lightens through moisture loss.

When they are thoroughly dry, place the seeds in a small, rigid container, such as a plastic film canister, lined with tissue. Carefully fill the remainder of the container with crumpled tissue to prevent the seeds from rattling around inside and being damaged (fig. 5.10). Always avoid using cotton wool because its fibers can snag on rough areas of the seeds and break them. If cotton must be used, wrap it in a piece of tissue first. Store the container in as dry a place as possible.

It is helpful to the expert studying the seeds to have a sample of the surrounding soil for comparison. This sample should be 25 cc to 50 cc and should be dried thoroughly before it is packed in a clean polyethylene bag. Follow the collecting and packing procedures set forth in the section on soil samples. Do not pack the soil sample together with the seeds.

Shell

Shell is the rigid, hard exterior covering of land, freshwater and marine mollusks; it consists almost exclusively of calcium carbonate. The shapes and colors of shells have always been attractive to humans, and worldwide use has been made of all kinds of shells since the earliest of times. Whole shells have been used as money and ornaments and as containers for food, drink, cosmetics, and pigments. Shells have also been worked and modified to make decorative ornaments of all kinds: inlay, cylinder seals, beads, and gorgets, to mention but a few.

Shell is usually found in good condition unless it has been buried in extremely acidic soils. Under these conditions, shell will become very friable and powdery as the acid dissolves the calcium carbonate, which is then washed away.

If an object made of shell is sound, there should be no problem in removing it from the ground following general lifting procedures. First, carefully clean around the object and remove all the surrounding dirt, using a wooden tool or stiff brush; a metal tool will easily scratch and abrade the shell. Gently undercut the object; when it is completely free, pick it up and place it in a paper envelope or unsealed polyethylene bag until it can be properly packed.

Sometimes a shell object is found to be extremely friable and will need to be consolidated before it can be safely lifted from the ground. To consolidate dry shell, use a 3% to 5% solution of Acryloid B72 in either acetone or toluene. If the shell is damp, use a PVA emulsion diluted 1 to 4 with water.

Carefully clean the surface to which the consolidant will be applied. Use a soft brush, making very sure not to scratch or abrade the shell in the process. Remove as much of the surrounding dirt as possible to prevent large lumps of dirt from being consolidated to the sides of the shell. Apply the consolidant with a brush, allowing it to soak in. Continue applying consolidant until it is no longer absorbed by the shell. Avoid a buildup of consolidant; there should never be a thick, glossy layer of consolidant on the surface. Allow the consolidant to dry thoroughly before attempting to lift the object. Any material still wet with consolidant is more fragile than it was before the consolidant was applied.

Shell objects found in good condition can be easily cleaned. First, carefully examine any unmodified shells for signs of paint. On some sites, complete shells used as pigment and cosmetic containers have been found with pigment still inside them (fig. 5.33). Some shells have been painted or stained with ocher. Do not wash any of these shells. Clean them only by gentle dry brushing, being careful not to remove the paint. If the paint comes off easily to the touch, do not attempt any further cleaning or consolidation. Pack the shell carefully as outlined below and take it to a conservator for treatment.

It is best to start cleaning any sound shell object with a wooden toothpick to ascertain the condition of the surface as well as the presence of paint. It is possible that a seemingly sound shell will have areas where the hard outer surface is flaking off to reveal a powdery layer underneath; this is especially true of worked shell. The shell beads shown in figure 5.34 have deteriorated along the natural laminations of the shell. The outer surface is gone and the remaining shell is powdery and soft.

Do not flick or pry off any lumps of dirt because they can pull off the surface of the shell with them. If necessary, soften them first by touching them with a brush filled with water. Then gently scrape them off using a wooden toothpick or a brush.

If sound and free of traces of paint, shell objects can be washed in water using a soft brush, if necessary, to dislodge dirt. After washing, allow the shell to dry thoroughly before marking and packing it. Small areas of dirt can be cleaned with swabs dipped in water. The swab should be moist but not dripping wet. Do not rub the surface of the shell with the swab as this motion can abrade the surface. Rather, gently roll the swab back and forth over the surface until the area is clean. Be sure to discard the swab for a new one as soon as it becomes dirty; a dirty swab can be very abrasive.

Broken pieces of sound shell can be joined with any of the adhesives recommended in chapter 3. Follow the joining procedure set forth in chapter 4. Any badly deteriorated shell should not be joined.

Cylinder seals are frequently made of shell. When excavated, they can be in poor condition with a flaking and powdery surface. If at all doubtful about the condition of the shell, do not make a rolling of the seal as the entire surface can be pulled off if the surface is friable; the seal must first be treated by a conservator. To make a rolling, see the procedure outlined in appendix I.

Shell can be packed in polyethylene bags as long as it is thoroughly dry. Delicate objects made of shell should be packed individually in polystyrene boxes that are well padded with acid-free tissue or polyethylene foam. Place the object in a depression in the padding and cover it with a flat wad of tissue or foam to prevent it from moving. If acid-free materials are not available, place the object in an unsealed polyethylene bag before placing it in a well-padded container. Shell should be stored in a dry area.

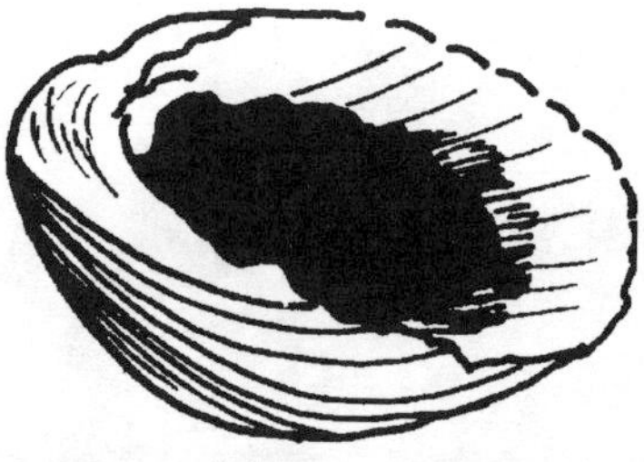

FIGURE 5.33 Mesopotamian cosmetic shell (cockle) containing a large piece of pigment

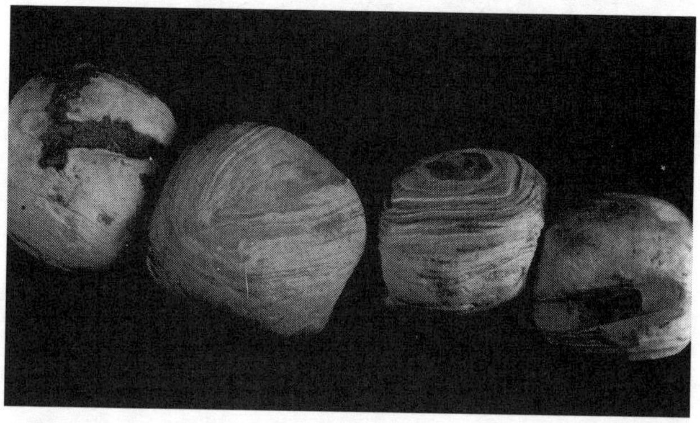

FIGURE 5.34 North American shell beads showing deterioration along the natural laminations of the shell. The outer surface is gone, and the shell is powdery.

Silver

Silver did not become common until quite late in the history of metals because its extraction from ore is a by-product of the smelting of lead, and an advanced technology was required to extract it. At first, only native (uncombined) silver was used. Since it was rare, silver was actually more highly valued than gold. Later, with advances in smelting techniques, silver became more common.

A lustrous white metal, silver is soft, very malleable, and ductile. It is capable of taking a high polish, but in the air it will easily tarnish to a dull, purplish gray. Silver is not as malleable as gold and, after prolonged hammering, it will become brittle and require annealing, or heating, to restore its malleability. Pure silver, like pure gold, is too soft for most practical purposes; so, it was commonly alloyed, especially with copper, to harden and strengthen it.

Silver can be extremely difficult to recognize when excavated. If it has a high copper content, it will be covered with the green corrosion products of copper and can easily be mistaken for copper or bronze. Pure silver can have a white, purplish gray, or black appearance.

Excavated silver is usually extremely fragile and brittle and is frequently cracked. If it is badly corroded, there may be little silver left and what is there may be mineralized. Because it is not always possible to determine the condition of freshly excavated silver, it is best to assume that it is fragile. It should always be handled carefully and as little as possible.

Never lift a silver object straight out of the ground as it will snap and break. Instead, lift it following general lifting procedures. First, carefully remove all dirt surrounding it. Loosen the dirt underneath to completely free the object. Gently lift the object out of the ground and put it directly into a well-padded, rigid container until it can be properly packed. Never place it directly into a plastic bag because it will still be slightly damp from the ground. This moisture will collect on the inside of the bag and re-wet the silver, which can initiate or exacerbate the corrosion process. If the bag sits in the sun, as it is likely to do before being taken to the dig house, this wetting process will be hastened.

Sometimes the silver is shattered or so badly corroded with deep cracks that the object must be backed to remove it safely from the ground. Follow the backing procedure set forth in chapter 4 using a 10% solution of Acryloid B72. It is not advisable to use an emulsion because the water in the emulsion could start or exacerbate the corrosion process. Any of the block lifting methods can be used to lift fragile silver objects.

No attempt should be made to wash or clean silver because even the slightest pressure can cause it to break. Because water and oxygen are the main causes of corrosion, silver objects should never come in contact with water.

Do not attempt to join silver fragments. It is very likely that the adhesive used will be stronger than the silver. If the object is handled excessively or carelessly after joining, the join will hold, but the silver can break in another place, usually on either side of the join. Furthermore, these joins must be taken apart later by a conservator before treatment can be undertaken. Small bits of the edges will inevitably be lost in the process, making subsequent joining difficult, if not impossible. Any joining, therefore, should be left for the conservator.

Silver objects should be packed individually in rigid polystyrene boxes that are well padded with acid-free tissue or polyethylene foam. Before padding it, fill the bottom of the box with a layer of silica gel. The gel can also be put into a perforated polyethylene packet to prevent it from coming in contact with the object. See the packing section in chapter 4 for directions on making silica gel packets. Place the object in a depression in the padding and cover it with a flat wad of padding to keep it immobile. Be very careful, however, that undue pressure is not exerted on the object when the lid is closed or the object will break. Seal the crack between the two halves of the box with tape to make the container airtight. Silica gel is effective only when used in a sealed, airtight container.

More robust pieces of silver can be stored in unsealed, perforated polyethylene bags; these are then placed, along with silica gel, in a metal or plastic container with a tight-fitting lid. The container should be further sealed with tape.

Silver should be stored in as dry a place as possible and taken to a conservator for treatment at the earliest opportunity.

Soil Samples

Soil samples are frequently collected from archaeological sites for several reasons. Soil analysis can indicate the contents of a vessel, hearth, or floor; aid in interpreting stratigraphy; and help to solve various stratigraphic problems, such as whether a ditch is manufactured or natural. More broadly, analysis of soils from ancient land surfaces can yield information about the climatic conditions that prevailed when these soils were formed and the sites inhabited. In turn, this can furnish important information about the climate and environment in which ancient humans lived. This information can be further amplified by studying the pollen found in soil samples.

The size of a soil sample depends on the nature of the soil and the method of analysis to which it will be subjected. Sometimes single samples are sufficient, but frequently comparisons must be made between levels, so that a series of samples taken from one section is needed. As a general rule, a reasonably sized sample should weigh approximately 250 g. Ideally, any sample taken should be sufficiently large to provide for the initial experiments (as well as repeated experiments should they be necessary) with some left over for future reference. It is always easy to throw away unwanted sample residue, but difficult, if not impossible, to retake samples.

Before taking a sample from a section, first carefully clean down the section. To prevent contamination between the layers, work horizontally across the section rather than vertically; working vertically can transfer material up and down the section. Clean the trowel blade after each scrape. Also, make sure all the layers are cleaned before sampling starts to prevent the sample from becoming contaminated by loose material dropping from above. All tools and containers used should be free of all organic material, grease, oils, lubricants, and preservatives.

To take the sample, start at the lowest level to be sampled. With a clean trowel or spatula, cut a block of soil from the section, being sure to stay within one level, and put it directly into a clean polyethylene bag without touching the sample. Repeat this procedure for each sample, working up the section. Be very careful to clean the trowel or spatula between samples.

Before sealing up the bags, it is necessary to allow the samples to dry out. The risk of microbiological growth is high if the sample is packed damp and storage conditions are not ideal. Allow the bags to stand open for as long as needed to dry out the samples; use a clean spoon, if necessary, to stir the soil to facilitate even drying. Do not allow dirt or dust to blow into the bags while the samples are drying. Loosely cover them with cloth to keep the samples from becoming contaminated.

Once the soil is dry, seal the bags tightly with tape and store them in as dry a place as possible. All labeling should be placed on the outside of the bag. Do not put a paper or cardboard label inside the bag where it can encourage fungal growth.

Samples taken from the insides of vessels should be treated in the same way as section samples. If possible, empty the contents directly into a clean polyethylene bag. If this is not possible, use a clean spoon to loosen and scoop out the contents, being careful not to touch the sample. Dry and store the sample as described above.

Ideally, soil samples meant for pollen analysis should be taken by the analyst, who will then be aware of the conditions under which the samples were taken. If the archaeologist does the sampling, the same sampling procedure described above applies. The size of the sample, however, need not be as large as that required for chemical and physical analysis. In fact, too large a sample can include more than one horizon and, therefore, be meaningless. Pollen analysis requires only what will fill a small matchbox or film canister.

Samples collected for pollen analysis can become contaminated from the atmosphere as well as from the higher levels of the section. To prevent contamination from upper levels, the sampling precautions mentioned above should be followed. Once the sample is taken, immediately seal the container to prevent any modern airborne pollen from contaminating the sample.

If a waterlogged sample is taken, it should be kept wet. Pack it carefully in a clean plastic container, a plastic film canister, or three well-sealed polyethylene bags, leaving as small an air space as possible.

Stone

Thousands of different kinds of rocks and minerals exist, but only a small portion of them were used in antiquity. Such stones as flint, obsidian, and soapstone are known from sites all over the world. Limestone, marble, alabaster, and serpentine are common from sites in the Mediterranean; carnelian, lapis lazuli, and turquoise were used in the Middle East. Jade, malachite, turquoise, and rock crystal were worked extensively in the Americas, as well as in the Far East. A wide variety of gemstones were used, as well, to make beads, seals, and jewelry.

A wide range of properties can be found among the different varieties of stone used in antiquity: brittleness, texture, and color, to name but a few. Limestone, sandstone, and soapstone, for example, are reasonably soft and easily worked, while granites, marbles, and basalts are much harder, requiring more sophisticated working techniques.

Most excavated stone objects are found in good condition, especially if made of a hard stone, and require no special handling. Stone objects can be removed from the ground following general lifting procedures. Carefully clean around the object to remove all surrounding dirt. If a metal tool is used, make sure not to scratch the surface of the stone. Undercut the object; when it is completely loose, lift it gently out of the ground. If the object is small and fragile, place it into a well-padded, rigid container until it can be properly packed. If the object is small but sound, it can be placed in an unsealed polyethylene bag or a paper envelope. A large stone object should be placed in a basket, bucket, or other suitable container so that it can be handled and moved without damaging its surface.

Sometimes stone objects are found in an extremely weakened condition with a friable surface. This stone will probably require consolidation. If, however, it can be safely lifted out of the ground, it is best to leave the consolidating process to a trained conservator. Lift the stone and allow it to dry out slowly and evenly. Make no attempt to clean it. Pack it carefully in a rigid container well padded with tissue or polyethylene foam. If it seems necessary, cover the padding with a large sheet of smooth tissue before placing the object in the container to prevent the crumpled padding from snagging on the stone's fragile surface. Take the object to a conservator for treatment as soon as possible.

If the object cannot be lifted safely without further strengthening, consolidate the stone using a 3% to 5% solution of Acryloid B72 if the stone is dry or a PVA emulsion diluted 1 to 4 with water if the stone is damp. Before consolidating the stone, carefully clean the surface to which the consolidant will be applied. Use a soft brush, making sure not to scratch or abrade the stone. Remove as much of the surrounding dirt as possible to prevent large lumps of dirt from being consolidated to the sides of the object. Apply the consolidant with a brush, allowing it to soak in. Keep applying the consolidant until it is no longer absorbed by the stone. Allow the consolidant to dry thoroughly before attempting to lift the object. Any material still wet with consolidant is more fragile than it was before the consolidant was applied.

Before washing or cleaning any stone object, examine it carefully for traces of paint. If paint is found, do not attempt to clean the stone; even dry brushing can remove the paint. Pack the stone carefully in a well-padded, rigid container and take it to a conservator for cleaning.

No attempt should be made to clean *ostraka*, which are pieces of limestone with ink drawings or inscriptions on them found mainly in Egypt. Because the ink is almost always water soluble, ostraka must never be washed. If it is absolutely necessary to clean them, remove the dirt around the drawing with a soft brush or wooden toothpick, being extremely careful not to damage or disrupt the ink in any way. Alcohol applied locally with a brush can help to soften the dirt but should not come in contact with the ink. It is best, however, to have a conservator clean ostraka because the stone frequently contains soluble salts and has flaking ink; therefore, extensive treatment is required. On the ostrakon shown in figure 5.35, small mounds of soluble salts can be seen pushing up areas of pigment and stone surface.

Pack ostraka individually in rigid, well-padded containers, making sure that nothing rubs against the drawings. Keep them in as dry a place as possible until they can be treated by a conservator.

As long as the surface of the stone is sound, it can be cleaned easily with water and a stiff brush. Alabaster, however, is reasonably soluble in water and should be cleaned only by dry brushing (fig. 5.30). Alabaster can be cleaned with swabs of water, if necessary, but be careful to dry the alabaster as quickly and thoroughly as possible. The swab should be moist enough to remove the dirt but not dripping wet. Do not rub the surface with the swab because this motion can abrade it. Instead, gently roll the swab over the surface until the area is clean. As soon as a swab becomes dirty, discard it for a new one because a dirty swab can be extremely abrasive.

No effort should be made to clean objects made of mica. The edges will undoubtedly be very fragile and weak, and the paper-thin layers can easily be broken off. Pack the object carefully as described above for ostraka and leave the cleaning to a conservator.

Stone, especially marble, is often found encrusted with insoluble salts or a mixture of insoluble salts and dirt that will not come off in water. These encrustations may obscure detail and decoration and are unsightly, but they do not otherwise harm the object (fig. 5.36). Do not use acid to remove these encrustations because it will attack the stone as well as the encrustation. Do not pry or flick them off because they can pull off areas of the stone's surface. These salts must be removed mechanically. Using a scalpel or a knife, slowly and gently cut off the encrustation. Hold the blade as parallel to the stone surface as possible and be extremely careful not to scratch or damage it. If the encrustation consists of more than thin, sporadic patches, do not attempt to remove it; take the object to a conservator for cleaning.

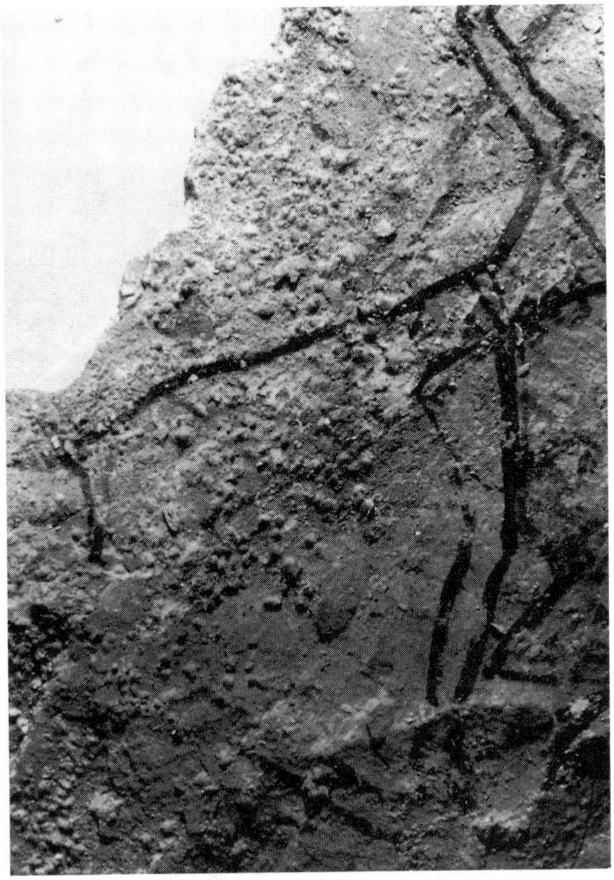

FIGURE 5.35 Detail of Egyptian ostrakon with soluble salts. The little mounds all over are salt crystals pushing up areas of pigment and stone surfaces

Minor broken fragments of stone can be joined with any of the adhesives recommended in chapter 3. Any complicated joining, however, should be left to a conservator. Follow the joining procedure set forth in chapter 4. If the pieces are large and heavy, do not attempt to join them because a stronger adhesive or doweling may be necessary.

If a white crystalline efflorescence begins to appear on a drying stone, the stone probably contains soluble salts. Stone from poorly drained sites on the sea or from saline desert areas is most susceptible to this condition. These salts have been absorbed by the stone from groundwater during burial and will cause considerable damage if not removed (fig. 5.35). Their removal, however, is not generally undertaken in the field unless a conservator is present. These salts may be all that is holding the stone together, and so do not attempt to remove them. Allow the stone to continue to dry

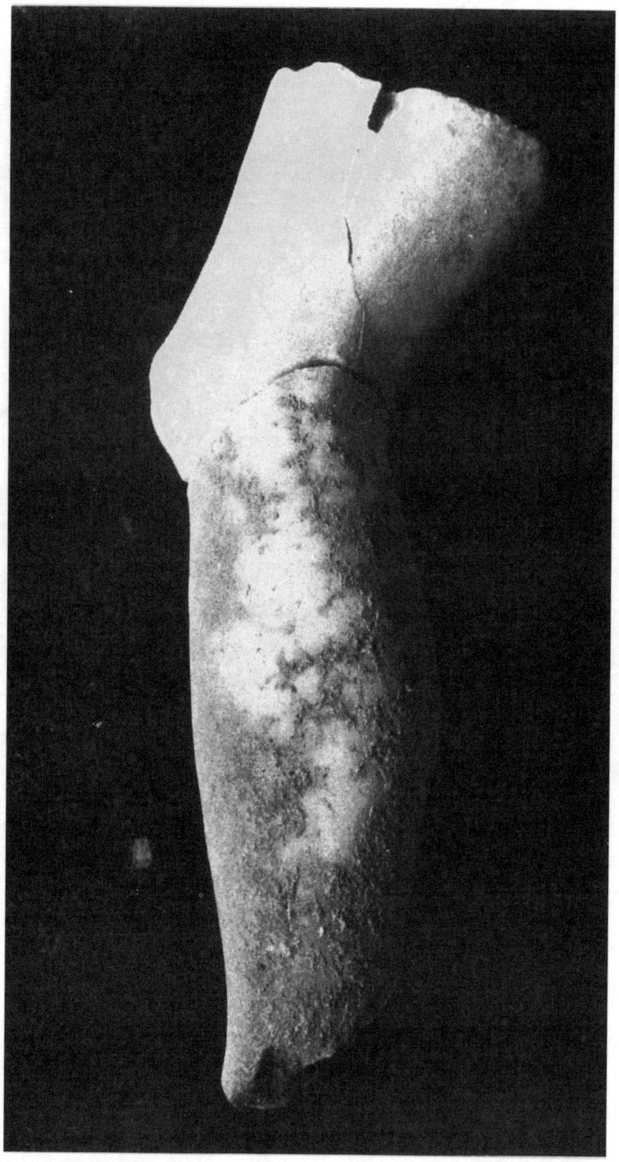

FIGURE 5.36 Insoluble salt encrustation on a Greek marble sculpture fragment.

out slowly and then keep it as dry as possible. Take it to a conservator as soon as possible.

If a stone has an inscription, it is frequently desirable to make an impression, or squeeze, of it for further study. The various procedures for making squeezes are set forth in appendix I. Do not make a squeeze of a stone surface that is not in good condition because the squeeze can pull off the surface.

Stone can be packed in polyethylene bags or in rigid boxes well padded with tissue or polyethylene foam. It is recommended, but not necessary, that this tissue be acid free. Avoid using newspaper because it is very dirty and will become brittle and disintegrate rapidly, no longer providing padding and cushioning.

No special storage conditions are necessary for stone, although stone known or suspected to contain soluble salts should be kept as dry as possible and not be subjected to drastic changes in relative humidity. If the storeroom is very damp, pack the stone, along with silica gel, in airtight containers.

Objects made of shale can present unusual problems on sites in northwestern Europe because shale is frequently found wet or waterlogged. If allowed to dry out, the shale will shrink, crack badly, and eventually split into thin layers. The extent of the cracking and splitting will depend on the orientation of the bedding of the layers in relation to the shape of the object, as well as on the degree of drying. Regardless of the bedding, however, disintegration will result if the shale is allowed to dry out. If the shale cannot be removed from the ground as soon as it is discovered, it should be immediately covered with mud or wet polyethylene foam, followed by several sheets of thick polyethylene. If necessary, spray the shale with water from time to time to prevent its drying.

Before lifting a shale object out of the ground, carefully clean around it to remove most, but not all, of the surrounding mud. Do not use a metal tool because it can easily scratch and abrade the soft shale surface. Undercut the object and gently lift it out of the ground along with the mud immediately surrounding it. Place it directly into three polyethylene bags and seal well. If support is needed, wrap it first in damp polyethylene foam. Do not use paper or cloth because they may rot before the object reaches a conservator. Place the sealed bags in a sealed container half filled with water. Keep the container in a cool place until the object can be taken to a conservator for treatment.

A shale object can also be packed in a rigid plastic container with a tight-fitting lid. Pad the container first with damp polyethylene foam. Fill the remainder of the container with more damp foam to prevent the object from moving. If the object is not taken almost immediately to a conservator, check it frequently to make sure that it does not dry out. Add more water to the container, if necessary.

Tablets

In Sumeria, Babylonia, and Assyria, clay was used to make writing tablets. Round, square, and rectangular tablets of wet clay were ruled and inscribed with a sharp instrument. The tablet was then set in the sun to harden. While all tablets were sunbaked, some, in fact, were further hardened by actual firing in a kiln. There is, therefore, tremendous variation in the hardness of excavated tablets. Clay tablets are also known from sites on Crete, mainland Greece, and in the Balkans. These tablets seem to have been only sunbaked, although some were inadvertently fired when the building in which they were stored burned.

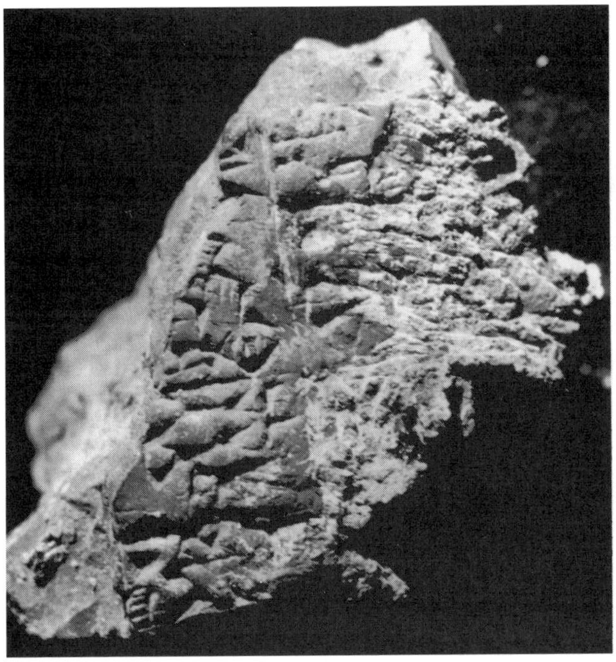

FIGURE 5.37 Detail of Mesopotamian tablet showing deep impressions of the writing.

Since tablets are made of unbaked clay, everything said in the section on unbaked clay holds true for tablets. However, they represent a special case and deserve individual treatment.

Before lifting a tablet from the ground, carefully clean around it to remove all surrounding dirt. Use only a wooden tool or a soft brush to do this because the edges of the tablet can be very soft; metal tools will scratch them. Carefully undercut the tablet, leaving several millimeters of dirt adhering to its underside. When it is completely free, gently lift it out of the ground and place it directly into a rigid, well-padded container.

If the tablet is broken, be extremely careful to remove all the fragments. Even the smallest fragment could be vital to the text when the tablet is joined together. Sieve all the soil from the immediate area after lifting the broken tablet.

If a tablet is found in the ground in a fragile condition, it may need to be consolidated before it can be removed. It is not advisable to use an aqueous consolidant because the water in it may cause the tablet to disintegrate. If the clay is damp, allow it to dry out slowly and then use a 3% to 5% solution of Acryloid B72 in toluene. In this instance, toluene is preferable to acetone because it is less volatile and will allow for better penetration of the resin, thus minimizing color change in the tablet's surface. Be sure to record the fact that the tablet has been consolidated, including the trade name and grade of the consolidant used. Make sure this information accompanies the object to the museum. Tablets are frequently fired in a laboratory or museum later so that they can be easily handled. The fact that a tablet has been consolidated or the specific consolidant used may affect the firing process, so this information is important.

To consolidate the tablet, carefully clean the surface to which the consolidant will be applied. Use a soft brush, making very sure not to scratch the tablet, especially the inscribed surface. Remove as much of the surrounding dirt as possible to prevent large lumps of dirt from being consolidated to the edges of the tablet. Apply the consolidant with a brush and allow it to soak in. Continue applying consolidant until it is no longer absorbed by the tablet. Avoid a buildup of the consolidant; there should never be a thick, glossy layer of the resin on the surface. Allow the consolidant to dry thoroughly before attempting to lift the tablet. Any material still wet with consolidant will be more fragile than it was before the consolidant was applied.

Although fired tablets usually can be safely washed in water, it is best to avoid any washing since it is difficult to distinguish fired from unfired tablets. Unfired tablets should never be immersed in water because they can dissolve into a lump of mud.

Before lifting a tablet, carefully remove as much superficial dirt as possible using a soft brush. Do not try to remove any persistent lumps of dirt by prying or flicking them off. Insoluble salts may well be mixed with the dirt, and they can adhere very tightly to the surface. If flicked off, they can easily pull off areas of the tablet's surface. The area of the inscription is especially delicate and vulnerable because the surface of the clay has been unevenly disrupted (fig. 5.37). Areas will have been undercut by adjacent indentations from the writing, and small cracks may have developed around these indentations as the tablet dried. Any undue stress put on the lumps of dirt, insoluble salts, or the tablet's surface around the writing can easily cause small fragments of the inscription to break off. For these reasons, only superficial dirt should be removed in the field. Detailed cleaning should be left for a conservator. For optimum results, a conservator and an epigrapher should work closely together on the cleaning of a tablet.

Frequently, tablets are found encrusted with insoluble salts or a mixture of insoluble salts and dirt that will not come off in water. Such encrustations cannot be removed with acid unless the tablet has been fired. If there is absolute certainty that the tablet has been fired, it can be cleaned with dilute acid following the procedure for cleaning unglazed pottery set forth in the section on pottery. Be sure to soak the tablet a minimum of one hour before immersing it in acid and rinse it thoroughly afterward.

Do not join fragments of tablets in the field. More often than not, tablets contain soluble and insoluble salts that will have to be removed. If the tablet has already been joined, it will have to be taken apart before treatment can proceed. If an irreversible adhesive is used, this separation may be difficult, if not impossible (fig. 1.1). Since the edges of the tablet are soft, small chips and bits along the joins will invariably be lost in the process. Such losses in the inscribed areas could be quite important. For these reasons, leave any joining to a trained conservator. Wrap the fragments very carefully in soft tissue, pack them together in a rigid, well-padded container, and take them to a conservator for treatment.

Tablets found in the Middle East almost invariably contain soluble salts. In fact, salts may have already badly damaged the surface of the tablet during its burial. The surface of such tablets will be very powdery and flaky, and portions of the surface may be missing even before the tablet has been excavated. As tablets dry out after being excavated, the presence of salts may become evident when a white efflorescence begins to appear on the surface and in cracks. Sometimes large crystals of salt appear. These salts have been absorbed by the porous clay from groundwater during burial and will cause considerable damage if they are not removed. The removal of soluble salts, however, is generally not undertaken in the field unless a conservator is present. Because salt removal requires soaking the tablet in water, unbaked tablets must be fired before soluble salts can be removed. Frequently, the salts are actually holding the tablet together; therefore, the tablet must be treated before salt removal can be attempted.

Tablets should be packed individually in a rigid container well padded with tissue or polyethylene foam. It is not necessary that this tissue be acid free. Place the tablet in a depression in the padding and cover it with a flat wad of tissue or foam to prevent it from moving. Make sure, however, that undue pressure is not exerted on the tablet, especially the inscribed surface, when the lid is closed.

Tablets should be stored in as dry a place as possible and be taken to a conservator for treatment at the earliest opportunity. It may be necessary to pack tablets containing soluble salts in an airtight container together with silica gel.

Terracotta

Terracotta refers to clay that has been fired to a temperature between 600°C and 1000°C. It is fired at a lower temperature than earthenware and, as a result, is softer and more porous. The term *terracotta* is often mistakenly used to refer only to a fabric that is reddish-brown in color. Terracottas, in fact, are found in a wide range of colors from pale pink to deep brown. The actual color depends on the amount of iron oxides and other impurities present in the clay and the firing temperature to which the clay is subjected.

Terracotta, as an architectural and sculptural material, was known from the earliest times: from pre-Dynastic Egypt, Assyria, and Persia to pre-Columbian America. As an architectural material, its first important use was in Greece; it was also important to the Etruscans and Romans. Its golden age, however, occurred in Renaissance Europe.

Terracottas found in an archaeological context display as extensive a range of hardness as of color. The hardness of an individual terracotta depends on the temperature to which the clay was fired, as well as the burial conditions to which it was subjected. Terracottas frequently have little mechanical strength, especially when they have been modeled by hand, because they can be riddled with air pockets. The most notable characteristic of terracotta is its porosity, which enables it to absorb staining material quite readily.

When found in the ground, terracottas can be treated much the same as other forms of pottery, although a few important differences should be kept in mind. Before lifting terracottas, clean around them with particular care, using only a soft brush or wooden tool. Terracotta is especially soft when damp and can be damaged easily.

Because of its extreme porosity, terracotta can cause problems if consolidation is necessary. Consolidants can, and usually do, change the surface color of the terracotta. It is impossible, therefore, to consolidate only small areas; the entire piece must be consolidated to keep the color of the entire terracotta uniform. Unless absolutely necessary, consolidation should not be undertaken in the field. It is preferable to subject the terracotta to a minimum of gentle handling and careful packing and leave the consolidation for a trained conservator.

If consolidation must be done in the field, use the following procedure. If the terracotta is wet, a PVA emulsion diluted 1 to 4 with water is appropriate. If the terracotta is dry, it can be consolidated with a 3% to 5% solution of Acryloid B72 in toluene. Toluene is less volatile than acetone and will allow deeper penetration of the resin, which will help to minimize color change. Clean the surface to be consolidated with a soft brush, being very careful not to scratch the surface. Remove as much of the surrounding dirt as possible to prevent large lumps of dirt from being consolidated to the edges of the object. Apply the consolidant with a brush, allowing it to soak in between applications. Continue to apply the consolidant until it is no longer absorbed by the terracotta. Try to avoid a surface buildup; there should never be a thick glossy layer on the surface. Such a layer will darken the terracotta and cause it to look as though it were made of plastic. Allow the object to dry thoroughly before attempting to lift it. Any material still wet with consolidant is more fragile than it was before consolidant was applied.

Terracottas were often decorated with paint. On some objects, paint was applied directly to the clay surface. On

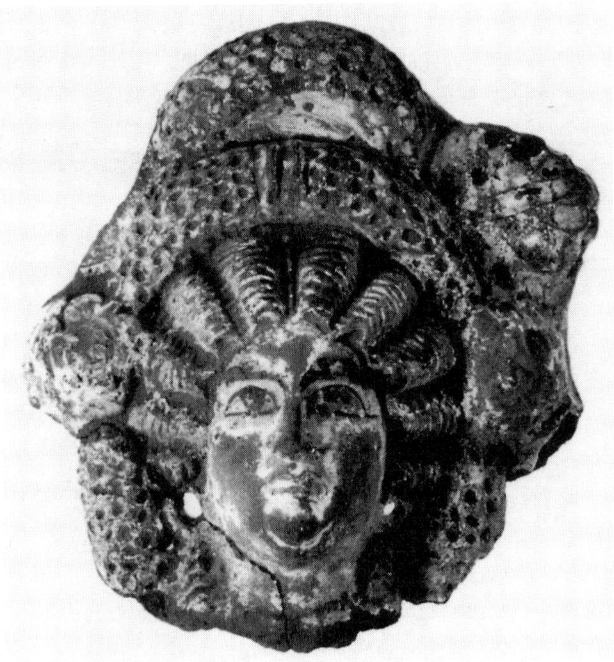

FIGURE 5.38 Fragments of terracotta figurine from Egypt showing traces of white gesso all over and traces of paint on the eyes and upper right portion of the headdress.

others, a white *gesso* ground was first applied to the terracotta which was then painted. The gesso ground served to even out differences in the color of the clay and brighten up the colors of the paint. On excavated terracottas, this paint has usually disappeared along with much of the gesso ground, but it is not unusual to find gesso, often with traces of paint, still in the cracks and indentations of a terracotta. Always be on the lookout, therefore, for traces of paint (fig. 5.38). When cleaning a terracotta, be very careful not to mistake any remaining gesso and paint for dirt and remove them. Generally, gesso is considerably whiter in color than dirt but, if it is covered with dirt, it may be difficult to distinguish.

If insufficiently fired, terracotta can be soluble in water to varying degrees, and so it is best to avoid washing it. Gentle dry brushing with a soft brush should be sufficient to remove superficial dirt, but be very careful not to scratch or abrade the surface of the terracotta, which can be quite soft and powdery. Impressions, frequently stamped on bricks, can be damaged by vigorous brushing. Always err, therefore, on the side of undercleaning. Overcleaning tends to wear down details, causing the terracotta to lose the crispness of the original mold. Also, be careful not to remove the seam lines from molds that appear as fine raised lines, usually along the sides of a figurine, or other evidence of molds.

Do not pry or flick off any lumps of adhering dirt as they can pull off areas of the surface, gesso, and paint with them. Soften them by touching them with a brush filled with alcohol, and then gently scrape them off with a soft brush or wooden tool. If this procedure does not suffice to remove them, make no further attempt to do so; instead, leave them for a conservator to remove.

Unlike unglazed pottery, terracotta covered with an encrustation of insoluble salts cannot be cleaned with acid. Such encrustations can be removed only with a scalpel. Because the surface of terracotta is very soft, this mechanical cleaning is difficult and is thus best left to a conservator.

Broken fragments of terracotta should not be joined in the field unless a conservator is present. Since the edges are soft and powdery, it can be difficult to achieve a good bond. Subsequent handling can cause the join to give way, and invariably bits of the edges will be lost, making joining later more difficult and unsightly. In addition, any excess adhesive will stain and discolor the surface of the terracotta, as will any later efforts to remove it with a solvent. It is best to leave any joins to a conservator.

When marking terracottas, be sure to follow the procedure set out in chapter 4 and write the number only on a patch of lacquer. If written directly on the terracotta, the number will be incised indelibly into its soft surface. In addition, the ink will be absorbed into the porous material and become impossible to remove (fig. 4.13).

If the terracotta comes from a poorly drained site on the sea or from a saline desert area, it will probably have absorbed soluble salts. These salts can cause considerable damage if they are not removed. Such removal, however, generally is not undertaken in the field unless a conservator is present. Any terracotta known to contain (or suspected to contain) soluble salts should be kept in as dry a place as possible and taken to a conservator for treatment at the earliest opportunity.

Terracotta fragments can be packed in polyethylene bags as long as they are thoroughly dry. More delicate objects should be packed individually in rigid containers carefully padded with tissue or polyethylene foam. It is not necessary for the tissue to be acid free. Place the terracotta in a depression in the padding and cover it with a flat wad of padding to keep it from moving.

Terracottas should be stored in a dry place. If the storeroom is quite damp, it may be necessary to store terracottas with soluble salts in an airtight container together with silica gel.

Textiles

Textiles is a general term for all cloth or fabric and covers a wide range of materials, techniques, and objects. It usually refers to fabrics formed with twisted or spun threads that are woven together, but knitting, quilting, and other methods of fashioning cloth and garments are also known. In antiquity, both animal and vegetable fibers were used to make cloth, the most common being wool, silk, cotton, and flax.

Wool is the fine, soft, curly hair of sheep that is capable of being spun and felted. The tiny scales all over the surface of the fibers give wool its sticky, cohesive quality—a property discovered very early, which accounts for the early importance of sheep. The hair of alpaca, vicuña, certain goats, and a few other animals has this same property and was thus exploited by humans in antiquity. Wool can be distinguished from other fibers by its characteristic acrid smell when burned. As it burns, it forms small beads of carbon.

Silk is the fibrous material produced by the silkworm *Bombyx mori* to form its cocoon. It resembles wool in structure but, unlike wool, the fiber used for weaving is made of two intertwined threads. The silk industry is very old in China and was a closely guarded secret. It eventually spread to Japan and India, but was quite late in reaching Europe and the Americas. Although silk was first woven in Rome around 50 BC, the production of silk in Europe did not occur until silkworms were smuggled into Europe in the sixth century AD. Silk was introduced into the New World by Cortez in the sixteenth century.

Cotton is a vegetable fiber that was used very early in India, China, and South America, but not in Europe until the early Middle Ages. The fiber is made of the unicellular hairs attached to the seeds of various plants of the *Gossypium* genus of the mallow family. The hairs are flattened and twisted, a distinguishing characteristic of cotton. Cotton, like wool, can be easily spun. There are many species and varieties of *Gossypium* that yield fibers of varying lengths, whiteness, and fineness. South America, the West Indies, tropical Africa, and southern Asia are all home to various kinds of cotton. In general, Asian cotton has short fibers, whereas the American varieties are long. Peruvian cotton tends to be brownish.

Flax is a vegetable fiber procured from the flax or linseed plant, *Linum*, of which there are several species. Annual flax, *L. usitatissimum*, was cultivated for thousands of years in Mesopotamia, Assyria, and Egypt. Perennial flax, *L. angustifolium*, is a smaller plant than annual flax and was cultivated early by the Swiss Lake Dwellers. The stalks, the important part of the plant, are fermented to separate the fibers and then mashed to remove the unwanted woody material. Spun and woven flax is called *linen*. Linen was very important in ancient Egypt, and in Europe it was the most important vegetable fiber until cotton was mass-produced in the eighteenth century AD.

Like most other organic materials, textiles generally will be found only when unusual burial conditions exist. A very stable environment is necessary, one that is either very wet or very dry. In dry, arid climates, it is possible for textiles to be found dry. They are likely to be very stiff and brittle from desiccation and must be handled extremely carefully to prevent the fibers from breaking.

Before lifting a piece of dry textile, carefully remove all dirt surrounding it with a soft brush. Do not use a metal tool as it can abrade and break the textile fibers. Gently loosen the textile and, when completely free, carefully pick it up, fully supporting it from underneath. Place it directly into a well-padded rigid container until it can be packed properly later. Place a sheet of acid-free tissue, polyethylene, or polyethylene foam in the bottom of the container before putting in the textile. This step will allow the textile to be picked up and moved without actually being handled. If the piece is large or an awkward shape, picking it up may cause breakage. If this is likely to be the case, after loosening the textile, gently slide it onto a rigid support or carefully work the support underneath the textile. Keep the textile away from direct sun and take it to the dig house at the earliest opportunity.

Never try to wash a piece of dry textile or bring it in contact with water. The cleaning of archaeological textiles is a difficult job that should be left to a trained conservator. The fibers are almost certainly brittle and, if badly deteriorated, will break under only the slightest pressure. Even if the textile is seemingly sound and supple, avoid any undue handling or folding. Repeated flexing of even the soundest fibers can result in breakage. If the textile is crumpled or folded, do not try to unfold or flatten it; unless done properly, this action will invariably result in breakage. Wrap the textile carefully in acid-free tissue and store it flat in a rigid, covered container until it can be taken to a conservator. If the textile is crumpled, it may require support in the form of wads of tissue or rolls of polyethylene foam at vulnerable areas. Make sure that undue pressure is not exerted on folds and wrinkled areas when the lid is closed or the fibers can break. Textiles should be stored in a dry area away from direct sources of heat and light.

Textiles will also be preserved under very wet conditions. In general, animal fibers—that is, wool and silk—are more resistant to deterioration when buried, whereas vegetable fibers are more likely to be attacked by bacterial and acidic soil conditions. Thus, flax and cotton decay rapidly and are less likely to be found on an archaeological site.

Waterlogged textiles should be handled as little as possible because they are almost certainly extremely fragile. It is important that such textiles be kept wet from the moment of being uncovered until they can be treated in a conservation laboratory. If they cannot be removed from the ground immediately upon discovery, they must be recovered with mud and damp polyethylene foam or other absorbent material, followed by thick plastic sheeting, until they can be lifted. Spray the textile from time to time, if necessary, to keep it moist.

To lift the wet textile from the ground, first carefully clean around it to remove some, but not all, of the surrounding mud. Undercut the textile and, when completely free, gently lift it out of the ground. Place it directly into three polyethylene bags, along with its surrounding mud, and add 20 ml of 0.2% fungicide to the innermost bag containing the textile. Seal the bags and place them in a container half filled with water and more fungicide. Seal the container and keep it in as cool a place as possible until it can be taken to a conservator.

An alternate method of packing waterlogged textiles is to place them with their surrounding mud into a plastic container with a tight-fitting lid. Pad the container first with damp polyethylene foam. Do not use paper or cloth for padding as they will rot before the textile can reach a conservator. Add fungicide to the container and store it in a cool place. If possible, keep wet textiles refrigerated to help prevent microbiological growth. Make very sure, however, that the textile does not freeze. If refrigeration is used, it may not be necessary to use a fungicide. Consult with a conservator before adding any fungicide. A fungicide with a pH as near 7 as possible should be used. Because it is difficult to identify the fibers with certainty immediately upon excavation, use as neutral a fungicide as possible. Any textile packed with fungicide must be meticulously labeled to that effect to ensure the necessary safety precautions during handling.

One other unusual instance will preserve small fragments of textile. When a textile is buried in close contact with an object made of copper or copper alloy, it may be beautifully preserved. The metallic ions of copper inhibit the bacterial action that would otherwise destroy organic fibers. Aside from possibly being stained from the corrosion products, the textile fibers are usually in good condition (fig 5.15). The fiber's features will also be preserved if the corrosion products completely cover the fibers to form a negative cast replica. This commonly occurs when the textile is near an iron object (fig. 4.11). It is also possible for the corrosion products to slowly permeate the fibers and gradually replace them. The corrosion products assume the shape and form of the fibers and textile, making an exact positive replica of the design of the weave and the spin of the fibers. The fiber itself may or may not be preserved, but its morphological features will remain (fig. 5.16).

If well-preserved pieces of textile are found on metal objects, do not attempt to remove or clean them or the metal object. The fibers will undoubtedly be brittle and fragile and could easily break. Carefully pack the object following the packing instructions for metal objects and take it to a conservator for treatment. Replaced textiles, or *pseudomorphs*, on metal objects should also be left in place. Make no attempt to clean the metal. Pack the object carefully in the appropriate manner for that particular metal and take it to a conservator.

Even if the textile itself has not survived, traces of it often provide evidence of its existence at the site. Frequently, impressions of a textile can be found on potsherds (fig 5.31). Such impressions can provide a surprising degree of detail and information about the textile. Sherds containing such impressions should be set aside for expert study. It is also possible to make casts of these impressions which can be taken away from the site for further study. The procedure for making such casts is detailed in appendix I.

Unbaked Clay

Occasionally, figurines, jar sealings, bricks, and other objects made of unfired clay are found. At most, they were baked in the sun, a process that does not subject the clay to high enough temperatures even to begin fusing the clay particles. These objects, although hard, are literally made of clay. Such unbaked clay objects vary tremendously in strength, depending on the nature of the clay used, its density, and the extent to which it was sunbaked. Often, unbaked clay objects are quite strong and can be handled easily without danger. It is best to be cautious, however, and always handle unbaked clay objects very carefully.

These objects can be lifted out of the ground following general lifting procedures. Carefully clean around the object to remove all surrounding dirt, using only a wooden tool or brush to avoid scratching and abrading the soft clay surface. Undercut the object and, when completely free, gently lift it out of the ground. Place it directly into a well-padded container until it can be packed properly. Allow the object to dry out slowly and uniformly away from direct sources of heat, including sunlight.

Since the clay has not been fired and, hence, fused together, unbaked objects are frequently found in a very soft, friable condition. They will require consolidation before being safely lifted from the ground. Unless absolutely necessary, however, consolidation should not be undertaken in the field without a conservator present. Consolidants can, and usually do, change the surface color of unbaked clay. It is impossible, therefore, to consolidate only small areas; to keep the color of the entire object uniform, the whole piece must be consolidated.

If an object must be consolidated, the following procedure should be used. If the object is damp, use a PVA emulsion diluted 1 to 4 with water. Since such a thin solution is used, good penetration should result with a minimum of surface buildup. If the object is dry, use a 3%

to 5% solution of Acryloid B72 in toluene. Toluene, being less volatile than acetone, will allow the resin to penetrate more deeply before the solvent evaporates, thereby helping to minimize color change.

Clean the surface to be consolidated with a soft brush, being very careful not to scratch the surface. Remove as much of the surrounding dirt as possible to prevent large lumps of dirt from being consolidated to the edges of the object. Apply the consolidant with a brush, allowing it to soak in between applications. Continue to apply the consolidant until it is no longer absorbed by the clay. Try to avoid a surface buildup; there should never be a thick, glossy layer of consolidant on the surface of the clay. Allow the object to dry thoroughly before attempting to lift it. Any material still wet with consolidant is more fragile than it was before the consolidant was applied.

Objects made of unbaked clay cannot be cleaned in water because they will disintegrate. Gentle dry brushing should be sufficient to clean them, but make very sure that the brush does not scratch the surface of the clay. Do not pry or flick off any adhering lumps of dirt as they may take areas of the surface along with them. Soften any lumps of dirt by touching them with a brush filled with alcohol. If this procedure still does not remove them, gently scrape them off with a wooden toothpick, adding more alcohol if necessary. Be careful not to damage the clay surface in the process. Any heavy encrustations of dirt and/or insoluble salts will have to be removed mechanically with a scalpel and is best done by a conservator. Never attempt to remove such encrustations with acid because the object will dissolve into mud.

If the site is very saline, the clay undoubtedly will have absorbed soluble salts. These salts will cause considerable damage if the object is subjected to drastic changes in relative humidity. Because the removal of these salts requires soaking the object in water, the object must first be treated by a conservator. Any object known or suspected to contain soluble salts should be kept dry and be taken to a conservator as soon as possible.

Fragments of unbaked clay should not be joined in the field unless a conservator is present. The joining edges are likely to be powdery and soft, and good bonds may be difficult to achieve. In addition, any excess adhesive will stain and discolor the surface of the clay, as will any efforts to remove it later on with solvents. For these reasons, it is best to leave any joining to a conservator.

When marking unbaked clay objects, be sure to follow the procedure set forth in chapter 4; write the number only on a patch of lacquer. If written directly onto the clay, the number will be indelibly incised into the soft surface.

Objects made of unbaked clay should be packed individually in rigid containers well padded with tissue or polyethylene foam. It is not necessary for the tissue to be acid free. Place the object in a depression in the padding and then cover it with a flat wad of tissue or foam to prevent it from moving. The container should be stored in a dry place.

Wall Painting

In Mesopotamia, the Mediterranean, and Central and South America, plaster made with either mud, lime, or gypsum as a base was used as a finishing surface for walls. Mud plaster is literally a fine mud or clay that is applied wet to a wall and allowed to dry. It is only suitable for internal walls or external walls in an arid climate. Gypsum plaster is only suitable for an arid or semi-arid climate given that it is water soluble. Used extensively in ancient Egypt, it is prepared by burning gypsum to alter it chemically; it is then powdered. It is mixed with water, and sets by evaporation and chemical reaction. The making of lime plaster also involves burning the lime to alter it chemically. It is then slaked before it is ready for use. Lime plaster sets by evaporation and chemical reaction.

Generally, a thick, coarse layer of plaster was first put on the wall, followed by a finer plaster layer to which the paint was applied. Lime plaster, especially, has little strength of its own; so, frequently hair, straw, or other vegetal material was added to the coarse layer to give it body and strength. The pigments were mainly earth colors, that is, oxides of iron. Minerals such as lapis lazuli, malachite, and azurite were also used.

If the wall to which the plaster was applied is strong, the major cause of plaster deterioration is dissolution of its constituents. Both gypsum and lime will dissolve in acid rainwater, although lime plaster is the more resistant of the two. Dissolution is less of a problem with gypsum plaster, however, because it was generally used only in arid or semi-arid climates. Plaster will suffer also from the action of soluble salts and cycles of freeze and thaw, both of which will result in exfoliation of the surface.

Deterioration can be rapid if the wall support is weak or the structure in which the paintings are located has collapsed sufficiently to expose the wall and paintings to the elements. The wall support can develop cracks, erode away, or even collapse, forcing the plaster to fall off and shatter. Freezing and thawing can cause the plaster to buckle, crack, and fall off. Earthquakes, as well, are responsible for the collapse of wall supports and paintings. Once off the wall, plaster, when buried, is subjected to acid groundwater and other destructive forces that will result in its dissolution.

FALLEN PLASTER: Frequently, all that remains of a wall painting is pieces of plaster in a jumbled heap in the ground—with both large and small pieces lying flat, on end, face up and face down, and on top of one another. They can also be lying on top of other objects, such as stones or potsherds. Such plaster can be difficult to lift, and there is always the added complication of the plaster itself being weak and fragile. The shock of impact can have shattered the plaster so that, although it is seemingly intact, it is actually riddled with minute cracks and is extremely weak.

When such a jumble of plaster is found, it is first necessary to clean the entire area to determine exactly the amount of plaster, its condition, and positions. Using a soft brush, gently remove as much dirt as possible from the surface of the plaster to determine the shape of the piece. Be very careful, however, not to scratch or abrade the surface. Do not try to clean the painted surface; the paint layer can be extremely delicate and fugitive; and injudicious cleaning can inadvertently destroy or damage it. Gently remove the dirt surrounding each piece of plaster with a wooden tool or brush, being careful not to scratch or abrade the edges. Plaster, especially when damp, can be very soft and friable; the edges can easily crumble and the painted surfaces be scratched. Before lifting the plaster, record the position of individual pieces in situ with photographs and detailed sketches. Continue this documentation throughout the excavation and lifting process. Such records can be of great assistance to the later reconstruction efforts.

To help strengthen the plaster, allow it to dry out as much as possible before attempting to lift it. Test a small piece first to determine its strength. If it appears sound and does not crumble when lifted, it is probably safe to lift the pieces without backing them. More fragile pieces will require backing before lifting. Both techniques may be necessary to remove a jumble of wall plaster from the ground.

If no backing is required, carefully clean around each piece and undercut it with a sharp, flat tool after making sure that there are no other pieces immediately underneath. Do not pry the plaster out of the ground because this action will result in unnecessary breakage. When it is free, carefully transfer the plaster to a flat, rigid container for transport back to the dig house. Sometimes, instead of lifting the plaster, it is better to slide it onto a rigid piece of cardboard which can then be placed into a rigid container. Gently remove any lumps of dirt that prevent the plaster from lying flat. Make sure all pieces of plaster found together, including the very smallest crumbs, are lifted and kept together. Keep the plaster out of the direct sun and take it to the dig house at the earliest opportunity.

If individual pieces or small groups of pieces appear too fragile to be lifted unsupported, use the backing technique in chapter 4. If the plaster is still damp, use undiluted PVA emulsion; if dry, use a 7% to 10% solution of Acryloid B72.

If a large jumble of plaster is found where it is difficult to isolate single pieces or small groups of pieces for piecemeal removal, or if all the plaster is extremely fragile, it may be necessary to remove it as a whole, using one of the block lifting techniques outlined in chapter 4.

Even seemingly strong plaster should be handled very carefully. Generally, there are many minute cracks in the plaster, some of which develop as the plaster dries. Pieces can suddenly break into many smaller fragments, crumbling along breaks. For these reasons, avoid any unnecessary handling. As soon as it comes out of the ground, place the plaster on a rigid piece of cardboard or wood. Keep it on this support at all times to provide an easy, safe means of picking up and moving the plaster without handling it.

If the plaster is fragile or the paint is water soluble, do not attempt any cleaning, but immediately pack it and take it to a conservator for treatment. If the plaster is sound, it can be cleaned with soft brushes. Be very careful not to abrade the painted surface or to crumble the edges. Do not pry or flick off any lumps of dirt, especially if they are hard, as they can take portions of the painted surface along with them. Soften the lumps first by touching them with a brush filled with water and gently remove them with a wooden toothpick or a soft brush. If this process does not suffice, make no further attempt to remove the lumps.

If the painted surface is extremely sound and the paint is not soluble in water, the plaster can be cleaned with swabs dipped in distilled water. Test each color for water solubility in the following manner. In an inconspicuous spot, roll a damp swab gently over the surface. If any color is transferred to the swab, the paint is water soluble. If this testing indicates that water can be used safely, the plaster can be cleaned with swabs dipped in distilled water. Never immerse the plaster in water. The swabs should be damp, but not dripping wet. Never rub the surface of the plaster with the swab as this motion can abrade the surface; instead, gently roll the swab over the surface until it is clean. As soon as a swab becomes dirty, discard it for a new one because a dirty swab can be very abrasive.

Often, the coarser plaster behind the fine, painted layer is crumbly and must be consolidated. This can be done by applying a 3% to 5% solution of Acryloid B72 with a brush to the coarse plaster. The consolidant should be absorbed readily by the porous plaster. Avoid getting consolidant on the painted surface because it can darken and intensify the paint colors. The painted surface should not be consolidated until it has been thoroughly cleaned by a conservator.

Broken fragments of plaster can be joined together with any of the adhesives recommended in chapter 3. Only small pieces, however, should be joined. Any complicated joining should be left for a conservator because large, joined sections require support.

All plaster should be packed flat, in layers, in rigid

containers that are well padded with tissue or polyethylene foam. Use pieces of foam to separate and support the layers. Small wads of tissue or foam can be used to fill in empty spaces to keep the plaster from moving. Store the plaster in a dry place.

IN SITU WALL PAINTINGS: In situ wall paintings present the same problems as mosaics. They form an integral part of an immovable architectural whole; to remove them is to destroy that whole. Ideally, wall paintings should be left in situ, but to do so poses difficult problems for it presupposes the careful preservation of the structure, the construction of protective enclosures (roofs, and the like), all of which are expensive and not always included in the excavation schedule or budget. The treatment chosen, then, depends on a variety of factors, including the long-term future of the site, the preservation and protection of the building, its geographic position, the climate, guardianship of the site, and the time and money available.

One can justify the removal of a wall painting only if the building and/or paintings are in danger of destruction if left in situ. It cannot be stressed enough that the transfer of wall paintings is a difficult and time-consuming job, only the first part of which takes place in the field. The actual lifting must be followed by backing, cleaning, and mounting in a conservation laboratory by trained conservators.

There are instances, however, when paintings are removed even though the structure will not be destroyed and the paintings will ultimately be left in situ. If the structure is in good condition but the plaster and paint layer are not, the painting will frequently be removed, treated, and replaced on the wall. This procedure can also be done if the structure requires restoration work. These procedures, however, are generally performed in conjunction with an architect and a conservator.

If wall paintings are likely to be found and it is known that, if found, they will have to be lifted, it is imperative that a conservator be present as a member of the excavation staff. It is also important that the necessary funds be in hand for the proper treatment of the paintings. If wall paintings are found unexpectedly and no conservator is present, they should be carefully covered up, or backfilled, until the services of an experienced conservator can be obtained to remove them.

Whether to be backfilled or removed, wall paintings should be uncovered for as short a period as possible. If the paintings are left exposed for any length of time, the movement of soluble salts and the speed of drying out can cause the plaster to crack, damaging the paintings irreparably. If there are numerous paintings, do not expose them all at once or faster than they can be safely dealt with individually. It may be necessary to erect a temporary shade over them with a tarpaulin, for example, to help retard the drying process.

As wall paintings are uncovered, it is common for the paint to appear to fade. What is actually occurring is that a layer of carbonates on the surface becomes opaque as it dries out, obscuring the paint. Groundwater has percolated through the wall over time, dissolving some of the plaster, which was converted to bicarbonate. This bicarbonate migrated through the wall and converted to a solid carbonate layer on the surface of the paint. Although this layer obscures the paint, it serves, in fact, to protect the paint layer. While it is possible to restore the intensity of the paint layer when in this condition by wetting the surface with water, it is inadvisable to do so repeatedly because the plaster will crack, and any soluble salts present will be set into motion, possibly causing irreparable damage to the surface.

Before backfilling can take place, a flat piece of expanded polyethylene or polystyrene foam approximately 4 to 5 cm thick will be needed. It should be big enough to completely cover the painting with a margin of 3 to 5 cm on all sides. To keep it upright, make interlocking supports of the same material (fig. 5.39). If expanded foam is not available, wood can be used. To backfill a wall painting, use the following procedure:

1. Fill the trench, or area around the painting, with earth to a level just below the bottom of the painting and tamp it down well.
2. Cover the painting, the wall, and the ground immediately in front of the wall with a layer of 0.5 mm plastic netting. Do not use a solid sheet of plastic as it can impede the natural seepage and drainage of ground water; where it lies horizontally, it will collect groundwater. Plastic will also encourage condensation under it which, in turn, can encourage microbial activity. Netting facilitates the removal of the backfill later on and in no way should impede the movement of groundwater.
3. Position the sheet of foam to form an upright partition approximately 20 cm away from and parallel to the wall painting (fig. 5.40).
4. Cover the ground inside the partition with vermiculite while simultaneously filling the area on the other side of the partition with earth. In this way, the space within the partition is entirely filled with vermiculite while the rest of the area is filled with earth (fig. 5.40). Ideally, only vermiculite should be used to cover a wall painting. Other materials—for example, sand—are too hard and sharp to be placed in contact with delicate painted surfaces. Sea sand should always be avoided because it

is contaminated with soluble salts. If vermiculite is not available, it may be necessary to use dirt from the site. Sieve it first to remove any stones and other materials that might harm the painted surface.

5. Once the partition has been filled, continue to fill the remainder of the trench with earth to a height at least 15 to 20 cm above the surrounding ground level to allow for settling.

Any backfilled wall painting should be checked at least annually to make sure that erosion or settling of the fill is not endangering the painting and to prevent any harmful plant or animal life from becoming established.

If the painting is on a wall that has been completely excavated and is therefore freestanding, or if the site is a rescue excavation, backfilling will not be practical or effective. In such instances, removing the painting from the wall may be the only way to preserve it.

The following removal techniques are not necessarily those that can be executed competently by inexperienced people. At the best of times, these techniques are tricky and unpredictable and should be undertaken by an experienced conservator. There are occasions, however, when, to save the paintings, inexperienced people must do the job. For this reason, the following removal techniques are given. They are all operations for at least two people. When the actual lifting takes place, it is wise to have additional people on hand.

There are three different methods for transferring a wall painting: block, *distacco,* and *strappo*. The block method involves removing all or part of the wall support with the plaster and paint layers. Although this is the least destructive and therefore most ethically responsible method, it is difficult logistically because the block can be extremely heavy and unwieldy and requires a great deal of planning and heavy equipment. For these reasons, it should not be attempted by untrained people and will not be dealt with here.

Both the distacco and strappo techniques require two kinds of cloth facings—one very fine, the other considerably heavier. See the section in chapter 3 on lifting materials for a discussion of suitable fabrics. The fine facing comes in contact with the painted surface, whereas the heavier facing is applied on top of the fine facing. Facings should be larger than the painting; allow at least 10 cm of extra material extending out around all edges. Eventually, this extra material will be fringed and doubled back on itself so that when attached to the painting, the margin will be reduced to approximately 5 cm. Before use, all facing materials should be carefully washed to remove any dressings on them. Cut off all selvedges (side edges) and make a fringe about 5 cm long on all edges of the facing by pulling out threads (fig. 5.41A).

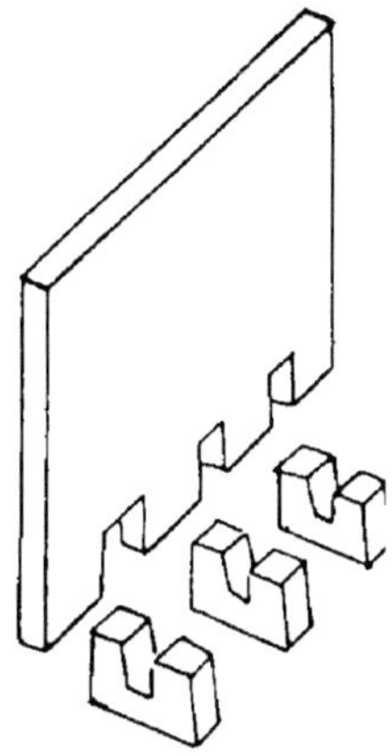

FIGURE 5.39 Partition for backfilling a wall painting. *After Mora 1984*

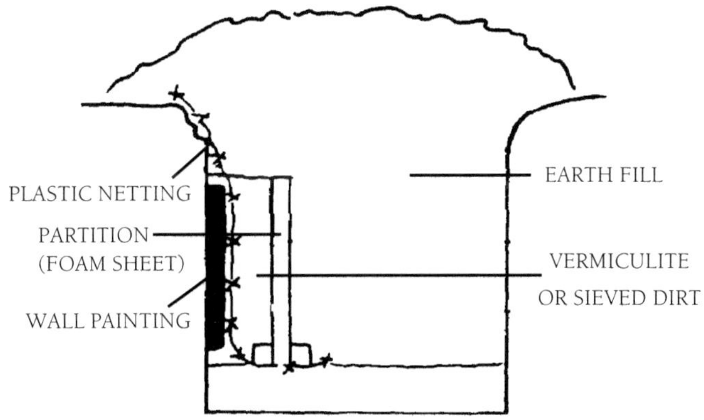

FIGURE 5.40 Method for backfilling a wall painting. *After Mora 1984*

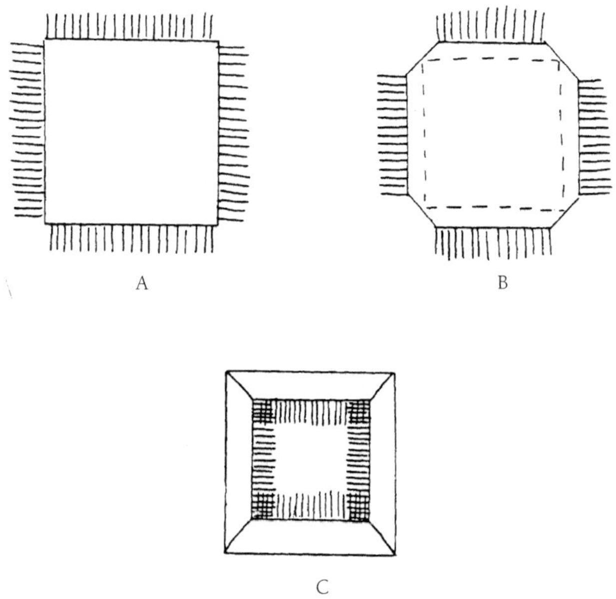

FIGURE 5.41. Facings for lifting a wall painting. A, selvedges have been cut off and edges fringed 5 cm; B, mitered corners after the facing has been applied to the wall painting (dotted line indicates fold line for doubling back the fringed edges of the facing); C, fringed edges have been folded back and adhered to the facing.

If it is necessary to use more than one piece of facing for a painting, the edges that will overlap should also be fringed about 5 cm. When the facings are applied to the painting, overlap only the fringed areas to avoid a harsh line being impressed into the painted surface. A layer of Japanese tissue can be used as a first facing to avoid impressions of the facings, but it is not recommended because it can be difficult to remove.

The traditional adhesive for applying the facings to the painting is animal glue to which molasses or honey and vinegar have been added. The molasses or honey makes the glue more flexible and prevents it from shrinking and pulling off the paint layer. The vinegar acts as a fungicide. Any of the PVA emulsions recommended in chapter 3 can also be used undiluted, especially if the area is damp. Animal glue cannot be used on a damp painting.

To prepare for use, mix 3 kg of animal glue with three liters of water. Allow it to soak for 12 to 24 hours, then boil it for an hour in the top of a double boiler. Add 2 liters of vinegar. If the stacco method is to be used, add 0.75 kg of molasses or honey to the glue. When ready for use, the consistency of the glue should be slightly thicker than milk. Inexperienced people tend to use glue that is too thick; add more water, if necessary, to achieve the right consistency. The glue may be made in smaller quantities as long as the correct proportions are maintained.

Before anything is done to the painting, regardless of which removal method is to be used, a good, full-scale sketch and/or tracing of the painting should be made. These sketches, augmented with a full photographic record, should clearly show the general scheme of the painting, any areas of weakness in the plaster, flaking paint, missing plaster, and so forth. Photographs and drawings can be useful guides later in the removal process when one may need to know where important figural areas are located or where there may be missing sections of plaster. They are also indispensable to the conservator.

No matter which method is used, as the painting is uncovered it should be protected from sun and wind to help retard the drying process, which can cause considerable damage. A tarpaulin or tent erected temporarily over the painting can offer considerable protection, allowing the painting to remain uncovered for proper documentation before lifting takes place. Even so, the painting should be left uncovered for as short a time as possible. If there are numerous paintings, do not expose them all at once or faster than they can be safely dealt with individually.

DISTACCO METHOD: The distacco, or stacco, method involves removing the paint and fine plaster layers along with all or part of the underlying rough plaster. For this method to work, it is essential that the plaster be in excellent condition with the paint layer well attached. If either is in bad condition, the following method should not be attempted:

1. Make a tracing and/or full-scale drawing of the painting and photograph the painting.
2. Test all colors, using the following procedure, to determine whether they are soluble in water. Dampen a cotton swab with water; it should not be dripping wet. Roll it gently over the painted surface in an inconspicuous spot. For obvious reasons, avoid any figural or prominent areas. If any color is transferred to the swab, the paint is water soluble. Test each color in the same manner using a clean swab for each. If PVA emulsion will be used as the facing adhesive, the paint should be tested for fastness to alcohol as well as water. Repeat the above procedure using alcohol instead of water on the swab.
3. Clean the surface of the painting carefully with a soft brush. If the paint is not water soluble, it can be cleaned carefully with swabs dipped in distilled water. Do not rub the surface with the swab. Rather, gently roll the swab over the surface, making absolutely sure that the surface is not abraded in the process. As soon as the swab becomes dirty, discard it for a new one; dirty swabs can be extremely abrasive.
4. The painting should be consolidated only if the paint is water soluble or the paint layer is powdery and flaking badly. The choice of a consolidant will depend on the adhesive used to hold the facings to the painting. The consolidant must not be affected by this adhesive or its solvent. If PVA emulsion will be used as the facing adhesive, consolidate the painting with a 3% to 5% solution of Elvacite 2013. If animal glue is to be used, consolidate with a 3% to 5% solution of Acryloid B72. To disrupt the fragile paint layer as little as possible, apply the consolidant with a sprayer. If a sprayer is not available, a brush can be used. Pay especially careful attention to any flaking, powdery, and soft areas of plaster and areas of water-soluble paint, making sure that they are well consolidated. If not properly consolidated, considerable paint can be lost when the facing is removed. Allow the consolidant to dry thoroughly before proceeding further.
5. Working from the bottom up, cover the painting with as even a coat of the prepared animal glue (or PVA emulsion) as possible. This coating protects the surface of the painting from receiving an imprint of the facing's texture.
6. With two people holding the fine facing in front of the

painting, slap the middle of the facing against the painting. Push the facing onto the surface of the painting with the hands, working out in all directions from the center. Be careful not to distort the weave of the facing or to trap any air bubbles between the facing and the paint layer. Good contact is achieved when the glue fully saturates the facing.

7. Miter the corners of the facings and then fold the edges back in the following manner. Cutting diagonally, remove the corners of the facings, including the fringe (fig. 5.41B). The cut should be made just short of the corner of the painting. Fold the edges back on themselves to form a mitered corner, making sure the fringed edges are glued down to the painting (fig. 5.41C). The fringed edges will prevent a hard line from being impressed onto the surface of the painting. The folded edges should give a 5 cm double layer of facing that is free of glue. This doubling serves to strengthen the edges for the lifting process and provides a means of grasping the painting. If the painting is quite small, it is not necessary to double the edges in this way.
8. Apply the second, heavy facing in the same manner as the first, using a minimum of glue. The second facing should be fringed, mitered, and turned back as well.
9. Allow animal glue to dry for two days. If PVA emulsion is used, allow at least two days for drying.
10. Using a sharp spatula, scalpel, or knife, cut along the side and bottom edges of the plaster section to be lifted. Leave the top edge uncut to ensure support for the painting until the last moment.
11. Using a padded mallet, start at the bottom of the painting and hammer all over the surface. Start gently and increase the force of the blows, if necessary, to loosen and separate the plaster from the wall. It may not be necessary to do much hammering.
12. Have a board which is slightly larger than the painting ready, especially if the painting is large. Cover the board with a sheet of polyethylene. If possible, attach a ledge approximately 1 to 2 cm high along the bottom edge of the board to catch the painting as it comes off the wall.
13. The painting should swing away from the wall after the hammering. If plaster still adheres to the wall, free it with a long, flexible blade, such as a spatula, working up behind the painting.
14. At this point, have several extra people ready to prevent the painting from falling. When it is completely free, swing the painting out from the wall. Position the board underneath it and cut along the top edge of the plaster. When detached, carefully slide the painting onto the board.
15. Gently invert the painting so that it is lying on the board with the facings down.

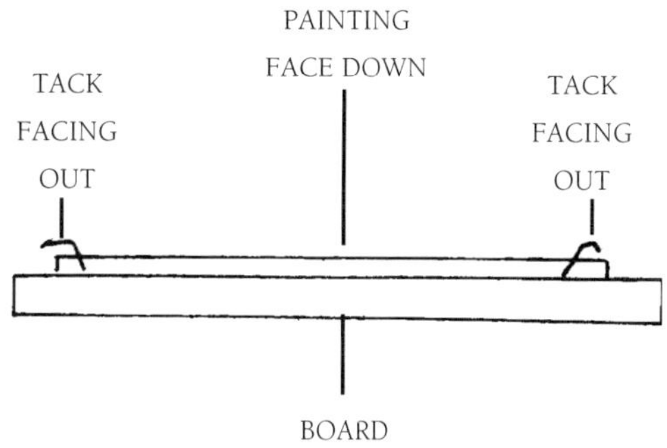

FIGURE 5.42 Method for tacking down a lifted wall painting to support.

16. To prevent the painting from pulling up and wrinkling as the glue dries and contracts, tack the 5 cm facing overlap down to the board at even intervals. Make sure that the tacks are in securely and that they bend outward to counteract the pull of the contracting glue (fig. 36). Tacking will also prevent the painting from sliding off the board.
17. Any large protruding areas of rough plaster can be shaved down gently with a rasp as long as this procedure does not interfere with the bond of the facings. This step will reduce the weight of the painting.
18. Cover the painting loosely with cloth or plastic and take it to a trained conservator for treatment as soon as possible. Be sure to submit a record of what was done to the painting, including a list of all materials used by trade name and grade. Also include a copy of all tracings, sketches, and photographs, as well as the results of the solubility testing of the pigments.

STRAPPO METHOD: The strappo method involves removing only the paint layer. Although not as ethical or responsible as the stacco method, it is much more convenient because the detached painting can be rolled up, and large areas can be removed in one piece. If there are several paint layers one on top of another, the strappo method can be used to separate them.

The same cloth facings can be used as for the stacco method. However, a slightly different adhesive is needed, one that will contract strongly. Use the recipe given above for animal glue with vinegar but omit the molasses or honey. Although animal glue is the best adhesive for applying the facings, undiluted PVA emulsion will also work well. In either a hot or a very cold climate, PVA emulsion may be preferable because animal glue may dry out too quickly if conditions are too hot or not at all if they are too cold and wet. Any of the PVA emulsions recommended in chapter 3 can be used. If there will be a long delay between lifting the painting and having it treated by a conservator, it is best to use PVA emulsion because, unlike animal glue, it will not continue to contract.

Follow steps 1 through 4 for the stacco method. If it is necessary to consolidate the painting, use the consolidant sparingly. A heavy consolidant buildup might interfere with the contact of the facing with the painted surface. Continue with steps 5 through 14:

5. Coat the painting with the prepared animal glue (or PVA emulsion) working from the bottom up and making sure to apply as even a coat as possible. Do not allow drips of animal glue to dry on the surface because as it dries and contracts, the glue can pull off the paint layer.
6. Several people should be on hand to help apply the facings and lift the painting.
7. Have two people hold the fine facing very taut in front of the painting so that there is at least a 10 cm overlap all around. Push the facing down onto the painting surface with the hands. When on the wall, the facing should be under tension; therefore, it is important that the people holding the facing do not let go. Working out from the center, smooth the facing onto the painting, stretching it as much as possible without distorting the weave of the fabric. It is imperative that there is excellent contact between the facing and the painting; do not trap any air bubbles under the facing.
8. When the fine facing is on the wall, cut, miter, and fold back the edges of the facing in the manner set forth in step 7 of the stacco method (fig. 5.41 B, C).
9. Apply the second, heavier facing in the same manner as the first, adding more glue, if necessary. Cut, miter, and fold back the edges of the facing.
10. Allow the glue to dry for four days so that it will contract. PVA emulsion should dry for at least two days.
11. Holding the double edges, start pulling at the facings, giving little jerks all along the bottom edge; then, gradually start working up the sides. Constantly look underneath the painting to ensure that the paint layer is coming away with the facing. The paint should come away from the wall fairly easily, although it will make a horrible noise. As the painting begins to pull away, use a palette knife, scalpel, or spatula, if necessary, to free any areas of the painting that are sticking to the plaster. If the painting is large, it will probably be necessary to have on hand a wooden pole or cardboard cylinder upon which to roll the painting as it comes free from the wall. The length of the pole should exceed the width of the painting by 10 cm or so on each end. When rolling up the painting, be sure to use a separator, such as a sheet of polyethylene, between the roll and the painting to keep the glue from sticking to itself or other parts of the detached painting.

    A shadow of the painting may be left behind on the wall, but if you have applied the facings properly, the upper layer of paint will have been removed. These shadows may just be traces of paint or they could be the cartoon or setting out lines for the painting. If the latter is the case, these lines could be of importance and should be fully documented with drawings and photographs.
12. Carefully lay the detached painting with the facings down on a large, flat board covered with polyethylene sheeting. If the painting was rolled off the wall, carefully unroll it onto the board. If PVA emulsion was used, the painting can remain rolled up, if desired.
13. To prevent the painting from moving and warping as the glue contracts, it is necessary to tack it down to the board at 6 cm intervals through the facing overlap. If the painting is large, it may be necessary to tack through the painting itself as well. If this is done, be sure to avoid figural or other important areas. Use the sketch, tracing, or photographs as a guide for the placement of the tacks. Make sure that the tacks are secure and that those on the edges bend outward to counteract the pull of the contracting glue (fig. 5.42). If PVA emulsion is used, it is not necessary to bend the tacks.
14. Loosely cover the painting with cloth or plastic and take it to a conservator for treatment as soon as possible. Be sure to submit a record of what was done to the painting, including a list of all materials used by trade name and grade. Also, include a copy of all tracings, sketches, and photographs, as well as the results of the solubility testing of the pigments.

Wood and Related Materials

Wood has been used since the earliest manner of constructions and objects. Other portions of trees and shrubs have also been used, for example, roots and bark. Although some of these examples are not strictly speaking wood, everything said below about wood pertains, and they can be included in this section. There is a certain amount of overlap with materials dealt with in other sections, and they too can be relevant. For example, twigs were used to make wickerwork and baskets; so, the section on basketry might provide additional useful information. In the same way, the section on papyrus might be relevant to certain kinds of bark.

Wood is the hard, fibrous substance—mainly xylem—that comprises the greater part of the stems and branches of trees and shrubs beneath the bark. Being an organic material, when buried it normally decays because of chemical and biological activity. For wood to be preserved, exceptional circumstances must exist: a very stable environment that is either very wet or very dry.

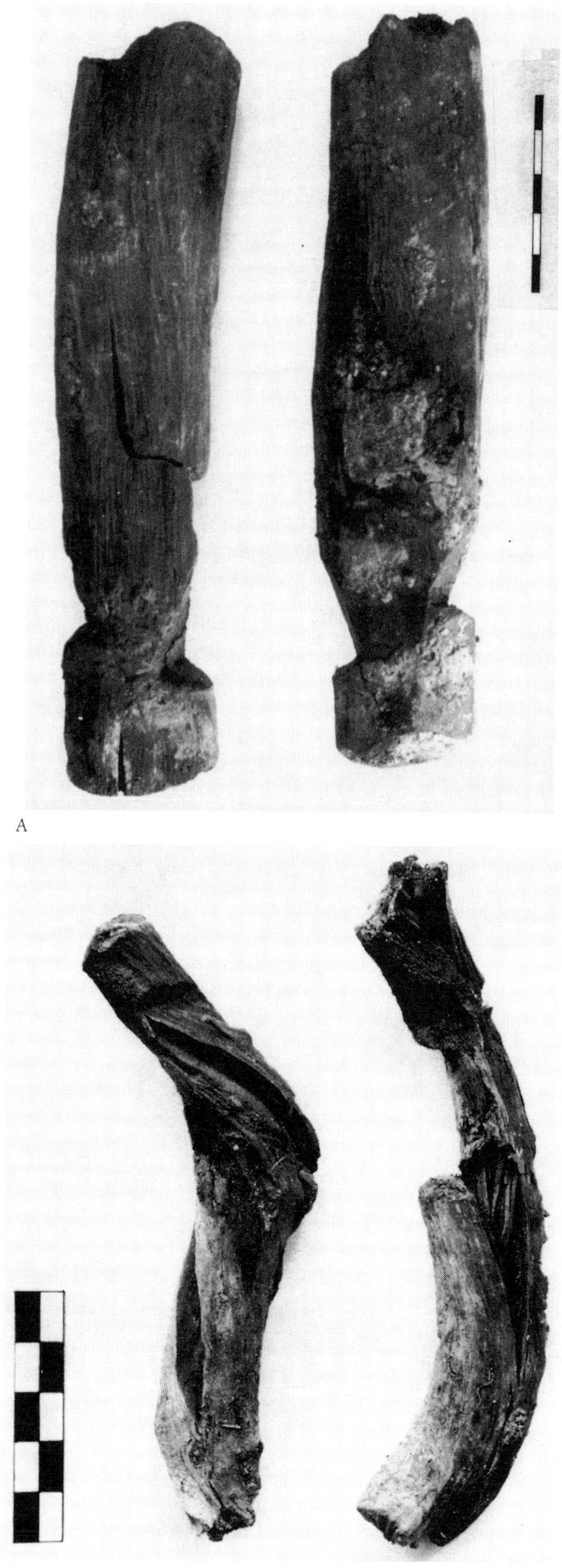

A

B

FIGURE 5.43 Effect of air drying on wet wood from Greece: A, when excavated; B, 32 years later.

In hot, arid climates, it is possible for wood to be found dry. It is not completely understood why such good preservation results. Certainly, it is partially because of a lack of moisture, but mainly it results from unknown factors that prevent the survival of decay-causing bacteria. Such wood will be in a weakened condition from extreme desiccation and must be handled carefully at all times.

Before lifting a piece of dry wood, carefully remove all surrounding dirt with a soft brush or a wooden tool. Do not use a metal tool because it can easily scratch and abrade the surface and edges of the wood. Undercut the wood and, when completely free, gently pick it up, supporting it from underneath, and place it into a well-padded, rigid container until it can be properly packed.

Dry wood must be kept dry; it will swell, warp, and possibly disintegrate if it gets wet. Never wash dry wood; clean it only with gentle dry brushing, being very careful that the brush does not damage the surface of the wood. Do not pry or flick off large lumps of adhering dirt because they might easily pull off some of the surface. They can be softened by touching them with a brush filled with alcohol and then be scraped off carefully with a wooden tool or a soft brush. If this method does not suffice to remove them, make no further attempt to clean the wood. Leave the lumps for a conservator to remove.

If the wood is extremely fragile, it may need to be consolidated before it can be safely removed from the ground. A 3% to 5% solution of Acryloid B72 should be used. Clean the piece of wood carefully with a soft brush. Remove all dirt surrounding the object to prevent lumps of dirt from being consolidated to the sides of the object. Apply the consolidant with a brush, allowing it to soak in. Keep applying consolidant until it is no longer absorbed by the wood. After applying the consolidant, cover the wood with a sheet of polyethylene to retard the rate of evaporation. This will minimize stress on the structure of the wood as the consolidant dries, thereby minimizing the chance of warpage. Allow the consolidant to dry thoroughly before attempting to lift the wood. Any material still wet with consolidant is more fragile than it was before the consolidant was applied.

Any piece of wood to be used for radiocarbon dating must not be contaminated with fungicide or consolidant.

Pieces of dry wood should be packed individually in a rigid polystyrene box that is well padded with acid-free tissue or polyethylene foam. Place the object in a depression in the padding and cover it with a flat wad of tissue or foam to keep the object from moving. Be sure that undue pressure is not exerted on the wood when the lid is closed or the wood may break.

Store the wood in as dry a place as possible away from direct sources of heat and light and take it to a trained conservator as soon as possible.

Wood will also be well preserved under extremely wet conditions. When waterlogged, bacterial and chemical degradation take place, destroying the cellulosic portion of the wood. The thicker lignin structures remain; as a result, the wood retains its shape and bulk as long as it is in the ground. It is in a very weakened condition; however, it is not necessary for this wood to be waterlogged to survive. It is difficult to determine exactly when wood is no longer just wet and has become waterlogged. Generally, waterlogging is thought to exist when the water absorption is sufficient to prevent the wood from floating.

It is important to handle wet and waterlogged wood with great care and as little as possible. Its surface is generally very soft and spongy. Some wood, being so full of water, may not be able to bear its own weight. If waterlogged wood is handled carelessly, it will be crushed and can break.

It is imperative that wet and waterlogged wood be kept wet from the moment it is uncovered until it is treated in a conservation laboratory. Even a few minutes drying out will cause irreparable damage. The pieces of wood shown in figure 5.43 provide an example of what will happen if wood is allowed to dry out. The pieces are shown when excavated and 32 years later. The piece of wood on the left shrank 15% in diameter and 38% in length, and the piece on the right shrank 30% in diameter and 28% in length. This wood was only wet when it was excavated. If fully waterlogged wood is allowed to dry out, it can lose up to 90% of its weight and 80% of its volume in a very short time, resulting in shrinking, warping, and cracking. The high surface tension of the water forces the weakened cell walls to collapse as the liquid evaporates, resulting in irreversible shrinkage and warpage. If a piece of waterlogged wood cannot be removed from the ground immediately after being discovered, it must be covered with mud or layers of damp polyethylene foam followed by thick polyethylene sheeting. If necessary, spray water frequently on the wood to prevent it from drying out. This procedure will also be necessary during the time when the wood is exposed for drawing and photographing in situ.

Waterlogged objects may be so degraded and fragile that they require support before lifting. Because of the wet conditions, consolidation is rarely successful, and so it is generally better to use one of the block lifting techniques set forth in chapter 4. When lifted, support the block carefully and prevent it from drying out by wrapping it tightly in wet foam or other absorbent material followed by plastic sheeting. Take the block to a conservator as soon as possible. It is best to attempt such lifting procedures only when a conservation laboratory is nearby so that the block can be taken there immediately upon removal from the ground.

Sound waterlogged wood can be lifted with few problems. Carefully clean around the wood to remove some, but

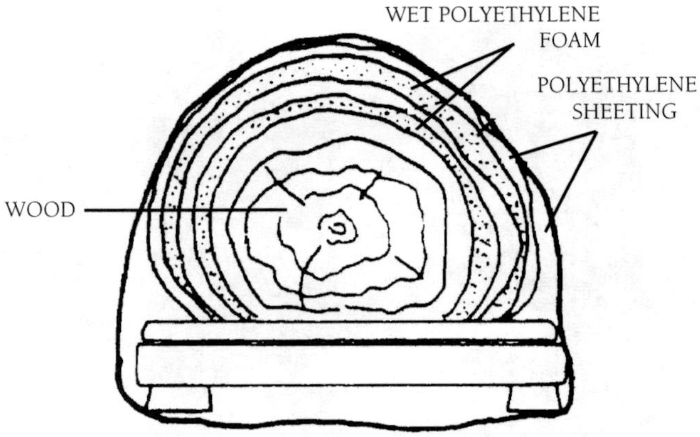

FIGURE 5.44 Method for packing a large waterlogged timber on a wooden pallet.

not all, of the surrounding mud. Undercut the wood and carefully lift it out of the ground together with the mud immediately surrounding it. It is important that the object be fully supported from underneath when it is picked up. Place the wood immediately into three polyethylene bags and add 20 ml of 0.2% fungicide to the innermost bag containing the wood. Seal the bags and store them, in turn, in a sealed container half filled with water and additional fungicide. Keep the container in as cool a place as possible until it can be taken to a conservator.

An alternate method of packing the wood is to place it directly into a rigid plastic container with a tight-fitting lid. Pad the container first with damp polyethylene foam. Add rolls of damp foam, if necessary, to keep the object from moving. Never use paper or cloth to wrap the wood because it will rot before the wood can reach a conservator. Store the container in as cool a place as possible.

Keep the wet wood refrigerated, if possible, to prevent microbial growth. Make sure, however, that the wood does not freeze. If refrigeration is used, it may not be necessary to use fungicide. Check with a conservator before adding any fungicide. Any wood stored with fungicide should be meticulously labeled to ensure that the necessary precautions are taken during handling.

Some waterlogged wood (generally large pieces such as building timbers) cannot bear their own weight and must be lifted on a rigid support. Suitable pallets can be made with planks of wood cushioned with sheets of polyethylene foam (fig. 5.44). Wrap the wood in several layers of damp foam, securing it with ties made from strips of polyethylene. Do not use string because it can cut into the soft surface of the wood. Wrap the entire bundle in sheets of polyethylene, ending with a final layer of heavy-gauge polyethylene. Place the bundle on the wooden pallet and secure it with polyethylene ties.

The wrapped, lifted timbers must not be allowed to dry

out. As soon as possible, place them in a large tank full of water to which fungicide has been added to make a 0.2% solution. The care of such timbers requires a great deal of thought and planning; therefore, large timbers should not be lifted until all aspects of lifting, transport, and storage have been carefully worked out and suitable storage tanks are ready to receive them.

If several large structural timbers are found waterlogged, it may not be feasible to save them all. A sampling system may have to be devised. Lifting and conserving such large waterlogged pieces is a difficult, lengthy, and expensive process. If it is known or suspected that a site contains quantities of waterlogged material, excavation should not take place without a trained conservator present. If such material is uncovered unexpectedly, cover it up again carefully and consult with a conservator to devise a method of dealing with the wood before excavation resumes.

No attempt should be made to clean any waterlogged wood. The surface of the wood is extremely soft and spongy and can be damaged easily, even by the softest and gentlest of brushing. Any cleaning should be left to a conservator.

Wood will also be preserved in the form of charcoal if it was burned with a minimum of oxygen. Frequently, burned wooden beams are found, along with charred wooden objects, seeds, and pieces of wood. Carbonized wood is very resistant to chemical and biological activity and is usually preserved quite well. Although it can be surprisingly strong, it should always be handled carefully. If the charcoal is to be used for C^{14} dating, observe the proper sampling procedure set forth in the section on radiocarbon sampling.

If the charred object is not to be used for dating, it can be lifted as outlined above for dry wood. The charred surface of the object will be very soft, especially if it is damp. Be very careful when cleaning around it. Allow the charred wood to dry out slowly and evenly away from sunlight and other direct sources of heat. When thoroughly dry, pack the charred object carefully in a well-padded, rigid container as outlined above for dry wood. Make no attempt to clean the charred wood. Store it in a dry place, and take it to a conservator for treatment.

Appendixes

I: Making Impressions

SIMPLE IMPRESSIONS can be made in the field using several different methods, depending on the condition, size, and composition of the material containing the inscription. More detailed molding processes should not be attempted in the field. Impressions can only be taken on good, hard surfaces. If the surface is friable, powdery, or painted, it must be consolidated first. This procedure is best left to a conservator.

Clay

If a quick impression is needed to read a seal, for example, it can be done easily using modeling clay or plasticine (fig. A.1). The resulting impression will be the reverse of the original. Use the following procedure to make a simple clay impression:

1. Roll a piece of modeling clay the size of a small egg into a ball, making sure there are no cracks on the surface.
2. Flatten the ball to form a disk using a piece of glazed tile, glass, or other smooth surface that has been lightly brushed with talc to prevent the disk from sticking.
3. Lightly talc the top surface of the clay disk with a soft brush and blow off any excess. Lightly talc the surface of the seal in the same way.
4. Place the seal cleanly in the middle of the disk. Do not move the seal once it has been placed on the clay.
5. Press down gently on the seal making sure that it is evenly embedded.
6. Carefully pull the seal out of the clay. Be sure not to rock the seal in the process or an uneven impression can result.

The resulting impression can be handled, although the clay can become twisted and distorted with excessive or rough handling. If a permanent impression is desired, the above procedure can be followed using one of the modeling compounds that can be hardened by baking in an oven. Follow the manufacturer's instructions for baking time and temperature. If a permanent positive of the original seal is needed, the clay impression can be used as a mold. The procedure for making the cast is the same as that for making coin casts, as outlined below.

Plaster

The following method is suitable for making small casts of surface impressions, for example, basketry or textile impressions on potsherds or inscriptions on tiles. Since the impression is a negative, the resulting casts are positives of the original.

1. Make sure the area to be cast is thoroughly clean.
2. Soak the sherd in water until it is wet all the way through. If it is not sufficiently wet, water from the plaster will be drawn into the pottery, resulting in weak plaster. In addition, particles of plaster will be drawn into the pores along with the water, producing staining.
3. With a brush, thoroughly coat the area to be cast with a dilute solution of liquid soap. Make sure all recessed areas are covered. Tip or blow out excess soap; do not leave any puddles.
4. Prepare a plaster of Paris mixture and, while it is still quite runny, paint a thin coat of it on the surface of the area to be cast. Use enough plaster to fill the shallow depressions of the detail. Gently tap the sherd on the table to remove air bubbles.
5. When the mixed plaster has thickened slightly, pour it onto the sherd. As the plaster begins to set, add more until it is approximately 1 to 2 cm thick all over. The cast is likely to break if it is any thinner than 1 to 2 cm. The edges can be evened off carefully with a knife when the setting plaster is the consistency of butter.
6. Allow the plaster to set fully before attempting to remove it from the sherd. This step can take from fifteen minutes to one hour, depending on the ambient temperature and humidity. It is not necessary for the plaster to be completely dry before removing it, although the drier it is, the stronger it will be. To remove the cast, invert the sherd. If the plaster cast does not fall off readily, tap it gently in your cupped hand or pry it off gently with a wooden tool.
7. Allow the cast to dry completely.
8. Thoroughly wash the sherd to remove all traces of soap and plaster.

Latex

Rubber latex provides an alternate means of taking impressions. The resulting *squeeze* is flexible and lightweight; so, impressions of large inscriptions can easily be taken. The method is also suitable for taking small surface impressions on pottery, tiles, and stone. The impression is a negative of the original. Latex can be used only on extremely sound

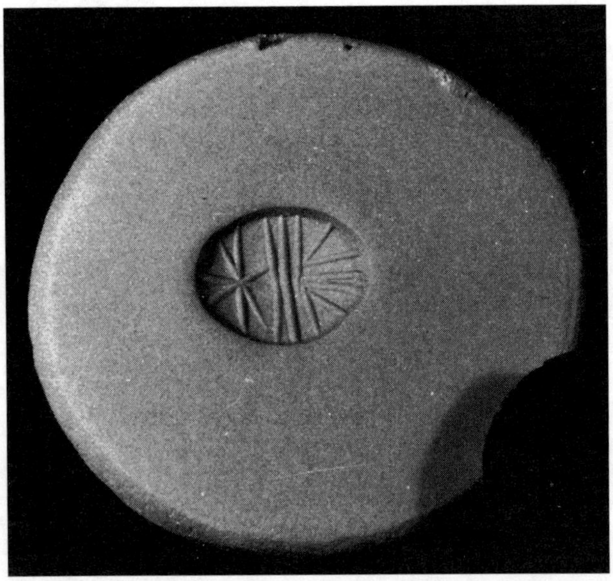

FIGURE A.1 Near Eastern seal impression with modeling clay.

surfaces. If the surface is soft, friable, or powdery, the latex can pull off parts of it as the rubber dries and shrinks. A latex squeeze is perishable; it is especially vulnerable to atmospheric pollutants containing sulfur. Use the following procedure for making latex impressions:

1. Dust the surface of the stone or object lightly with talc to ensure the release of the latex.
2. Because latex is very hard on brushes, you can prolong the life of a brush by dipping it into detergent before beginning to use the latex.
3. Using undiluted latex with a brush, apply a fairly thin coat to the surface, being sure not to allow it to build up in deep cuts of the inscription. If the surface is vertical, always start at the bottom and work up to avoid drips and dribbles that will disrupt the face of the squeeze. Latex contracts strongly as it dries. Thus, if too thick a layer is applied, it will pull up from the surface to create air pockets in the squeeze.
4. Allow the first coat to dry thoroughly before proceeding in order to avoid the danger of pulling up the partially dried latex with the brush and balling it.
5. Apply a second coat of latex and allow it to dry thoroughly.
6. Coat a strip of the surface with more latex. Take a strip of bandage several centimeters longer than the surface to be covered, including the sides, and place it on the wet latex starting at one side. As you lower the bandage onto the wet latex, gently tamp it down into the latex with a brush, working from one side to the other. Try not to trap any air bubbles as the bandage is applied; to release inadvertent air bubbles, pull back the bandage while the latex is still wet. With a brush, gently push the bandage down into all the cuts of the surface. Add more latex, if necessary, to ensure that the bandage is thoroughly saturated and has good contact with the surface. If the relief is deep, it may be necessary to snip the bandage with scissors to release tension and ensure good contact. If an entire side or surface of an object is to be done, take the squeeze over the edges by at least an inch so that it can be used as a simple mold at a later date, if so desired.
7. Continue to cover the entire surface with strips of bandage in the same manner, being sure to overlap them by at least 1 cm on each edge.
8. Apply a second layer of bandage strips in the same manner, but at right angles to the first layer. It is not necessary to wait for the latex to dry between application of the two bandage layers.
9. Allow the latex to dry thoroughly. It is dry when it has lost its milky color, a process that generally takes 12 to 24 hours.
10. To remove the squeeze, gently but firmly pull it away from the surface of the stone. Do not use sharp tools to help free the squeeze because they may cut the latex.
11. Dust the squeeze with talc to prevent it from sticking to itself. It is best to store latex squeezes in a dark place protected from light and atmospheric pollutants.
12. Brushes can be cleaned with dilute ammonia. The latex will ball up on the brush and can then be pulled off.

Paper

The method given here for paper squeezes is generally best suited for making small impressions that will fit on one sheet of paper; it is possible, however, to take larger impressions by using overlapping sheets. If overlapping is necessary, allow for at least a 2 cm overlap. This method, which requires a strong, robust surface, is suitable for inscriptions on stone and will produce a negative of the original.

A thick paper is needed for taking squeezes. See chapter 3 for a discussion of suitable papers.Use the following procedure:

1. Wash the surface of the stone and thoroughly wet it down.
2. Place the sheet of paper over the inscription. If the surface is vertical, have an assistant hold the paper in place.
3. Wet the paper thoroughly by squeezing a sponge filled with water over it.
4. Using a brush with short, densely packed bristles and a long handle, hit the paper against the surface of the stone. Continue hitting the paper, forcing it into all the cuts of the inscription until the entire surface has been thoroughly covered many times, but not so much as to turn the paper into a mushy pulp or to tear it. To finish

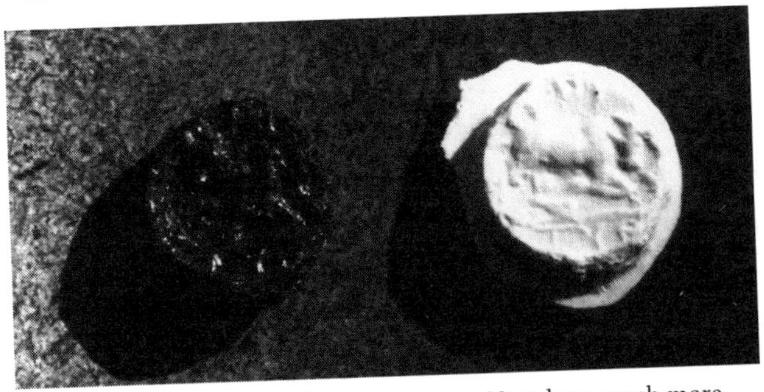

FIGURE A.2 Roman coin and its plaster cast. Note how much more detail is visible on the cast.

the squeeze, you can go over the inscription with your fingers, but there is a danger of creating what is not there in areas where the inscription is indistinct.

5. As you work, the paper can be rewet with a sponge if it begins to dry out.
6. When finished, either leave the paper in position to dry or gently ease it off the surface by supporting it with newspaper. Lean your arm against the paper to further support the squeeze as it comes off. Allow the squeeze to dry on a flat surface.

Coin Casts

When coins cannot be taken out of a country for study or will otherwise be inaccessible, numismatists rely on casts. Casts are easy to make and when a production line is set up, large numbers can be made quickly and efficiently. Many published photographs are of casts rather than of actual coins because casts remove the distraction of color differences and show detail more clearly (fig. A.2). This method is ideal for small seals as well as coins, but any small surface could be cast in this way. The resulting cast is a positive of the original.

While plaster of Paris can be used, a fine dental plaster will produce a better cast with finer definition of detail. Use the following procedure for making coin casts:

1. Make sure that your hands, work area, and modeling clay are clean. If white modeling clay is used, any dirt that might affect the quality of the cast will be readily apparent.
2. For each mold, take a piece of modeling clay the size of a small egg. Carefully roll it into a ball so that there are no cracks on the surface. Between two pieces of glass, glazed tile, or other smooth surfaces that have been lightly brushed with talc, flatten the ball to form a disk no less than 2 cm thick. Make sure the top surface is absolutely clean.
3. Lightly talc the top surface of the clay with a fine, soft brush and blow off any excess talc. If there is deep detail on the coin, it is wise to talc the surface of the coin lightly, too.
4. Place the coin cleanly in the middle of the disk. Do not move the coin once it has been placed on the clay.
5. Cover the coin with your thumb and gently press it into the clay, making sure it is evenly embedded. The coin should be flush with the surface of the clay. If the coin is smaller than your thumb, use the tip of the forefinger.
6. To remove the coin, place the disk coin-side down in your cupped left hand. Without bending the disk, tap it smartly directly behind the coin with the three middle fingers of the right hand. The coin should pop out cleanly. If not, tap again. Never bend the mold to remove the coin as this motion will distort the impression.
7. In a strong, raking light, check the impression carefully for imperfections. If necessary, repeat the above six steps to achieve a perfect impression.
8. Using a soft brush, carefully paint the impression with a 1 to 1 mixture of alcohol and water, making sure the entire mold is covered. A dilute solution of liquid soap can also be used. Tip or blow out any excess liquid; do not leave any puddles.
9. Mix up a fine dental plaster to a consistency slightly thicker than milk. With a soft brush, paint the mold with enough plaster to fill the shallow depressions of the detail.
10. Pick up the mold between the thumb and third finger and gently, but firmly, tap it against the table to remove air bubbles.
11. Fill the mold with plaster so that it rises slightly above the surface of the clay. It is better to err on the side of too much rather than too little plaster. Allow it to set fully. Depending on the temperature and humidity, this step can take from ten minutes to one hour.
12. Remove the cast as in step 6 and inspect it against the original for imperfections and air bubbles.
13. Remove the sharp edge, or flashing, around the cast with a sharp knife and bevel the edges.
14. Repeat for the reverse of the coin.

If many casts are being made simultaneously, inscribe the number of the coin on the back of the mold with a pointed object, (do not use a pencil because the lead will dirty the clay). When the plaster has set, the number can be transferred to the cast before removing it from the mold.

Cylinder Seal Rollings

Before making an impression, or rolling, of a cylinder seal, make absolutely sure that the surface of the seal is strong enough to withstand the rolling process. If there is any doubt about the condition of the surface—if it is powdery or friable—do not make a rolling because the entire surface

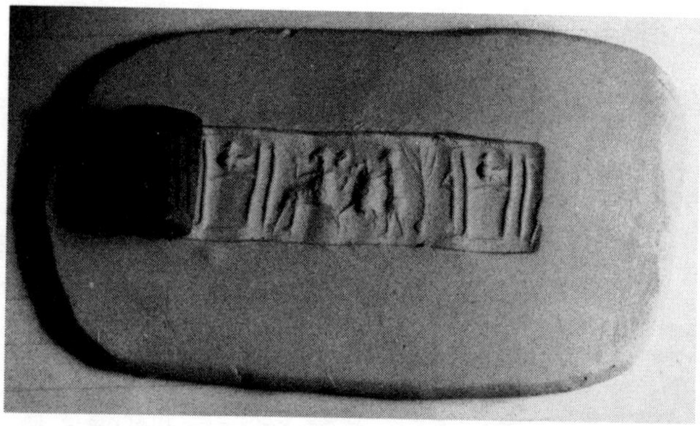

FIGURE A.3 Method for making a cylinder seal rolling.

can be pulled off. The seal must be treated first by a trained conservator. Since the seal is a negative, a rolling will give a positive impression.

If only a photograph is needed, white modeling clay can be used. If a permanent impression is desired, use one of the modeling compounds that can be hardened by being baked in an oven. Follow the manufacturer's directions for baking time and temperature. Use the following procedure to make a cylinder seal rolling:

1. On a clean surface, roll out a strip of clay that is at least 1 cm thick, that is considerably wider than the height of the seal, and that will accommodate at least one and one-half to two circumferences of the seal. Make the surface as smooth and flat as possible. A rolling pin is good for this, but any smooth cylinder, such as a glass or a metal can, works well. Or, the clay can be covered with a piece of plastic, and a broomstick or other cylinder with a less smooth surface can be used.
2. Lightly talc the surface of both the clay and the seal with a soft brush, being sure that the talc is distributed into all the depressions of the design. Blow off excess talc.
3. Place the seal cleanly on one side of the clay. Do not move the seal once it has been placed on the clay.
4. Gently, but firmly, press the seal evenly into the clay. At the same time, slowly roll it along the surface of the clay, maintaining as even a pressure as possible at all times to avoid undulations in the impression. The depth to which the seal is pressed into the clay depends on the depth of the incised lines on the seal. It must be deep enough to pick up all detail clearly, but not deep enough to distort the impression.
5. Continue rolling until there is a complete impression of the seal's surface with an overlap of at least 1 cm at the ends (fig. A.3).
6. Remove the seal cleanly by carefully lifting it. Lifting can also be accomplished by inserting a toothpick into the holes of the seal and then pulling it up gently.
7. Carefully inspect the rolling against the seal for imperfections and distortion.

II: Making Up Solutions

A SOLUTION is a liquid in which a solid has been homogeneously dissolved. When a liquid dissolves a solid, the liquid is referred to as the *solvent*, and the solid is called the *solute*. In making a solution, no chemical action takes place; it is purely a physical process.

The concentration of a solution is expressed as the amount of solid per unit volume of solution. Thus, a 10% solution means that 10 g (weight) of a solid were dissolved in enough solvent to make 100 ml (volume) of solution; it should be written correctly as 10% weight/volume or w/v. A 7% solution means that 7 g are dissolved in enough solvent to make 100 ml of solution and so forth. The simplest and easiest method for making up a solution of 5% Acryloid B72 in acetone is:

1. Measure out 100 ml of a liquid and place it in a jar. Mark the level of the liquid with a piece of tape on the outside of the jar. Pour out the liquid.
2. Measure out 5 g of Acryloid B72 and place it in the jar.
3. Add acetone to the jar until it is level with the tape.
4. Cover the jar securely and allow it to sit. Swirl or stir the solution frequently to facilitate the dissolving process. It will take time for the Acryloid to dissolve.

When making up solutions of consolidants, it can be difficult to get the resin into solution. There is a tendency for it to sit on the bottom of the jar in a viscous mass. This is especially true when higher concentrations of solution are being made. To avoid this problem, place the weighed out resin in the middle of a small piece of gauze bandage. Pull the corners together and tie them securely with a long piece of string to form a little bundle. Suspend the bundle in the solvent, hanging the end of the string over the rim so that it is caught when the lid is screwed on (fig. A.4). Swirl the solution from time to time until all the resin has been dissolved, then remove the flattened bundle. Untie the string, flatten the gauze, and allow it to dry out so it can be reused.

If the climate is very hot and dry, the seal of the jar may not be tight enough to prevent the slow evaporation of the solvent. As a result, the solution will slowly get thicker. To help prevent this from happening, cover the mouth of the jar with a piece of polyethylene before screwing on the lid. The piece of polyethylene should be considerably larger than the mouth of the jar to ensure that a good seal is achieved (fig. A.4).

If larger or smaller quantities of a solution are needed, the same proportions as used originally must be kept to maintain the percentage of solution. That is, if you double the amount of solution, you must double the amount of the solute as well. If you wish to triple the amount of solution, you must triple the amount of the

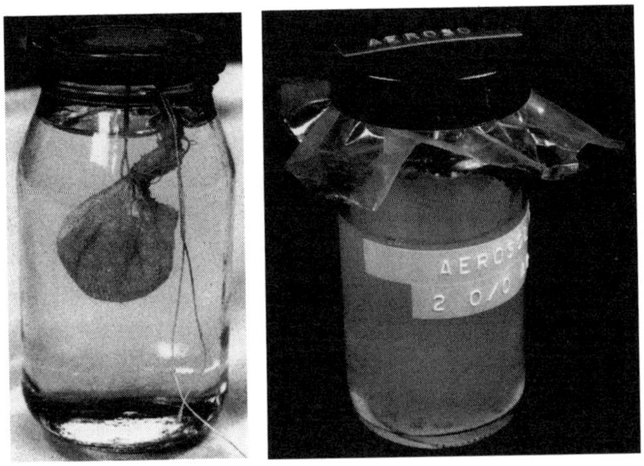

FIGURE A.4 ***Left***, making up a consolidant with bundle of resin suspended in solvent; ***right***, jar of consolidant with a plastic inner seal to help prevent evaporation of solvent.

solute, and so forth. Conversely, if you want to halve the amount of solution, you must halve the solute. Thus, for a 5% w/v solution, you want:

- 2.5 g dissolved in acetone to make 50 ml
- 5 g resin dissolved in acetone to make 100 ml
- 7.5 g resin dissolved in acetone to make 150 ml
- 10 g resin dissolved in acetone to make 200 ml
- 20 g resin dissolved in acetone to make 400 ml

Diluting a Solution

Sometimes it is necessary to dilute a solution. You may have purchased a resin or fungicide in solution or have made up a solution and wish to dilute it. To do this, it is necessary to know the concentration of the already existing solution. Since you will not necessarily have this information, it is easiest to assume that the solution is 100% and dilute it accordingly.

To dilute a solution, you must add more solvent. The amount needed is inversely proportional to the amount by which you wish to dilute the solution. Thus, if you wish to halve the concentration, you must double the amount of solvent; to dilute the solution by one third, you must triple the amount of solvent.

For example, a 10% solution means that 10 g of solid were dissolved in enough acetone to make 100 ml of solution. If you wish to dilute this to make it a 5% solution, the amount of the solute remains the same (10 g), but more solvent must be added to reach the desired concentration. Since you are halving the concentration going from a 10% to a 5% solution, you must double the volume of the solvent, add enough solvent to the already existing solution to make 200 ml of solution. This procedure will give you 200 ml of a 5% solution. If you wish to make a 2.5% solution, you must quadruple the amount of solvent. This will give you 400 ml of a 2.5% solution.

Increasing Solution Concentrations

To increase the concentration of an existing solution, add more resin. The amount of resin needed is directly proportional to the amount by which you wish to increase the concentration. To double the concentration, double the amount of resin; to triple the concentration, triple the amount of resin. If you have a 10% solution, for example, that you wish to increase to 20% and you have 10 g of resin in 100 ml of solution, double the amount of resin to double the concentration: add 10 more grams of resin to the already existing solution—creating 100 ml of a 20% solution.

III: Sources of Conservation Supplies

Acryloid B72, Rhoplex AC33, Acrysol WS24
Rohm and Haas
Independence Mall West
Philadelphia, Pennsylvania 19105

Paraloid B72, Primal AC33, Primal WS24
Rohm and Haas (U.K.), Ltd.
Lennig House
2 Mason's Avenue
Croydon CR9 3NB England

PVA AYAF
Union Carbide
270 Park Avenue
New York, New York 10017

CM Bond M3
Conservation Materials, Ltd.
1395 Greg #10
Sparks, Nevada 89431

Mowilith 50, DMC2
Farbwerke Hoechst Ag.
6230 Frankfurt (Main) 80
Postfach 800320 Germany

Vinamul 6815
Vinyl Products, Ltd.
Mill Lane
Carshalton, Surrey England

Elvacite 2013
E. I. DuPont de Nemours, Inc.
Wilmington, Delaware 19898

HMG Adhesive
Henry Marcel Guest, Ltd.
Collyhurst
Manchester MI0 7RU England

Duco Cement
Devcon Corporation
Danvers, Massachusetts 01923

Durofix
Rawlplug Company Ltd.
Rawlplug Works
Humber Road
London NW2 6HN England

UHU, UHU Hart
Lingner and Fischer GmbH.
D-758 Bühl/Baden Germany

Plasticine
Harbutt's Plasticine, Ltd.
Bathampton
Bath BA2 6TA England

Klean Klay
Art Chemical Products
Box 678
Huntington, Indiana 46750

Sculpy Modeling Compound
Polyform Products Corporation
9420 Byron Street
Schiller Park, Illinois 60176

Panacide
BDH Chemicals
Poole, Dorset BH12 4NN England

Topane WS
Imperial Chemicals, Ltd. (ICI)
Millbank
London SW1P 4RG England

444 Madison Avenue
New York, New York 10022

Dowicide A, Dowicide 1 Ethafoam (polyethylene foam)
Dow Chemicals USA
Midland, Michigan 48640

Dow Chemical Europe SA
8810 Horgen Switzerland

Tego 51
Th. Goldschmidt
Ag. Chemische Fabriken
43 Essen 1
Postfach 17 Germany

Silica gel bricks
W.L. Gore and Associates, Inc.
100 Airport Road
P.O. Box 1550
Elkton, Maryland 21921

IV: Organizations and Publications

THE FOLLOWING ORGANIZATIONS can provide helpful information concerning conservation and conservators. While they may not be able to recommend specific conservators, they can either refer your queries to conservators or provide you with a list of conservators in your area.

Each of these organizations, with the exception of ICCROM, publishes its own journal. The two most likely to be of interest and contain useful information are *Studies in Conservation*, published by IIC, and *The Conservator*, published by UKIC.

International Institute for Conservation (IIC)
6 Buckingham Street
London WC2N 6BA
England

American Institute for Conservation (AIC)
3545 Williamsburg Lane
Washington, D.C. 20008

International Institute for
Conservation/Canadian Group
Box/C.P. 9195
Ottawa K1G 3T9, Ontario
Canada

United Kingdom Institute for
Conservation (UKIC)
c/o Conservation Department
Tate Gallery
Millbank
London SW1P 4RG
England

Institute for the Conservation of Cultural Material
(ICCM)
P.O. Box 2046S
Melbourne, Victoria 3001
Australia

ICCROM
13 Via di S. Michele
Rome 00153
Italy

Bibliography

Beck, Curt W.
1982 Authentication and conservation of amber; Conflict of interests. In *Science and technology in the service of conservation*. IIC Washington Conference, 104–107. London: International Institute for Conservation.

Bourque, B. J., Brooke, S. W., Kley, R., andMorris, K.
1980 Conservation in archaeology: Moving toward closer cooperation. *American Antiquity* 45 (4): 794–799.

Brady, George S., and Clauser, Henry R.
1979 *Materials handbook*. 11th edition. New York: McGraw Hill.

Brothwell, D. R.
1981 *Digging up bones*. Oxford: Oxford University Press.

Brothwell, D. R., and Higgs, Eric, editors
1973 *Science in archaeology: A survey of progress and research*. 2nd edition. New York: Praeger Publishers.

Burleigh, Richard
1974 Radiocarbon dating: Some practical considerations for the archaeologist. *Journal of Archaeological Science* 1:69–87.

Chaplin, Raymond E.
1971 *The study of animal bones from archaeological sites*. London: Seminar Press.

Clark, Grahame
1986 *Symbols of excellence: Precious materials as expressions of status*. Cambridge: Cambridge U Press.

Cockburn, Aidan, and Cockburn, Eve, editors
1980 *Mummies, disease and ancient cultures*. Cambridge: Cambridge U Press.

Commoner, Lucy
1984 Personal protective equipment for conservators. *Journal of the American Institute for Conservation* 23:153–158.

Cornwall, I. W.
1958 *Soils for the archaeologist*. London: Phoenix House.

Coy, Jennie
1978 *First aid for animal bones*. D.O.E. Faunal Remains Project. Hertford: The British Archaeological Trust.

Dimbleby, G. W.
1967 *Plants and archaeology*. London: John Baker.

Dowman, Elizabeth A.
1970 *Conservation in field archaeology*. London: Methuen.

Escritt, J., and Greenacre, M.
1972 Note on toxic gases in polyurethane foam. *Studies in Conservation* 17:134.

Forbes, R. J.
1950 *Metallurgy in antiquity*. Leiden: E. J. Brill.
1957 *Studies in ancient technology*. Leiden: E.J. Brill.

Frank, Susan
1982 *Glass and archaeology*. London: Academic Press.

Gedye, Ione
1975 Pottery and glass. In *The conservation of cultural property*, 109–113. Paris: UNESCO Press.

Grierson, Philip
1975 *Numismatics*. Oxford: Oxford U Press.

Helbaek, Hans
1973 Paleo-ethnobotany. In *Science in archaeology: A aurvey of progress and research,* edited by D. R. Brothwell and Eric Higgs, 206–214. New York: Praeger.

Hodges, Henry
1964 *Artifacts*. London: John Baker.

Janaway, Robert
1983 Textile fibre characteristics preserved by metal corrosion: The potential of SEM studies. *The Conservator* 7:48–52.

Jones, Julie M.
1980 The use of polyurethane foam in lifting large fragile objects on site. *The Conservator* 4:31–33.

Keene, Suzanne
1977 An approach to the sampling and storage of waterlogged timbers from excavations. *The Conservator* 1:8–11.

Koob, Stephen P.
1986 The use of Palaroid B-72 as an adhesive: Its application for archaeological ceramics and other materials. *Studies in Conservation* 31:7.

Larson, John
1980 The conservation of terracotta sculpture. *The Conservator* 4:38–45.

Leigh, David
1978 *First aid for finds*. 2nd edition. Hertford: The British Archaeological Trust.

Lucas, A.
1948 *Ancient egyptian materials and industries*. 3rd edition. London: Edward Arnold.

Michels, Joseph W.
1973 *Dating methods in archaeology*. New York: Seminar Press.

Mora, Paolo
1984 Conservation of excavated intonaco, stucco and mosaics. In *Conservation on archaeological excavations*, 97–107. Rome: ICCROM.

Muhlethaler, B.
1973 *Conservation of waterlogged wood and wet leather*. Paris: Editions Eyrolles.

Muir, G. D., editor
1977 *Hazards in the chemical laboratory*. 2nd edition. London: The Chemical Society.

Novis, W. E.
1975 The lifting of mosaic pavements. In *Conservation in archaeology and the applied arts*. IIC Stockholm Conference, 143–145. London: International Institute for Conservation.

Pascoe, Michael
1980 Toxic hazards from solvents in conservation. *The Conservator* 4:25–428.

Philippot, P., and Mora, P.
1975 The conservation of wall paintings. In *The conservation of cultural property*, 169–189. Paris: UNESCO Press.

Plenderleith, H. J., and Werner, A. E. A.
1971 *The conservation of antiquities and works of art*. 2nd edition. Oxford: Oxford University Press.

Powell, Kathleen, and Wilkie, Patricia
1976 Labeling and tagging for artifact identity survival. In *Pacific Northwest wet site wood conservation conference* 1:81–90. Pullman, Washington: Washington State University.

Price, J. G.
1975 Some field experiments in the removal of larger fragile archaeological remains. In *Conservation in archaeology and the applied arts*. IIC Stockholm Conference, 153–164. London: International Institute for Conservation.

Robinson, Wendy S.
1981 *First aid for marine finds*. Handbook in Maritime Archaeology, no. 2. London: National Maritime Museum.

Rosenfeld, Andrée
1965 *The inorganic raw materials of antiquity*. London: Weidenfeld and Nicholson.

Ryder, Michael L.
1968 *Animal bones in archaeology*. Oxford: Blackwell Scientific Publications.

Sanford, Elizabeth
1975 Conservation of artifacts: A Question of Survival. *Historical Archaeology* 9: 55–64.

Sax, N. Irving
1978 *Dangerous properties of industrial materials*. 5th edition. New York: Interscience Publishers.

Scichilone, Giovanni
1984 On-site storage of finds. In *Conservation on Archaeological Excavations*, 55–63. Rome: ICCROM.

Scott, David A.
1983 The deterioration of gold alloys and some aspects of their conservation. *Studies in Conservation* 28(4):194–203.

Sease, Catherine
1984 First aid treatment for excavated finds. In *Conservation on archaeological excavations*, 31–50. Rome: ICCROM.

Sheppard, John C.
1976 Influence of contaminants and preservatives on radiocarbon dates. In *Pacific Northwest wet site wood conservation conference* 1: 91–96. Pullman, Washington: Washington State University.

Singer, C., Holmyard, E. J., and Hall, A. R., editors
1954 *A history of technology*. Oxford: Oxford University Press.

Singley, Katherine R.
1981 Caring for artifacts after excavation: Some advice for archaeologists. *Historical Archaeology* 15 (1):35–48.

Spriggs, James
1980 The recovery and storage of materials from waterlogged deposits york. *The Conservator* 4: 19–24.

Spriggs, James, and Van Byeren, Thad
1984 A practical approach to the excavation and recording of ancient Maya burials. *The Conservator* 8: 41–46.

Stolow, Nathan
1979 *Conservation standards for works of art in transit and exhibition*. Paris: UNESCO.

Tintori, Leonetto
1963 Methods used in Italy for detaching murals. In *Recent advances in conservation*, edited by G. Thomson, 118–122. London: Butterworths.

Tubb, Kathryn Walker
1985 Preparation for field conservation in the Near East. *The Conservator* 9:17–21.

Webb, Virginia
1978 *Archaic Greek faience*. Warminster: Aris and Phillips.

Werner, A. E. A.
1975 The conservation of leather, wood, bone, ivory and archival materials. In *The conservation of cultural property*, 265–290. Paris: UNESCO.

Western, A. C.
1973 Wood and charcoal. In *Science in archaeology: A survey of progress and research*, edited by D. R. Brothwell and Eric Higgs, 178–187. New York: Praeger.

Index

Illustration references are in italics.